PRAISE FOR *LEGACY MINDSET*

"Powerful and inspiring, Korey Shaffer's soul-stirring book, *Legacy Mindset*, movingly describes his extraordinary journey from the depths of despair to finding a profound purpose in helping his fellow brothers-in-arms and their families. It is a story of debilitating emotional wounds and their miraculous healing. It is also a tale of taking personal responsibility and asking for help. After I finished his remarkable book, I left with a deep appreciation for the man Korey is and all that he has accomplished in the face of extreme difficulty. This book is a must-read."

—**Colonel Bruce Hurd, Retired US Air Force Veteran, Bestselling Author of** *Aim Point: An Air Force Pilot's Lessons for Navigating Life*

"Korey teaches us to go all in for something you believe in with the mindset of 'sink or swim.' This story is a divine appointment . . . An incredible book."

—**Colin Wayne, Retired US Army Veteran, CEO of Redline Steel**

"In *Legacy Mindset*, Korey Shaffer masterfully intertwines his personal experiences with universal lessons, guiding readers on a journey of emotional and psychological growth. Through raw honesty and practical insights, Shaffer challenges readers to transform their pain into purpose, fostering empathy and resilience. This compelling narrative is a must-read and testament to the power of vulnerability and the impact of leaving a lasting legacy."

—**Renee Nickell, Gold Star Sister and Author of** *Always My Hero*

Legacy Mindset

LEGACY MINDSET

Take Charge of Today
— and —
Build Extreme Resilience

KOREY SHAFFER
FOUNDER OF TIL VALHALLA PROJECT

BROWN BOOKS
PUBLISHING GROUP

© 2024 Korey Shaffer

All rights reserved. No part of this book may be used or reproduced in any manner without written permission except in the case of brief quotations embodied in critical articles or reviews.

Legacy Mindset
Take Charge of Today and Build Extreme Resilience

Brown Books Publishing Group
16250 Knoll Trail Drive, Suite 205
Dallas, Texas 75248
www.BrownBooks.com
(972) 381-0009

A New Era in Publishing®

Names: Shaffer, Korey, author.
Title: Legacy mindset : take charge of today and build extreme resilience / Korey Shaffer.
Description: Dallas, Texas : Brown Books Publishing Group, [2024]
Identifiers: ISBN: 978-1-61254-694-0 (hardcover) | LCCN: 2024940964
Subjects: LCSH: Shaffer, Korey. | Resilience (Personality trait) | Self-actualization (Psychology) | Self-control. | Pain--Psychological aspects. | Determination (Personality trait) | Intuition. | Discipline. | LCGFT: Self-help publications. | BISAC: SELF-HELP / Motivational & Inspirational. | SELF-HELP / Personal Growth / General.
Classification: LCC: BF698.35.R47 S53 2024 | DDC: 155.24--dc23

ISBN 978-1-61254-694-0
LCCN 2024940964

Printed in the United States
10 9 8 7 6 5 4 3 2 1

For more information or to contact the author, please go to www.KoreyShaffer.com.

To my wife Tiffany, whose unwavering faith and relentless support allowed me to pursue my dreams and discover the value I could bring to others.

To my newborn Cayden, for giving me a purpose that has ignited my wildest imagination.

To my dad, who showed me what it meant to be a true father, and taught me that my ever-racing mind is a gift, not a curse.

To my mom, who taught me compassion and raised three young kids to thriving adults as a single parent.

To my brother and sister, who taught me what it meant to be a big brother.

To the military personnel who fight battles overseas and at home.

To the first responders who allow us to sleep soundly at night and live boldly, knowing they are only a call away.

Finally, this book is dedicated to everyone who has ever doubted their worth. To those who battle daily with their mental health—you are not alone. This is for all the dreamers, the warriors, and the unsung heroes. Your strength and resilience inspire me every day.

TABLE OF CONTENTS

Acknowledgments	xi
Prologue: Rock Bottom	xiii
How to Use This Book	xxvii
What Does It Mean to Have a Legacy Mindset?	xxix
Chapter 1: Against the Grain	1
Chapter 2: Your Intrinsic Worth	11
Chapter 3: Good Pain, Bad Pain	19
Chapter 4: Reflection that Matters	29
Chapter 5: Assign Value Accordingly	37
Chapter 6: Law of Attrition	55
Chapter 7: Law of Attraction	71
Chapter 8: Mental Discomfort vs. Mental Anguish	85
Chapter 9: Forced Discipline	93

Chapter 10: Adapt and Thrive	103
Chapter 11: Speak Up	117
Chapter 12: Empathy is a Tool	137
Chapter 13: The Forge of Adversity	151
Chapter 14: The War Within	167
Chapter 15: Wake-Up Call	181
Chapter 16: The Price of Perfection	193
Chapter 17: Turning Points	203
Chapter 18: Harnessing Momentum	215
Chapter 19: Untested Valor	231
Chapter 20: What Lives On	243
Chapter 21: The Breaking Point	255
Chapter 22: Keep Moving Forward	267
The Mission of Til Valhalla Project	277
Afterword	279
About the Author	281

ACKNOWLEDGMENTS

There are too many people to acknowledge individually, but I credit my successes, both current and future, to everyone who has supported me, including you—the reader. Without the backing of my staff at Til Valhalla Project, as well as my family, friends, and supporters, I would just be a guy with big dreams. It takes a collective effort to turn those dreams into reality.

I want to thank Russell Brunson, Grant Cardone, Dean Graziosi, David Goggins, Tony Robbins, Napoleon Hill, Jocko Willink, Andy Frisella, Colin Wayne, JoAnne (Jo) Bass, and many more sources of inspiration. I have followed you and learned from you all along the way. Your teachings and guidance have been invaluable.

Great thanks to Barry Schrader, my current VP, for taking care of the team for the better half of a year while I focused on writing and got my footing as a new dad. Your dedication and mission-driven leadership have been a cornerstone of our success.

To my wife, Tiffany, thank you for allowing me to put in 18-20 hour days over the past ten years without ever once telling me that I work too much. Your unwavering support and belief in me have been my greatest strength.

To my publishers, and specifically Brunella Costagliola, Ben Davidoff, and Jennie Knupple, for going above and beyond during my constant fears and knee-jerk decisions to ensure this book was as impactful as possible.

Catterlin, thank you for being a leader through some of the most transformational and scariest times of my life.

Here's to you, Dunston, for showing me how to lead by respect and not by fear.

And to my entire 2/7 Marine family who molded me into who I am today, thank you.

Thank you all for being part of this journey.

PROLOGUE: ROCK BOTTOM

"Shaffer, Dunston is gone."

I hadn't heard Corporal Catterlin's voice in almost a year, but there was no mistaking his tone through my old, beat-up work phone from the Marine Corps. I knew better than most what he sounded like when he was joking, serious, or scared. Though the speakers were muffled from years of abuse and countless drops, the somberness in his voice was unmistakable. He had been my team leader in Afghanistan—I trusted him with my life—and his tone was sincere, but I had just woken up. Despite all the signs, I remained doubtful and thought, *I must have heard him wrong.*

"What do you mean *gone?*" I asked. "What the hell happened to him?"

"He killed himself, brother," Catterlin said. "He's gone."

I swear I could hear my heart break. The world slowed, my vision began to tunnel, and everything started to feel hazy—a bad dream coming to life. Unrealistic thoughts flooded my brain like a fire hose trying to contain a wildfire. *Not Dunston*, I thought. *Something must be wrong. The police must be confused.* I imagined, or maybe hoped, it was one of those disputable cases—that he fell overboard while on one of his notorious fishing escapades, and they called off the search for some indiscernible reason. Or maybe he hit the road in his dark blue 2012 Honda Civic we worked on together and kept driving, not telling anyone where he was going. I searched for anything that would deny the hard evidence of my new reality. Anything that could help me make an argument for an alternative—one that resulted in him being okay.

It can't be real, I told myself.

Dunston was a Marine and my best friend throughout our service. He was only one year out at this point—the same as me. And he had just started picking up the pieces of his life outside the corps, finding his value as a security guard. I had just spoken to him two weeks prior about getting my security license, too, thinking we could start something up together—something that would allow us to work together again.

"Shaffer?" Catterlin said. "You there?"

"I'm here, I'm . . ." I couldn't get the words out. "Thanks for letting me know, brother."

I hung up, and everything seemed surreal. The morning light breached through the curtains, the fan above my head whirred, and the reality of his absence started to settle in. A man who had honorably served. A man who did everything his nation asked of him. A man with brothers who loved him, who would die for him.

Gone.

Images flashed through my head. His face. His smile. His laugh. He's the one who gave me hope when I joined the Marines. When I had no friends and feared leadership, he showed me through kindness and empathy that respect is stronger than fear. He offered to be my gym partner when the other seniors wanted nothing to do with us "boots." (A "boot" was a derogatory term that was frowned upon, used to describe new Marines that hit the Fleet Marine Force [FMF]. It was intended to put you in your place and remind you that you were inferior to those who had more time in service.) When I went through a breakup, he helped me remember who I was before and told me it would all be okay, as long as we took care of our mind and body.

He encouraged my work at the gym to protect and strengthen my mental and physical health as a young Marine—using the weight room and conditioning as an outlet for my internal demons. When that wasn't enough, we drowned out the bad thoughts together with a shared love for metal music. We loved all kinds, from 1980s to current, but we found it particularly funny when we would jam to White Chapel, Slipknot, or other hardcore bands because of the "What the hell are you listening to?" comments we would get from other Marines walking by. We spent hours and days in training talking about life, goals, and those big, unrealistic dreams. Most of all, he showed me what true leadership looked like . . .

I was just getting back into the gym for the first time as a new Marine. My favorite exercise was the bench press—a simple move that was easy to measure progress from. But when I finished my pre-workout, got in my gym gear, and finally sat on the bench ready to push weight, I did nothing. The entire time I just sat there getting in my own head, saying things to myself like, "Man, you're about to push a lot less weight than you're used to," or "Don't push yourself too hard, you have to train tomorrow." I know now that I was scared to acknowledge how much weight and muscle I'd lost after joining the Marines with the overtraining, dietary restrictions, and more running than I had ever done in my life. But I knew if I never tried, I wouldn't be able to realize that loss. So, I just sat there and stared around the Marine-packed gym, watching everyone else but me put in the work.

Fifteen minutes passed. I decided that getting to the gym in the first place was enough progress for today. *I'll do better tomorrow.* I stood up to pull the weight off the bar, then—*SMACK!*—what felt like two bear paws struck my shoulders, latched on, and started to shake me back and forth. I froze in fear. *Did I do something wrong? Is some senior about to call me out?*

"What's up, Shaffer?!" someone shouted in my ear—with an unmistakable Wisconsin accent.

I immediately laughed and turned around. *I knew it was you.*

"What's up, man?! I'm just getting ready to leave. Want the bench?"

Dunston looked at me confused. I assumed he saw me enter the gym just minutes ago. "How much did you hit on the bench today?" he asked, looking at the two hundred twenty-five pounds I had on the bar.

"Well, I didn't," I said timidly, quickly following up with, "I didn't have a spotter."

"Well, s—t. Get your a— on that bench. We're working chest today!" He shouted with excitement, smacking my shoulders again.

Yippee . . .

I laid down on the bench, sure that I was about to absolutely embarrass myself. *I haven't lifted this much weight since high school.*

"How many you goin' for?" he asked.

"I'll be lucky if I don't die before I—"

"Bulls—t. Plant your feet. Add a slight arch to your back, and when you feel that bar hit your chest, explode with everything you have. I got you."

I grabbed the bar and paused for a second to think about the weight, if I was ready to lift it—but before I could sink too far into my mind, I hear Dunston say, "Ready? Go!" as he lifted the bar off the rests.

Sink or swim . . .

"Holy sh—t, this is heavy," I said, wanting some empathy. But all I got in return was . . .

"DOWN!"

I closed my eyes, not giving myself time to think, and as the weight went down I felt it hit my chest—

"AND PRESS!"

With my eyes still closed, the weight started to feel a lot lighter—and I got the rep with what felt like ease.

"EASY!" Dunston shouted, giving me confidence as I opened my eyes and racked the weight.

"Dunston! Did you touch the bar?"

"Not at all, Shaffer, that was all you."

"Yeah, right." *No way.*

"Well, get your a— back down and do it again with your eyes open. Same form, same strategy. Give me everything you got."

With a boost of confidence, I laid back down.

"READY? GO!"

I lifted the weight off the bar and saw that Dunston's hands were clear of the bar.

"DOWN!"

Again, I felt the weight hit my chest.

"AND UP!"

I pushed with everything I had, and to my surprise, it went up with ease.

"NICE! AGAIN!" he shouted as I hit the top of the rep.

I began to panic . . .

"LET'S *GO*, SHAFFER!"

I gritted my teeth. *One more . . .*

The weight stalled on the way up and I was confident that I was about to go back down, but Dunston put his hands under the bar without touching it and shouted. "UP, UP, *UP!*"

I racked the weight.

"*That's* what I'm talking about!" he shouted while smacking my back. "Good job, Shaffer."

I smiled from ear to ear, just thinking about how excited he was for my success.

"I can't believe I got that twice in a row," I said through a laugh.

"Better start believing, Shaffer."

Damn, that felt good.

I stepped aside so Dunston could go for the same weight; he unracked it and I watched him warm up with ten reps without breaking a sweat—without even celebrating his own success.

Humble giant . . .

Staring at the sun-washed ceiling, listening to the steady hum of the fan, I realized I couldn't return that gift. The opportunity was gone forever.

And if he's gone, what chance do I have?

I had the urge to call Dunston right then to prove that the world was playing a cruel joke on me. I scrolled over his number and the picture of him in 29 Palms Marine Corps base, all geared up. To hear his voice, to let him know all these stories and how they impacted and shaped me—how they helped me. I pressed call and immediately hung up before it even went through. I didn't want it to become real. He died never hearing any of those words from me, and it's killed me every day since.

The truth is, I didn't expect to speak to Catterlin that day, or the next day, or the next week. After leaving the Corps, we didn't do too much communicating outside of some shared Facebook posts. It was honestly sad considering how close we were when serving together. I couldn't have been awake for more than a minute, listening to the sound of the unbalanced fan rock back and forth, drowning out the ringing in my ears, when I quickly grabbed my phone off my old beat-up nightstand—like the millennial I am—to check my Facebook store that specialized in 3D-printed items and decals (admittedly unsuccessfully) to see if any new sales had come in.

My wife Tiffany was still asleep beside me. I thought to wake her so we could start the day together, but I scrolled through my feed instead. The first thing I saw was a post from Marino Vilano (I knew him only as "Vilano" in true military fashion)—a service picture of him and Dunston.

"The only photo I have with you, brother. Love you, bro. Rest easy, warrior. We'll see each other again one day."

Then another.

"Semper Fi, brother. I miss you already."

And finally, one from Catterlin.

"Never above you. Never below you. Always beside you. I'll never forget the great times we had and how you were part of a rare breed of Marines. Never afraid to speak the truth, and always a true friend. Until Valhalla, brother."

Until Valhalla, brother. The phrase stuck in my head. Something we always say for our Fallen* brothers and sisters in arms. An allusion to Norse warriors and their mythology: *I'll see you again in the halls of the slain.* Many of us in the military idolize the Vikings for their ruthless and relentless behavior. We connect with their belief that dying in the line of battle and laying down your life for a brother in arms is an act of glory that earns each warrior a special place of Honor in the afterlife. Though we cannot say that we shared the same morals as the Vikings, their warrior's ethos hit home to the infantry.

---

* I make it a point to capitalize words like Fallen, Hero, Heroes, and Honor to pay tribute to those who have served. By emphasizing these terms, which are often used to describe individuals who have sacrificed for our freedoms, I aim to bring attention to their significance.

Unfortunately, "Until Valhalla" is something my unit had already said too many times.

When my infantry unit 2/7 (2nd Battalion, 7th Marines) returned from Afghanistan, we suffered mass suicides by military standards. Before my enlistment, 2/7 went through hell on their 2008 deployment, killing over one hundred enemy fighters and losing Marines killed in action (KIA) in Sangin Valley, a well-known hellhole plagued by violence within the Helmand province of southern Afghanistan. The suicides were so prevalent that they nicknamed this unit the "Forgotten Battalion," because of the casualties both overseas and back in the States. There were so many casualties, in fact, that the remaining Marines did not deploy to a combat zone again. If you are unfamiliar with how the military works, that's extremely uncommon—our contract states that we are set to redeploy every six to seven months. But not them; they got a four-year pause. That effectively meant the four-year contracts of all the Marines who remained were over.

We were the 2/7 replacements, leaving in September 2012 and returning in March 2013 after a seven-month deployment. Our combat encounters differed significantly from 2/7 in 2008, but sadly the suicide rate remained the same, losing over a dozen warriors in a short window after our return. Dunston was now among them.

It felt like our unit was cursed.

"Til Valhalla." It tinged wrong when I whispered the words out loud. A shiver-up-the-spine kind of feeling. Like an anvil on your chest and a weight that settles deep in your gut.

When a Hero dies overseas fighting for their nation, they're recognized for it. We hold them on a well-deserved pedestal for serving their country with Honor at the highest level and paying the ultimate sacrifice for our freedom. We edify them as the Heroes we desire to be, the ones with a servant's heart, always ready to lay down their life at a moment's notice for others in need.

I pictured Dunston's face.

What happens when you serve your nation Honorably, fighting the war out there only to return home and lose the war in your mind? How are those Heroes Honored? We all know these Heroes. We've seen them. Returning veterans trying to make ends meet, to find a renewed sense of purpose. A family, a job, or a home. Some are begging on the street, going through the motions of their daily battles, remembering how they fought, and reminding themselves to keep fighting. But there's no wall for them to be remembered by; no statues, no placards, nothing. Just grieving families left to pick up the pieces of a system that failed our troops mentally and physically.

They held Dunston's funeral in his hometown a week later. And for months after, I just kept sinking. Tiffany watched, unsure of what to do, as I kept drinking and fading further into an empty shell of who I used to be. I had never made drinking a habit prior to my deployment, I didn't believe in it, and within a month or two out of service, I picked up the bottle and didn't put it back down. After hearing about Dunston, it might as well have been strapped to me.

All I could picture was him slowly fading from our minds and lives like a drunken thought, his memory and legacy lost to time.

But the thought of his legacy fading was unbearable. I had to do something to make sure that wouldn't happen. I needed to Honor Dunston the way he deserved to be. As his face started to become hazy and his voice and his laugh unclear, I needed something to keep me grounded so I could keep him close to me. I didn't want to be eighty years old and say, "who?" when my grandkids mentioned his name as we flipped through an old military photo album. I needed something that would remind me day in and day out who he was—the man and leader and friend I remembered. So, I made a choice that seemed small at the time.

"I need to build a plaque for Dunston," I told my wife, Tiffany.

"A plaque?" she answered, confused by my meaning.

"Something *in memoriam*, you know? Something to remember him by."

She looked up at me, her light brown eyes giving me full attention. Without hesitation, she replied: "Let's get the materials."

In a moment, we were in the car, and she drove me to the craft store. She drove me because I would still have episodes, conditioned responses to what I saw on the road that put me in a dangerous mental state–A pile of trash on the road equaled a potential IED (improvised explosive device), a motorcycle a potential VBIED (vehicle-borne improvised explosive device). Either that or I had been drinking, and I refused to get behind the wheel even after just one sip.

Her driving me, her encouragement when I had the idea, was the sort of unconditional love that kept me going and gave me hope—and it's something I didn't tell her enough at the time. Tiffany's support made the plaque possible. Knowing I had the most loyal wife by my side made me feel like every move was a win. Just her compassion, when I honestly didn't feel like I deserved it for what I had put her through, gave me the confidence that we could bring Dunston the Honor he deserved.

At that time I was an associate at AutoZone and living at my father's house, so I didn't have much money. When we got to the store, I realized I only had enough cash for one piece of pine wood. I grabbed the best piece I could find and took some extra countertop samples to meld together.

When we returned home later that evening, I went straight to my dad's garage. Once there, I laid out the pieces and started drinking—a *lot*. I told myself it was so I could access my emotions and permit myself to feel—to let it all out to make the best memorial I could and connect with Dunston. I told myself whatever a struggling alcoholic says to get another drink. But at that time, I needed it to work. I needed it to do anything rather than stand still and let his memory fade.

Need is a strong word, and a problem for another day, but at 5:26 p.m. on September 2, 2016, I started making my first plaque four months after Dunston had passed. I wish I could remember the entire building process; the hand-sanding of the wood, the stain filling the engraved design, the cutting of the plexiglass, the smell of the laser burning the pine, or even the pile of mistakes I woke up to the next morning—but it was like I was on autopilot.

I pushed through until I knew Dunston was being Honored with something he deserved. Standing in front of my cheap workshop table, grinding away in my dad's cluttered garage, I was hell-bent on making this memorial unique. Nothing was organized and the table was a complete mess. But I felt like it was just Dunston and me in there; him helping me with my demons while I Honored him after he fell to his.

Tiffany brought me a photo of Dunston to place on the memorial. Seeing his face made me smile, remembering all the times we made absolute fools of ourselves in the barracks: screaming along with his favorite hardcore metal songs; singing, jumping from the racks; dancing around like two kids at a concert; and spending late nights under the stars, talking about what we would do when we finally got out of the Marine Corps. Trusting he'd have my back like I had his. It all came flooding back and hit me like a freight train.

But I wasn't done yet. I had to choose to keep going.

When it came to the last line on his nameplate, which would tie the memorial together, the only thing that seemed fitting was "Til Valhalla, Brother." *I'll see you again in the hall of the slain.*

I wrote a personal message to him on the back of the granite nameplate and glued it onto the plaque, never to be seen or shared. It sealed my final message to him in stone. Finally, with everything set in place, I gazed at the plaque, immensely proud of what I had created, and hoped he would be proud too. The entire night was pure therapy. Dried-up tears riddled the table, each a memory and a message of how much I missed him—closure in knowing that I was making a difference in my Fallen brother's legacy.

Then, right there on the workshop table, I passed out.

When I woke up, I saw the plaque finished on the table. The engineer and perfectionist inside me said it was god-awful. The Marine inside me cried for my brother. And whoever I happened to be, tossed up in that strange mix, didn't want to look at it for another minute.

I thought of his family and friends. *What do they have to keep his legacy alive? Who is going to make sure they know that we will never forget? Even after days turn to decades, how will they know we remember Dunston for the Hero he is? It's not fair,* I thought. *Why should I have something like this on my wall while his family and friends don't?*

I had my time with him. He stood over my shoulder while I built the plaque. He stayed there as my guardian, guide, and leader. But every time I looked at it, it hurt too much. Because I've found that what hurts the most is when you see how much value someone brings to the world but they can't see it themselves.

I still wish I had the courage to tell Dunston what he meant to me. As a leader, a friend, and a brother.

But I couldn't see any good memories when I sobered up that morning. I could only focus on his final moments. How I failed him, how a system failed him—how we all failed him. Guilt surrounded me; I never told him what he needed to hear—that he was one of my best friends and drove me to success in more ways than one.

Corporal Benjamin Dunston, it said below the picture of him on my plaque.

His smile started to morph in my head; all I could see was the dichotomy between that photo and what his last three seconds on this earth looked like. At twenty-four years old, all I could envision were the worst images and thoughts—visions of him that weren't actually him. I didn't have the emotional maturity to compartmentalize my feelings positively, so everything was funneled back in a negative way. I turned the plaque over on my workshop table.

And that's when I decided to make a gesture that changed my life forever. A small choice that had a huge impact.

I felt the world needed to see what I had built, so I made a personal commitment to send the plaque to his family. But first I posted the plaque on social media. I don't know why I chose to do so—probably because I wanted to show myself and the world that I wasn't just standing still. Within a few minutes, my inbox filled with questions on how to get one of these memorials, even though the plaque (to me) looked poorly constructed.

Then a comment popped up: "Send one to his parents."

This message was worth its weight in gold because it validated my plan.

I found Dunston's mom on Facebook, which was easy from all the memorial posts, but specifically because someone tagged her right after I posted the plaque. In hindsight this wasn't the best approach, but considering this was my first rodeo, I think it's forgivable.

When I got into Facebook Messenger, I paused at the blank page. I didn't know if it was the right time to open up these emotions on either my side or hers. We were all grieving in our own way, and there was no rule book on when or how to deliver a memorial like this. (Now that we have built over 3,000 of these memorial plaques as of June 2023, it's safe to say our process is a little better ironed out.)

But at that moment, my nerves were firing. I started shaking. Thankfully, a lesson from overseas came back: "Speak up, even when you're scared." She knew who I was because we had all added each other's family on Facebook to stay connected after service—sharing posts, pictures, anything. But I had a hard time taking my own advice. Usually, I give myself three seconds to do something I don't want to. I've discovered that if I wait longer than three seconds, I tend to overthink the situation and not follow through—and I risk making a poor decision. This time, three seconds turned into three minutes. Three minutes to realize my fear was illogical, and I felt embarrassed that this plaque wasn't intended to be hers in the first place. That would have been far more noble. I summoned the fortitude, made the choice to hit SEND, and waited for her response. In a second, she responded that she'd "like to pay for it."

All I said was that I couldn't take money for it, but her response solidified something that would stay with me for years: No family should have to pay to Honor their Fallen Hero. They've already paid enough.

After receiving her address, I headed to the post office, gently packed up Dunston's memorial, and sent it away. As soon as it was out of my hands, I felt relief—closure—knowing he was on his way home, knowing his mom was receiving something that would keep his memory alive. And a few weeks later, she posted the plaque for the world to see. Then it was shared. And shared. And shared. My inbox flooded with people wanting their own. Families, friends, and loved ones wishing to Honor their Fallen Heroes who weren't Honored in the way they deserved.

Each plaque meant hundreds of dollars in materials, sanding, staining, and time. But I didn't want to say no to *anyone* trying to Honor a Fallen Hero.

I also didn't want to charge to keep their legacies alive.

So, despite being broke, I had to find a way to ensure that nobody paid for their Hero's memorial and that every Hero was Honored no matter how they passed away. Their service and willingness to serve was what mattered most.

It's how they lived, not how they died. I took on as many Fallen Hero memorials as I could.

Making my first memorial hurt—a lot. So many times in the process I wanted to stop, hoping someone else would come into the picture and offer a better, more impactful, more creative way to carry on these Heroes' legacies. When a loved one passes, people often bring all sorts of amazing ideas to the table, such as decals, statues, engraved stones, license plate covers—objects that commemorate their Fallen Heroes for the world to see. But for my fellow Fallen, no one ever did. I realized *it had to be me*. Though these plaques became my therapy, my mental health continued to decline, and making them only added fuel to the fire. With every creation the voices of my demons grew louder, and I could feel the weight bearing down on my shoulders as if I carried the souls of all those who came before me. The memories of everything I tried to forget overseas flooded back uncontrollably while I empathized with each Hero's last moments. The thought of how my fate was likely no different than theirs haunted me, sending a coldness into my bones . . . But when it came to Honoring Dunston, to Honoring them, I felt I had warriors at my side. The bravest service members on earth were in my corner. Heroes killed in action, lost to suicide, or taken in car accidents.

Yet, considering my alcoholism, PTSD, compressive spine injuries, traumatic brain injuries (TBIs), hearing loss, chronic migraines—sustained both during training and overseas—and all the while hopped up on VA meds and crafting like a madman, sometimes I wonder how I'm still here.

But I am.

Because all those plaques, I realized, were the impact of small choices. These memorials were making me recognize an internal war that I didn't fully realize was going on. On one hand, I was doing a great service by Honoring those Heroes. On the other, guilt and empathy for each of these Fallen men and women was so strong it made me question why I'm still here and they're not. But one side of the internal war was winning: my desire for service was superseding the guilt of my existence. I was starting to see the value of this work even if it was at my own mental expense.

Because the small choices in life started adding up. Whether it's creating a plaque, asking for someone to drive you, or sending a Facebook message, small choices make a difference. They help us continue moving forward, even when there aren't any signs that we should. They encourage us to be our own light in the darkness. And they allow us to be comfortable being *uncomfortable*, knowing a bigger plan is at play.

Because from that first small choice and gesture, I created a business with a mission I believed in. If my plan was to inspire veterans, I had to do it myself to show them it's possible. There are other grunts in the industry, but they had proven to be special from the start. Not me. From that small choice and gesture, I and my amazing team composed of dozens of veterans, first-responders, and patriots created something that has helped many more families of Fallen Heroes across the nation.

We founded Til Valhalla Project.

HOW TO USE THIS BOOK

Change starts small, and it stacks. Your first goal moving forward is to be honest about the challenges in your life, and even more open about ways to overcome them. Nothing happens overnight. No big revelation will suddenly send you down a new path. But one small choice after the other, one small step after the other—that's what brings the big changes.

In the coming pages, you'll encounter stories of my life, the people in it, and the lessons I've learned from the good and the bad. In every chapter, after I tell you about my life, I want you to dig down deep into yours. I'll ask you questions about your struggles, goals, and dreams, and together we can start creating a plan of action.

So bring a highlighter.

Bring a pen.

And let's uncover, build, and maintain our Legacy Mindset.

WHAT DOES IT MEAN TO HAVE A LEGACY MINDSET?

Adopting a legacy mindset means prioritizing serving others first, then living off the reciprocity of your service to propel you and your family toward success and well-being across generations. It involves taking daily steps toward greatness, driven not just by personal gain but by the ambition to elevate those around you.

Embrace a legacy mindset and observe how your purposeful actions create ripples of progress, forging a path to a brighter today and ensuring a prosperous future long after you're gone.

CHAPTER 1

AGAINST THE GRAIN

In a world where conformity thrives, dare to be the brushstroke that paints a unique masterpiece in ways perceived to be wrong by all.

For as long as I can remember, I have felt out of place.

I'm not going to pretend that I had terrible parents or wasn't loved as a kid, but I can tell you how my mind has structured itself since birth: to always look at the worst thing possible and dwell on it. I can't tell you why I did it—likely blaring signs of depression at a young age that I wouldn't address until I was older—but I can tell you that I was always on a path of self-destruction, going the wrong way on a one-way street and resenting any sign of structure.

As a kid growing up in Rhode Island, I was raised in lower-class areas, any place my mother could afford as a single parent. Throughout the majority of my childhood I thought that most people lived in poverty, struggled, fought to survive—I didn't know any better. I didn't know there was a better life out there for me, for all of us. Perspectives don't change until we leave our hometown, after all, and my inability to fit in was a constant battle for my family.

The first signs of my being an outsider started when my dad was still around. As a kid, I could not and would not pay attention to *anything* except what interested me—toys and testing boundaries. And my dad had the best toy in the house: a Super Nintendo under the old glass-front Zenith TV. We would sit down together, a flat gray controller with purple buttons in his hand, RGB cables sticking out from the front—almost as if it knew it would be a sign of nostalgia today—and I would watch him play. My dad's favorite game was Killer Instinct (an old fighting game). When I was old enough, he always wanted to play against me, encouraging me to fight back and win as we went head-to-head, one-on-one, mano-a-mano. But it was like pulling teeth to keep my attention. The countdown would appear on the screen—"3, 2, 1, FIGHT!"—and I'd immediately walk my character in the opposite direction. My dad would then have to follow after me, almost like someone at a bar trying to hassle and pick a fight. But I was busy testing the mechanics in a desperate search for limitations, comparing a handful of pixels to real life.

Can I jump over the ropes of the ring?
Nope, well that sucks.
Can I interact with the background?
Zilch. Then why is it even there?
If I land a hit, will the punches leave marks on the opponent?
Nada, well that's not realistic.
Do those marks make sense based on the point of impact or angle of trajectory?
Negative. Well, that's just lazy coding.

Of course, the language of my questions didn't form like that as a four-year-old kid, and the answer to all of them back in the day was almost always "no," anyway, because graphical fidelity, animations, and effects in the '90s were nowhere near today's standards. All I discovered was that hit markers never made sense, animations were flat and repetitive, the boundaries were rigid, and I couldn't leave the ring or make any daring moves outside the character's predetermined move set. Ultimately, I was disappointed, and it made games hard to enjoy. But I still just had to know: *What makes these things tick?*

Meanwhile, my dad stared at me, getting gradually more frustrated.

"Are we going to play the game, or what?"

What took us years to realize is that we had two entirely different definitions of "play." Our worldviews were different, and our interests were different. We were connected by wanting to spend time together—but he wanted to play the game as it was designed, and I wanted his company while testing the bounds of the game's design. Whether playing or testing limitations, it just isn't the same alone. And even if we didn't share the same definitions of "play" when it came to video games, we were both people with mechanical, analytical, and dissecting minds. My dad was a mechanic by trade, after all, something he'd pursued after working at the factory. And although it took him some time to discover this "pulling-teeth to keep focus" personality trait of mine, as well as what I considered "play," my mom already knew.

"You were the type of kid with a mind of your own, living in a world of your own," she said as I interviewed her for this book. "The type of kid who would find more interest in tearing things apart and taking a look inside than actually enjoying them as they were."

It was one of the things someone else had to tell you about yourself before *you* realized it, but once you do, a lot of other pieces start to fall in place.

I remember borrowing my dad's toolbox to take apart my brand-new toys. Both he and my mom might have wanted to persuade me to rethink my actions, looking at me and saying something like, "You know you're not going to get any more if you keep breaking them, right?" And giddy little me, recognizing this as an empty threat and ready to rip the wheels off my toy car, would say, "It's okay! I'll put it back together!"

Putting it back together rarely happened as I moved on to the next "how does that work?" project. Machines and their mechanics were my safe place. Taking things apart is where I felt most comfortable—but taking apart a brand-new toy when your parents hope it's the one that will beat last year's isn't a good feeling. It's the same as when you have a dog that tears apart the plush to get to the squeaker. "Mission accomplished," Spot barks. "Now what?"

The worst part is that I would be the one to get upset when they didn't get me the new expensive toy from the commercials. I couldn't realize then that my parents not buying toys wasn't a way of punishment but a function of finances. While living in Rhode Island, they worked split shifts in a Styrofoam factory. They traded schedules on graveyard shifts, and each pulled overtime every week just to afford the roof over our heads and food on the table. What kid has ever realized or understood that struggle when something shiny shows up on TV?

At the same time, I couldn't take apart and understand the inner workings of my parents' minds the way I could those toys. They lived in a hustle world. A world where everyone was asked to keep their head down, bottle their feelings, and push through. Because the sentiment was clear: *No one cares about you out here or owes you anything.* They had to provide for their families, and if you couldn't make the cut or if you went home, that spot would be filled the next day. So, every day and late at night, my parents would come home with a black tar-like soot covering their hands and faces. Some days it was so bad that you could see where they breathed in all the fumes from the light spots under their noses.

The impact of this kind of work stayed with them, too, carrying long-term effects as they began to age. Imagining now what they went through and my incessant asking for more still makes me cringe. Uneasy. I want to go back in time and say, "Mom. Dad. I know you're fighting to give me the best life possible, but it's not worth your health. I'll be fine." But we can't undo the past; we can only move forward with the present.

And in the present, those mechanical parts of my brain are still there. I'll pore over a sentence a hundred times with an itch that something isn't quite right. I'll reformat the document another dozen, even in an early draft. As I write these words on a laptop, I'm aware of the low-level programming and transistors, operating in a binary state, creating logic gates, interacting with the numerous hardware, moving through the data ribbon; the LED screen operating on a range from 0–255 pulse width modification (PWM) to display the words in front of me. And to be honest with you, I'm astounded by all of it. I can't create a laptop from scratch—likely one of those "how does it work?" projects that wouldn't get put back together even today—but knowing how this "toy" works is mind-boggling and relentlessly fascinating.

Something about taking things apart has taught me to see the whole picture. Each day we see the pieces, and from those pieces we make assumptions and educated guesses about the future. That became clearer when I once heard an old Chinese proverb—more accurately, a Taoist parable called "Sāi Wēng Lost His Horse."

The story goes a little something like this:

A farmer and his son owned a cherished stallion crucial for their livelihood. One day the horse ran away, and the neighbor lamented, saying, "Your horse ran away. What terrible luck!"

The farmer responded, "We'll see."

After some days the horse returned, bringing wild mares with it. The neighbor rejoiced, saying, "Your horse is back and brought others. What great luck!"

The farmer, once again, replied, "We'll see."

Subsequently, the farmer's son rode one of the mares, got thrown off, and broke his leg. The neighbor exclaimed, "Your son broke his leg. What terrible luck!"

The farmer's response remained, "We'll see."

Later, soldiers recruited young men for the military, but the farmer's son, still recovering, was spared. The neighbor marveled, "Your boy is spared. What tremendous luck!"

And the farmer, as always, replied, "We'll see."

The story goes on from there and could honestly continue for eternity with enough clever maneuvering. However, I found two significant takeaways:

For one, that is a very nosy, in-your-face neighbor. I'd recommend moving.

Two, taking things apart means seeing parts of a whole. If we zoom out, we can get a clearer picture of our lives. But when we're in it, we see pieces. We see the wheels of the RC car, the dismembered leg of He-Man, the controller on the Super Nintendo, or the RBG cords plugged into the old Zenith TV (ah, the nostalgia). We make judgments on our lives based on the pieces we're living in the present. We can't see the future and often forget or misremember the past. We think we'll keep missing our shots because we have been, or we'll keep coming up in the clear on blackjack because we're on a roll.

Neither is true.

The first time I heard the parable, I didn't believe that. It didn't hit home for me. It was only later on, when I saw a documentary about combat in Afghanistan, that I was able to connect to what the farmer meant. There was a Marine who was on the shorter side standing post during the Battle of Marjah in 2010, two years before my deployment. The documentary was filmed in the middle of intense combat there, and eventually cuts to the Marine providing security. He was shot roughly one inch above the rim of his helmet, dead square in the center. The shot was so dead center, in fact, that it hit the metal plate used to mount his night vision goggles, which is the only thing that saved his life. In the clip, you can see him smiling and chewing gum, laughing at his close call. I remember sitting there thinking:

"How many times in life did he wish that he were just two inches taller?"

These stories show us the importance of seeing the world from various angles and understanding how small details can shape significant aspects of our lives.

Everything is not always what it seems, and one day those pieces will fall into place. No one part of your journey ever tells the whole story, and you must be here to write the rest of it. The good, bad, lucky, unlucky; all of it. The choices to keep moving forward, to keep trying, to do just a little more today than we did yesterday—that's what matters. And so, if you feel yourself trapped in a series of misses, zoom out. Pull back and see where you're directing your focus. Is it on the failures? Is it on the near misses? Is it on the mistakes, the regrets, the fear of what might happen tomorrow if you take that big risk? Can you still see the forest through the trees?

If you come to me and say, "I can't do it. Everything I touch ends in failure. Every shot I make misses," you'll already know my answer.

"We'll see."

I'm kidding. I don't pretend to be as wise as the farmer, and the people and problems we encounter in life deserve a lot more care and attention than a "we'll see" response. But the sentiment still holds up, and learning it made me thankful for my incessant need to tear things apart. Because when it comes down to it, even with their workload and my need to destroy toys, I know my parents enjoyed spending time with me. They were resilient at work and at home. They would let me explore the hidden systems of whatever I could get my hands on (though I never took apart Dad's TV or Super Nintendo), and they didn't push too hard for me to get on the "right" path. Eventually, they embraced that I saw things differently and let me explore in ways that allowed me to be creative and (more often) destructive, within reason. But this doesn't mean it didn't get on their nerves sometimes!

Together, we can look at life as a complex and dynamic puzzle where the pieces may not always make sense in the moment. By taking things apart, whether it's toys or situations, we can learn to see the whole picture and appreciate the interconnectedness of different elements. The story of the Taoist parable, "Sāi Wēng Lost His Horse," should emphasize the importance of perspective and understanding that individual events don't define your entire journey. We should remember in times of adversity to zoom out, assess your focus, and recognize that challenges, failures, and near misses are just pieces of a larger narrative. The key is to keep moving forward, learning, and embracing the unique way each person sees the world, even if it doesn't align with societal expectations.

With all that said, society and school didn't have the same patience as my parents. And the lesson I had yet to learn is that it's a lot harder to understand people, classmates, and myself than it is to take apart a remote-controlled car.

Summary:

- Life events are interconnected and complex. Always remember to look at the bigger picture, and don't jump to conclusions about whether a situation is good or bad.
- Recognize that what might seem negative now could have positive implications in the long run, and vice versa.
- Don't be afraid to go against the grain in life; it might just be what makes you different enough to make an impact.

Chapter 1 Exercise

- Reflect on a moment in your life when you felt out of place or misunderstood. How did this experience shape your perspective or actions moving forward? Write about how you navigated this situation and any lessons you learned along the way.

_____

_____

_____

_____

_____

_____

_____

_____

_____

_____

_____

_____

_____

- Choose a recent challenge in your life that seemed only negative at the time. Write two narratives about this event: one from your initial perspective, focusing on the negative aspects, and another from a "we'll see" perspective, considering potential positive outcomes or lessons. Compare the two narratives to explore the impact of perspective on perception and resilience.

_____

_____

_____

_____

_____

_____

_____

_____

_____

_____

_____

_____

_____

_____

CHAPTER 2

YOUR INTRINSIC WORTH

Never measure your own value

against someone else's scale.

From the start of our lives, we're weighed and measured and, as the saying goes, most of us are found wanting. What we want for and what we want out of life may be different, but the scales don't seem to change. When we're born, Apgar tests conducted minutes after birth determine our health, measurements determine our size, and from infant to toddler to teen, milestones determine our progress. When we get to school, aptitude tests determine our intelligence, classes determine our abilities, and clothes define our friend groups. Later, money determines our status, and often our health, homes, or jobs determine our socioeconomic class.

We're conditioned to people telling us who we are and where we stand in society. We're conditioned to living our lives and creating our value based on the scales and predetermined factors that are constantly used to measure us.

How many followers do you have on social media?
How many likes did this post get?
That person went on a vacation. Can I afford one?
That person got married, and I'm still single.
That person is doing well in their career, and I'm broke.

When I was growing up, even if I was in the place I'd begged to be, it would never feel quite right. If I wanted to have a bunch of friends and changed myself to be accepted by them, it felt wrong. If I wanted to be big and strong to fit in with the muscleheads, I'd get big and strong and still feel out of place. If I wanted to join sports, I'd make the team and then feel like an outcast or a fraud because there was no true passion in it for me. I was searching for a place to belong, and I was measuring my success in that search on someone else's scale.

Nowhere was that clearer than when I started school. To no one's surprise (my parents, especially), I was not an easy kid to get along with on the playground. I would fake being sick and get myself out of class because the bullying, teasing, and not having friends became too intense. I was a loner, but not because I wanted to be. What I never realized then is that I have very particular and unpopular interests, and if you don't share my hobbies, I get very easily flustered on what to talk about.

Often times in school, during lunch, I would stand in line with the rest of the kids, food tray in hand, and just listen to what they were talking about.

"Did you see the new Tamagotchi? My dad bought me one last week."

"We're going to go play baseball after school!"

"I went to the mall yesterday and saw the coolest . . . !"

None of those topics or conversations sounded fun to me. So, when it came down to finding someone to sit with, I would just pick whatever spot was open and stay quiet. And for those few times when someone was brave enough to spark a conversation with me, it would quickly become apparent that we weren't going to be hanging out together after school.

"Hey Korey, do you like sports? We're going to play kickball at recess."

"No thanks," I'd say, "I think I'm going to play with my model cars if anyone wants to join."

To no one's surprise, I was met with awkward silence. I never had an acceptable hobby or interest that merited friends. Kids my age didn't like tearing toys apart or talking about engines and rockets.

Eventually I adopted the perception that was given to me. A switch inside me flipped, and I became that aloof loner that I felt others saw me as. I stopped caring about the repercussions of my actions. I wasn't interested in class so I didn't pay attention, turn in homework, or even show up. If I had friends, they never lasted long. If I hung out with family, I tried to get out of it. I became awkward, and that awkwardness led to me becoming the laughingstock, constantly made fun of for being overweight or low-income—just an easy target in general. I tried to play the part of the loner tough guy, thinking that's what my peers wanted, but everyone called my bluff.

I was the outsider who wanted to break in. I wanted to get my foot in the door. But no matter what I tried, I couldn't seem to, and these experiences began to take a negative toll on my mental health. I became even more acutely aware that I was different, and not in a good way. I wanted to understand these kids like I understood my toys. I tried to find a way to pick apart their brains so that I could say the right things and fit in, but it didn't work like that. They were a mystery to me, and I wasn't worth understanding to them.

In the third grade, I hated school and just wanted to stay home. It seemed like nothing I ever did was right by anyone's standards. If I tried to make friends, I would find out people were making fun of me. If I went to a friend's house, their parents wouldn't like me. If I tried hard in school, I still failed because I was easily distracted.

There's a memory that is burned into my brain. One day I was sitting in class, wrapping an elastic band around my hand, trying to make a pencil launcher. I almost had it ready to go—but I went to make one final adjustment and it slipped, and the pencil went flying right into the face of the girl next to me. I froze, wishing I could pause time and take it back. My face began to burn red with embarrassment and I thought to myself, "Maybe she will keep this between us?" She burst into tears as the entire rest of the class turned and stared daggers at me. No one said a word. They weren't surprised that the weirdo outcast screwed up again. I closed my eyes and wished with every fiber of my being that the floor would open up beneath me and swallow me whole. But it didn't. I just sat there, replaying it over and over in my head—the impact, the tears, the silent shaming. All these oddities of mine began to compound. I had missed many days of school from faking illness, my grades were so poor that my teachers took notice, and they already didn't like me because I was distracted and a class-disrupting nuisance. So they decided to hold me back in my grade.

I remember crying because I knew I had disappointed everyone around me, but I didn't know how to fix it. Feelings of helplessness began to overtake me, and I felt just plain stupid. For most of my grade-school years, I was put in special education classes, never knowing why I was being separated from the "normal" kids. Of course, my parents framed this as a good thing so I wouldn't be discouraged by my failure to adapt, but it was not such a good thing when I was called a "sped" (special ed) and people laughed at me. It made me feel like I had some incurable ailment. I enjoyed my interests, but to everyone else they were somehow wrong. I wanted friends, but it felt like I couldn't be myself in order to make them. I think we all feel that way at some point of our lives.

After receiving medication and participating in one-on-one sessions with the onsite guidance counselors, they decided to push me through to the fourth grade, if only because they didn't want to put up with me another year. I'd say this was also when my depression first emerged, amplified by the feeling of not belonging no matter how many places I tried to fit in.

Would you believe that it took almost twenty-six years for me to realize that all these so-called "weaknesses" were actually gifts in disguise?

There's a famous saying: "Everybody is a genius. But if you judge a fish by its ability to climb a tree, it will live its whole life believing that it is stupid." If there was any flounder trying to flap its way up a tree, it was me in those formative years. Our lives are based on set standards set forth by people that need something of us for their own (typically selfish) reasons, whether related to their job or physical appearance. But it's their standards, not yours—standards that drive us to constantly compare ourselves with others, despite often misperceiving the full truth of others' lives. None of these standards have you in mind; they just represent what you're told to want.

Everything in this world can make you feel inadequate if you let it. Comparison, as they say, is the thief of joy.

Every person's experience, good or bad, teaches lessons built especially for them, and you cannot measure yourself based on the lessons someone else has been given. Even if you relate to my stories, we've all led different lives. As much as I want to connect with you, my scale is not your scale. The goal is to set standards for what *you* want from life. Every day, it's you versus you. It's a challenge between who you are today and who you want to be, because only one version of you can exist in this lifetime.

Remember the farmer and his philosophy of "we'll see."

"We'll see" removes the illusory control that we feel we have in measuring and ranking everything in our lives. It doesn't discount a more significant part we may still have to play, but it does acknowledge that we're not in control of everything. I was held back in the third grade, causing me to graduate and enlist in the Marine Corps one year behind everyone else. This landed me in Afghanistan in 2012 versus 2011, a much more dangerous year with a higher death toll. What if that Marine who wished he were two inches taller had been me? It wasn't, but it might as well have been. And something I fear even more than death—what if I had never met my wife? One tiny change could have taken us on completely different paths.

Throughout my life, I've had a series of "why me?" moments—getting held back, getting placed in special ed, getting sent to California, getting deployed late, not going recon (Marines Special Forces Reconnaissance). Today, with hindsight being 20/20, each of these moments was a blessing I wouldn't change for the world.

But I'm getting ahead of myself.

The point is, if you have ever felt out of place in life, that you had no choice but to live by someone else's standards, remember that those standards are attempting—and failing—to control the chaos of the world with predetermined scales that place people in generalized categories. You don't need to seek validation from anyone who won't be in your will or at your funeral. Why seek attention from people who wouldn't notice if you disappeared tomorrow? Focus on impressing those who truly matter and have a place in your legacy.

I believe in the potential for greatness within everyone. There are so many beautiful souls out there. It's not about looks—it's about recognizing the potential within each person. It upsets me deeply to see someone who doesn't understand just how truly special they are because of societal standards. Don't be too hard on yourself for trying to live up to those flawed standards. We all do it, but you're still here, and that means you still have time to set your own.

Summary:

- Society imposes numerous scales to measure our worth, but these measures do not truly reflect our value as individuals.
- Develop your own metrics for success and happiness that resonate with your values and desires. Ask yourself what you want in life, whether its health, wealth, happiness, having healthy kids, owning a home, or something else. Tailor your goals and aspirations according to what truly matters to you rather than adhering to societal expectations.
- The only competition that matters is the one with yourself. Strive for personal growth and self-improvement rather than comparing yourself to others. Every day, focus on being a better version of yourself.
- As you read, try to maintain a "we'll see" mindset, which acknowledges the uncertainty and uncontrollability of life. This mindset helps you relinquish the illusion of control and understand that outcomes are unpredictable.

Chapter 2 Exercise

Listed below are a handful of internal standards by which people measure themselves and set goals for improvement. Circle the areas that are most important to you at this moment, then create a plan for how you can continue to reach those goals over the next thirty days. Write down the standards that you left un-circled and think about why these are not as important to you.

Achievement of Personal Goals

Creativity and Expression

Financial Independence and Security

Happiness and Contentment

Integrity and Ethical Behavior

Learning and Curiosity

Mental Health

Physical Health

Spirituality and Inner Peace

_____

_____

_____

_____

CHAPTER 3

GOOD PAIN, BAD PAIN

There's always an easier route, but that doesn't mean it will come with the growth you need.

In my life, I've experienced two distinct types of pain: destructive and constructive.

Destructive pain is the type that eats away at who you are and who you're trying to be. It's pain without a legitimate lesson; it just hurts. I concede that there is always a way to spin a bad situation with a positive outlook, but not everyone is able to shift their perspective so easily.

When we think of destructive pain, what may come to mind are stories we often cannot fathom for ourselves: a child with cancer, a loved one lost to a drunk driver, a family being separated, a dream job lost, a business failing. In such stories there may be a bigger plan at work, but these stories are just *too big* to possibly comprehend their threads.

Destructive pain can spark the worst in us—not only hate and disdain for humanity, for life in general, but all the parts of our mind that make us dwell on these feelings without offering any answers in return. People with enough emotional maturity, endurance, and foresight can transform these feelings into something constructive—maybe. But sometimes the lesson itself is just pain, and it sucks.

On the other side, there's constructive pain. This is the type of pain that comes with a sense of purpose and the potential for personal development. This pain could be considered uncomfortable, or the annoying "I'd rather be doing something else" sort of pain. The most straightforward example of constructive pain can be found in the gym; you don't go there expecting to be comfortable. You go there to face the resistance of the machines and gravity on your body and develop a mindset of *I will endure this pain now because a better, healthier version of me is on the other side.* You go there to *construct.*

It's pain that propels you toward a better tomorrow, even if it hurts like hell today.

The challenge most people face is an inability or unwillingness to separate the two types of pain. It's *pain,* after all. Meanwhile, we're hardwired to avoid pain and limit discomfort. So, the question is *How can we tell the difference?* And the other, far more difficult question to answer is *Can we extract something constructive from something destructive?*

When I was five years old, my parents, though never married, were still together. We all lived in a little apartment in Rhode Island, and both my parents worked grueling late-night shifts. It was clear to me that neither of them wanted to do that, that neither of them wanted the life they had. But they saw their circumstances as constructive pain, using it as motivation to provide stability for me and work toward making their next move. Situations like these, however, can also be fueled by a sort of broken optimism that obscures destructive pain, that makes life feel like an endless grind that never sharpens to a point.

The life my parents put together for me and my younger brother and sister was built out of love, but it came with a massive struggle for them. My mom loved us with all her heart, but when she got angry, we knew it. I would get my butt whupped because I would "talk back," completely underestimating the power of this five-foot-two Portuguese/Italian woman I called Mom. After enough whuppings, I had to learn something, anything constructive. I had to break it down, take it apart, and ask why. Why was she angry?

The answer should have been obvious, I was acting like an a–s.

My dad wasn't a big guy but his presence was loud, even when he was quiet. To this day he is one of the strongest guys I've ever met. But at five feet, ten inches and a buck eighty on his heaviest day, it made no sense. He could move and lift things that would give me a run for my money, even at the peak of my weight-lifting days. Add to that he always looked younger than his age, with a full head of black hair, a clean-shaven face, and sharp wrinkles whenever he got them. People joked that he was "growing back in time."

Maybe he was—the man never stopped moving.

You could spot my parents from a distance with their grease-covered work uniforms and the soot on their cheeks. When my dad shook your hand, you could feel the callouses—you could feel your hand swallowed up in them. The permanent darkening on their fingers and knuckles showed the toll their work had on their bodies. But that always made me respect both of them—people with no "wasted steps," always moving with a purpose.

The difference, I discovered, is what that purpose is.

At five years old, soon after my little brother had been born, I knew my dad wanted to get away. He wanted to leave our impoverished environment and start a new life with us in another state to focus on his passion—engineering. He was tired of the daily struggle, the destructive pain of sleeping three hours each night just to go back to work again, not seeing his family, not having any time left to enjoy himself. Punching in and punching out for years, decades, a lifetime.

Anger built up in my dad as he felt he could achieve so much more if he got away—if he got *out*. But that was not my mother's plan—she valued family more than anything else in the world. To risk something steady to gamble on something uncertain—a bird in the hand was worth two in the bush to her. And to be honest, I understood why.

They were my very own rock and a hard place.

Yet, somehow, my father convinced my mother to take that step and leave Rhode Island.

So what happened?

We moved to Jacksonville, Florida, to live with my grandmother and aunt. After my baby brother Justin had been born, and when my dad saw how fast our family was expanding, he knew we needed to make a change. It was no small feat to get my mom to leave Rhode Island. Even today, I don't know how he managed it.

However, in just a few short months in this new house, my parents' arguments and animosity grew. You could often hear my parents speaking loudly from across the house.

"*Tom, we need to get our own home, and I've still yet to find a job close enough.*"

"*Would you relax, Sandy? This is better for us as a family, just give it time.*"

I could almost hear my mom's eyes roll in disbelief as they walked into a room and shut the door to muffle their bickering.

She resented the move because the risk had yet to pay off, and he resented the lack of support for the same reason.

And me? I was caught in the middle.

Screaming matches became commonplace. So common, in fact, that I thought that's just how people communicated. I was five—it seemed to make sense. *To be heard, scream. I'd better write that down.*

And one day, I wanted to get in on that chaotic conversation.

It was early on a Saturday morning and I was sitting alone at the dining room table, munching on a bowl of cereal and watching *George of the Jungle* on VHS.

Suddenly, their loud conversation rapidly grew into an unintelligible screaming match in the other room.

I turned up the TV louder, trying to drown out the noise. Then the door swung open, and even turning the volume to the max couldn't drown them out. I couldn't hear the movie anymore, and my cereal was getting soggy. I was just trying to enjoy my Saturday morning. And that's when I did something that altered my entire life.

I shouted, "Dad! I can't hear the TV!"

In retrospect, it was a daring move. But I was desensitized, so I couldn't see what I did wrong. *I screamed to be heard.*

My dad's entire demeanor and body language shifted.

He got right up in my face, finger pointed at me, right between my eyes . . .

"Don't you f——ing tell me to shut up!"

To my recollection, I never said "shut up"—those words weren't even in my vocabulary at the time. But I'm sure with my tone of voice, that's exactly how he heard it.

Perception is often reality.

As my mom watched him charge a little too aggressively and get up in my face, she stepped in and pushed him off like a mama bear protecting her cub.

"Don't you talk to him that way!" she yelled, raising a hand like she was going to hit him.

In what felt like slow motion, my dad grabbed and bear-hugged her to stop the potential slap—before they both realized his mistake: that my mom was now pregnant with my little sister.

He set her down. The energy shifted.

You could hear a pin drop as they stared at each other.

I sat there, observing them, a sinking feeling in my gut indicating that something was wrong. Their body language relaxed, their once-red eyes turned somber, and, most notably, a heavy silence lingered in the air. *This isn't like the other times*, I thought to myself. In my young mind, I sensed that this marked a turning point for them, for me. It was as if they had snapped, much like a rubber band stretched to its limits. The tension had built up, reaching its breaking point, and just like that it whipped back to a state of ease—happy and relieved of the burden, yet damaged in the process. Witnessing this real-time unraveling between my parents, I started to cry.

I should have watched TV in my room.

I should have kept my mouth shut.

Was it worth speaking up? I didn't even get to finish the movie . . .

What are they going to do now? This is bad.

As the dust settled and with tears still in my eyes, the air remained heavy.

They separated right then and there.

Soon after, my mother took me, my brother, and my soon-to-be sister back to Rhode Island while my dad stayed.

For most of my life, I carried that guilt as destructive pain. I made myself the catalyst of my parents' separation and the arbiter of their unhappiness. And whether that resentment from them existed or not, whether it was directed at me or not—it didn't matter. The effects it had on me were real. I resented my mom for leaving because as a child, the person I connected with the most (especially on a mechanical level) had been my dad. Now I was going to be stuck with a mom a thousand miles away from my dad, a mom who didn't understand the way my little mind worked like my dad did, a mom unable to share any of those masculine moments with me as a young man. That was my dad's job, and he was doing it well when he was with me.

And deep down I knew their issues were with each other, not me. So why was I paying the price for it? It didn't seem fair to me.

But eventually I came to realize that this experience provided an enduring lesson: that of being *resilient*. We can't always control what happens in our lives, but what we can control is what we do with the adversities we face. My parents' separation drastically affected my life's trajectory, and no matter how hard I might have tried at five years old, I couldn't have changed that.

Who would I be at eighty years old if my parents had stayed together? And who will I be now, considering they didn't?

It doesn't matter. In that alternate reality, I'd be unrecognizable to myself today. The only thing that matters is making the best of whatever reality I'm currently in. Your story is being written one day at a time; it's up to you to adapt that narrative to whatever reality you're in and ensure that your story plays out with the best version of you.

As a child, however, I could not yet comprehend this truth. So, in true childlike fashion, I was willing to do anything to get my distant dad's attention while he stayed behind in Florida, starting the new life he had dreamed of—alone.

But as we all know, if left unguided, we can find attention in all the wrong places.

Summary:

- Destructive pain has no apparent beneficial lesson and only produces emotional or physical torment. Having the emotional maturity to turn destructive pain into constructive lessons is essential but seldom easy.
- Constructive pain inspires personal growth in some way; it is temporary discomfort that's a means to improvement.

- Understanding the difference between constructive and destructive pain is crucial for maintaining emotional well-being and supporting healthy decision-making.
- How you perceive and interpret others' actions or words can have significant consequences on your self-perception. Just as I incorrectly felt that my parents' separation was solely my fault, it's important to realize that perceptions are not absolute truths.

Chapter 3 Exercise

Write about a time in your life when you have turned destructive pain into a positive outcome.

Ex: If someone lost an arm in an accident, they could write a book or start a YouTube channel inspiring others who have been through similar experiences. That could lead to them being able to make an income through speaking engagements.

_____

_____

_____

_____

_____

_____

_____

_____

_____

_____

_____

_____

LEGACY MINDSET

CHAPTER 4

REFLECTION THAT MATTERS

You should not dwell on your past but revisit it as often as needed to validate that you're on the right track and create a positive connection with it. Don't regret—react.

My dad became a mechanic in Florida. He achieved what I thought was his dream, and I admired him for it. And the more I did, the more I saw him as a Hero, and the more I resented my mom and our life in Rhode Island. I no longer valued her opinion and no longer cared when people tried to correct me about it. In my mind, everybody was in my way, bad talking the man I thought to be the only positive influence in my life. The things I admired about my dad—his persistence, his mechanical mind, his goal setting—these were the things that people seemed to dislike the most.

Fleeting comments from my family would plague my brain for days at a time.

"Thomas worked too much."

"Family should come first."

"Your dad should be here, not chasing a dream."

But what I liked about my dad were the same exact things I liked about me, even if I didn't know it at the time. While we didn't always see eye to eye, I felt understood by him. The problem was, at that age I couldn't take the evidence, reexamine that scene at the breakfast table, and see why each person acted the way they did.

I was just too young. All I knew was that I missed my dad—a lot. We were *so alike*.

We shared a passion for engines, cars, guns, trucks, dirt bikes—everything mechanical. As he worked as a mechanic, I realized how much I admired his profession. There were respected mechanics in our apartment complex who helped people by getting their cars running so they could get to work—helping to solve some of their other problems, too, as a result.

I loved and respected the fact that we, as humans, could create these fantastic, miraculous machines with just our minds, hands, and a little ingenuity. As I heard more about my dad's life in Florida through his phone calls—"Looks like I'm going to buy a new home soon," "I just got a new car," "You can ride on my new motorcycle when you come visit"—it opened my mind to what is possible, breaking down my mental walls of poverty, making me think bigger than I ever had. I stared at the water-stained ceiling of our apartment, dreaming of going to space or building my own racecar.

Every summer when school was out, I would fly solo to Florida for a few weeks and spend time with my dad. When I saw him, the first things I would connect with him on were mechanical in nature. I would ask him, "Have you built anything new?" And he would give me a half-cracked smile and say something like, "You bet, I just got a new truck!" or "Sorry buddy, not this time." But when he did build or get something new, it was like show-and-tell. He would put me in his new truck and let me ask all the questions I wanted, or he would show me the old junkyard engine he was working on. I remember thinking, *Wow, my dad is a genius! I can't even remember where I put my shoes, yet Dad has nuts, bolts, tools, and car parts all over, and he knows how to bring them to life!* Dad would take me for rides in whatever his new "toy" was and we'd do burnouts and drifts in dirt lots and back roads. I just loved that we could have so much fun with things built from our bare hands; I was in awe.

Dad could restore a hopeless situation, like a car with an engine that sat for years collecting rust, to what it used to be—or something better. With a simple plan, structured thinking, some twists of a wrench, and precise timing, he would breathe life into that old car as it fired up for the first time in eons. And that made him my Hero.

And now that he was gone, living far away, everything seemed wrong. I remember sitting in my room and feeling like the house was empty even when everyone was home. I stared at the model cars I had on my old beat-up oak shelf and felt as if each one signified a lost connection. *I'm being punished,* I thought to myself, reflecting on the big fight between my parents. I looked away from the model cars and was reminded how completely alone I felt.

I looked at my feet dangling off the bed, dwelling on the fact that everyone else seemed completely fine with this new situation. Like nothing ever happened.

"F—k 'em," I said quietly to myself. "I guess it's just me."

Suddenly, I felt as if a weight lifted from one side of my body to the other; it was my sadness shifting over to anger. I hated how the world could be so cruel. I just wanted to run away and start over with new people I didn't have to decode, people who would understand me and empathize with me. In a last-ditch effort to save the last bit of faith I had in my parents getting back together, I sat there and thought to myself, *Maybe if I hurt myself really badly, they will have to work together to sort me out,* like I was a broken project they had to fix as a team. With these terrible thoughts rushing over me, I felt exhausted, that I was a burden just being idle. But nowhere in this plan was there a place for me to let anyone around me know that I was struggling in a healthy, productive way.

I fell asleep in broad daylight and when I woke up, I was not the same person as the day before. I was angrier, like when you wake up after something traumatic and remember that it wasn't a dream. This was the beginning of a new me—and it was not ideal.

As I got older, it only got worse. My feelings of hatred and disdain, even my suicidal tendencies that I learned to repress for fear of judgment quickly became things I didn't care if people knew about. My music tastes became deeper, darker, and more violent as I got into heavy metal and rap. I would sit at the dinner table with a CD player and my headphones on full blast, somehow playing louder on the outside of the headphones than inside, so that everyone could hear the cuss words, gunshots, and screaming from artists like Eminem and 50 Cent.

"Korey, I don't want you listening to that crap!" my mom would shout to try and break through the deafening loudness.

"Whatever, Mom, I like it," I'd reply, simultaneously thinking, *Really? All the s—t I'm going through, and you're going to try and take my coping mechanism away? What else do you want to take?*

My nasty responses were always met with an argument that separated me from my mom a little more each time. Afterward, I'd lock myself in my room and continue to listen to whatever I felt like, mostly music that reinforced my emotions that the world sucked. Over time my mom conceded. She was a single mom with three kids, and she couldn't dump all her energy into one child. But Dad wasn't there, so I didn't care.

When I got to middle school, I knew it was getting bad. Half of the time, I was bullied for being overweight and an outcast, and that manifested in me taking my anger out on some poor soul who was probably more similar to me than I realized, just so someone else felt like s—t too. My grades began to suffer, resulting in my mom having to beg the school for a "mercy pass" several times; I'd make myself unwelcome in class by drawing violent scenes depicting guns and gang violence; I'd get into trouble by experimenting with fire; and, of course, I'd hang out with the wrong crowd. I was constantly fighting for my dad's attention, and I intentionally got my butt kicked to get my mom's empathy—yet I'd still denounce both of them, claiming I didn't need them or anyone else. I tormented the people around me, including myself, just for a chance to let people know I was there—and I was hurting.

The message I was hearing from the universe seemed crystal clear: "Korey, you're a failure. Give up."

I'd like to give you the good news that I found the right path as a teenager and I've been on that path ever since—but it isn't true. From five years old until I hit the middle of high school, my pain continued to be destructive. I played the victim because, in many ways, I knew that I *had* gotten dealt some bad hands.

We have all been victims at some point in our lives. But we must remember that our lives are *ours*, the only ones we have, and that no one owes us an explanation for our circumstances; we have no one to look at but our own selves for a better life.

If we look for what we're owed, holding our hand out and waiting for the payment we feel we're due, we'll be holding our hand out for a long time—maybe forever. We all deserve help and kindness, but no one owes you either. No matter how hard your life is or how deserving you think you are, good things aren't guaranteed.

But boy, are we thankful when we receive it.

When we desperately *need* it.

Realizing that life doesn't owe us anything, especially love, was an important lesson, and I applied this logic later in life to my marriage with Tiffany when I made some ground rules before deciding to tie the knot. One of the first rules I set, all those years ago while I was stationed in California, was "If we ever disagree on something, we talk. None of that yelling nonsense, please." I followed up with, "If we don't want to end up like most couples, we can't do what most couples do." That lesson stemmed from that childhood breakfast table, but even as I said it I hadn't fully realized it.

You can't expect explanations for your circumstances, and you must embrace that adversity is part of the journey. Even some of the worst stories you can imagine can be transformed into lessons of gratitude and personal responsibility. We must learn from all the little pieces of our experience, appreciate unexpected sources of support, turn adversity into strength, and approach life with an open heart.

Summary:

- Life doesn't owe us anything; waiting for external factors to provide fulfillment or solve problems won't get you very far.
- Reflection on past experiences, even painful ones, can lead to personal growth and be a guide for making better choices in the future.
- Acknowledging the pain and adversities from your past is essential, but so is understanding the importance of moving forward and taking control of your life.

Chapter 4 Exercise

Reflect on a period in your life that felt overwhelmingly destructive. With the benefit of hindsight, can you identify any constructive outcomes or lessons learned from that period? How have these experiences shaped the person you are today?

_____

_____

_____

_____

_____

_____

_____

_____

_____

_____

_____

_____

LEGACY MINDSET

CHAPTER 5

ASSIGN VALUE ACCORDINGLY

The difference between who you are now and who you want to be tomorrow is what you do today.

At the start of this book, I talked about "legacy" as being that which lives on in the people whose lives we've impacted. The things that don't live on in quite the same way—that is, material possessions and wealth—I'd initially glossed over for good reason. My goal has been to first impress upon you that true value is found in our character and choices, but that doesn't mean possessions or wealth is meaningless. We call them *valuables*, after all, for a reason. The critical distinction, however, is in *how* we assign value to objects versus character and choices, and in what order we assign them in our priority list.

The trend of instant gratification and the "get results quick" mindset is prevalent in our society today, especially in those driven to make a drastic lifestyle change. When we want something, we usually don't want to wait for it; we want it now—so much so that we will work harder, pull out loans, stack up debt, try that weight loss supplement, and trade in our perfectly good cars for new ones. Anything we can do to close the gap between today and the future, we jump on it, even if it means borrowing happiness from tomorrow at a high interest rate.

Meanwhile, swiftly acting on what we think we want without first properly assigning values to it encourages us to make bad decisions. It's easy to get your priorities wrong, even when everything seems to be going right at first glance. We all want change to happen *now*, and we usually envision that change in the form of material possessions. Let's be honest, we have all dreamed of that one day when we're "rich" and can change our situation, whatever "change" means for you. Most of us wish we could have a bigger material impact on those around us. Who wouldn't want to help friends and family retire early or feed starving families, all without sacrificing their own lifestyle? That type of impact comes at one of only three expenses: the cost of your time, the cost of your money, or some combination of both—and most of us value what little time we have, so we wait until we have the money to truly give back at scale.

But with this goal often comes a very large oversight: changing anything starts with changing yourself. If you want a life you've never had, you must do things you've never done, and that starts with developing a priority list based on the *legacy mindset*. Having a legacy mindset is about learning to prioritize and assign value to serving people first, then living off the reciprocity it brings back to you and your family for generations to come. It calls to mind the adage that those who plant trees, knowing they will never sit in the shade, have at least started to understand the meaning of life.

So, when we begin assigning value, we must analyze exactly *why* things are valuable to us, or we risk making decisions that will not only set us back but crush our internal drive when we realize we've miscalculated what really matters.

Assigning proper value helps you develop a mind of your own instead of being influenced by what the rest of the world thinks is important. *Why do we want that car? Is it to drive, or is it to show off? Why do we want that vacation? Is it to experience a new culture and learn, or to take a picture of that scenic spot and remind everyone else they aren't there? Why do you want that high-level job? Is it to show the people in your life that you're capable?* Despite your answers to these types of questions, what's most important is that you identify your reasons for acting *before* you embark on the journey, even if they are selfish in nature.

We all hate liars, but for some reason when we lie to ourselves to justify something, we're okay with it—as long as the lesson that comes down the road doesn't punch us in the face. This leads to the universal pitfall of assigning value: most people do it too late. If you told me you wanted a big house, I would ask, "What are you willing to give up and sacrifice for this possession that you can't take with you? Your family? Your friends? Your mental health? Your comfort? Every goal has a cost, and you must be sure you're willing to pay that cost in advance."

This is something that I learned the hard way.

As a teen, when we still lived in our apartment, there was a place at the end of the train tracks called Blueberry Hill where people would go every weekend with their dirt bikes, four-wheelers, and go-karts. I never saw a blueberry, but there were colossal mountains of sand and dirt piled as high as the industrial complexes that hid them (and us) from the police. It wasn't necessarily illegal to be there, but generally speaking, it wasn't legal either. It was just one of those great spots, and as a kid on a beaten-down bike, I was extremely jealous of the kids who played there after school. I pedaled as fast as I could on rusted chains, uncovered seats, and loose handlebars to keep up with them, but with one turn of the throttle or foot to the gas, they left me in their literal dust.

Every weekend that I could, I would head down to the train tracks and try to join in. With two-wheels and no motor, that wasn't happening; I was merely a spectator to all the fun. And, likely out of jealousy more than anything else, I began to compare what I and my family had to what other people had, assigning value to their possessions early on. To me, possessions equaled freedom, and freedom equaled fun. Determined to reverse-engineer the other kids' seemingly stressless life, I started to study people's emotions and attached them to what they owned. If somebody had a nice dirt bike, I would take a mental note on how much they smiled or how friendly they were when they spoke. This wasn't just at Blueberry Hill, either. I watched people everywhere. I examined what they had and analyzed how they acted. I would compare seemingly happy people with nice things to other people who seemed genuinely unhappy—people all around me whose misery I felt, like my mom and dad and everyone else who lived in our apartments; the people who didn't have new dirt bikes but old cars, cars that sometimes crashed people's lives over their heads by refusing to start; people reliant on price-gouging mechanics because they couldn't miss a day at work. People who *just couldn't quite make it work.*

I was starkly aware of the split between the haves and have-nots, the big spenders and big-time brokes, the seemingly "rich" and the "poor."

If I saw someone come around our place with a little more money than most—the type who would drive a Hummer or a new Lexus—I tried to study them to see how they prioritized things like wealth, health, happiness, and relationships. And, if you can imagine my awkwardness at that age, I wasn't subtle. I would stand there and stare at them or analyze their car as I tried to take apart their engine in my head, even with the hood closed shut. Add in the fact that my entire family spent nights talking about how great those people were, how their cars were so lovely, how everything was going right for them. . .

I remember Mom saying things like, "Hey, son, when you get older, are you going to buy me a new car like that? Will you buy me a pretty place to live like they have?" I would say, "Of course," understanding how much my family prized such things.

I tried to reverse-engineer that kind of success by understanding these people's priority lists, but I couldn't see how they prioritized things. Was it wealth first, then family? Was it health, wealth, then family? Was it family first, then came all the good stuff? It doesn't matter if you have all the parts to an engine if you can't put the pieces together in an order that makes it work. But as a young teen I had to start somewhere, and there was no future to think of; there was only now.

So I made an extremely complex plan with the knowledge I had to work with:

Priority One (Monetary): Get money.
Priority Two (Possessional): Buy a dirt bike.

That was it. If I did that, I'd be one step closer to the success and smiles I was craving, no matter the cost. The only question was: *how?*

Despite the complexities of my life at the time—the missing father figure, puberty and depression in full swing, crippling self-doubt, bullying—my foolproof plan made me blissfully ignorant to my problems and helped me see a light at the end of the tunnel. I had a way out—cruising full throttle on a four-speed, clutchless-shifting, rocket-speed lime-green 90cc Baja dirt bike (a timeless beauty). But first I had to accomplish step one.

To make money, I needed a job. Not only would a job get me closer to my rocket, but it would help me get something for myself other than food stamps, WIC (Women, Infants, and Children) assistance, second- or seventh-hand clothes, and welfare program Christmas gifts. I'd had enough of all of them.

So, at thirteen years old, I said: "I'm getting my first real job so I can do whatever I want without anyone giving me permission. Take that, suckers!"

Or something to that effect. So, as I began asking around for jobs, my middle-school bus driver offered to take me under his wing on his side-income paper route and pay me under the table for $60 a week. It was going to be tough hours, but there weren't a lot of jobs for kids my age, so I accepted it, at least partly because he was the "cool guy" bus driver who would buy cigarettes and alcohol for the older kids. All red flags now, but nothing would get in the way of getting my own dirt bike.

My mom had to work late most days, and I was out of the house and on the 7:30 a.m. school bus before anyone noticed. That was a good thing and a bad thing. To me it was great because I had some time for true independence, to experiment with smoking and alcohol—something I saw a few of those successful people doing. Little did I understand at the time that "nothing good happens after midnight."

I was too young to notice all the signs then, but that bus driver would do things like talking to me with his hand on my inner thigh and leaving his hand under my seat so that whenever I threw the papers out of the car window I would sit on his hand, and he would do other creepy "oopsie" type stuff. As we drove, he would talk about having sex with his girlfriend, who I think was another bus driver—or a lie.

Looking back, he raised every red flag known to man (and apparently even child), but I managed to ignore them. My eye was on the lime-green prize, and he gave me the opportunity.

This creepy, horrible stuff went on for months, and eventually this guy made physical contact with probably every part of my body at least once. At that point I couldn't deny there was a problem, that what was happening was wrong. But still, I dealt with it. The "success" I saw for myself seemed attainable, and self-dignity was not yet on my priority list, or it was at least very far down. I just wanted the paycheck. I wanted the bike. I wanted a different life.

Looking back, the only thing I would've changed is turning that man into the authorities after I got my last check.

It was only later that the bus driver's brother, who turned out to be a family friend, informed me that his behavior was well-known and warned me to stay away from him. Regardless, driven by a depressive "tough guy" syndrome, I allowed this whole routine to continue for over a year, believing I could always escape if it got worse.

I'm honestly lucky it didn't. The bus driver started testing my limitations by telling me false stories about other kids who wanted to have sexual interactions with him. But I was too scared to lose what I was working so hard to achieve, so I still tolerated the situation.

Finally, I'd saved enough money to quit the paper route (unfortunately, I did still have to ride that same bus to school). I counted my cash that I kept in a box under my bed—$780. I felt the smile on my face begin to form, knowing that when I got to school the next day I would ask Chris, one of the kids with "successful" parents, who I knew had the Baja dirt bike, how he liked it, because "I'm getting one too." And I did. I offered him that subtle flex, and man, it felt great.

To my surprise, Chris said, "My dad just bought me a bigger one. I'm selling mine now."

"No way! Are you serious?"

"How about $400?" he asked.

"Hell yes."

"Awesome. My dad and I can bring it by your house this weekend."

I literally could not focus on school the whole rest of that week. *This must be what the "successful" people feel like all the time.*

Saturday finally arrived. A beautiful sunny day, and the perfect day to ride. You have no idea the feeling of success and achievement I had when Chris and his dad pulled up to our apartment in his nice new truck and unloaded the bike onto the street. I could see the lime-green sticking over the bed. *Woah, that's actually mine!*

And then I remember thinking to myself, *I don't think everyone has to go through adversities like that to get nice things, but I have a lot to learn.* The thought faded when it was time for me to review the details with them.

Chris's dad seemed genuinely happy to get me all squared away; it was that "successful" sort of happiness I'd come to admire. He even gave me some free riding gear to ensure I was safe. The stuff I wished I could afford was just being handed to me because they had the heart to give it freely. That stuck with me; I wanted to be like that. Chris's father also offered some good advice on bike upkeep as I handed him, not Chris, the $400.

"See you at the hill!" I shouted to Chris as they left.

I turned back and admired my new dirt bike, glistening in the sun, before I looked over the engine, started it, and just watched it run. *I did it. This is mine.* I got my helmet on, put up the kickstand, and took my lime-green beauty down the street to get a feel.

It was amazing. It was everything I ever wanted. The wind pushed against my body with every twist of the throttle, increasing speed with every shift. The power and freedom felt completely surreal. I wasn't having bad thoughts of hurting myself or others. I didn't think about my grades or what my parents would say about my new bike. I just rode and enjoyed every second of it—for about fifteen minutes.

I forgot to mention one small thing.

You see, when Chris's dad brought my new dirt bike over, he said, "Hey, this bike is quick. You really don't need to take it into fourth gear unless you're trying to go highway speeds. Just stay between gears one and three, and you'll be good."

If he had known my obsession with discovering things for myself, of taking things apart and seeing how they tick, he wouldn't have said anything at all. So, as I cruised, I glanced down at the shifter. *Fourth gear, huh? That sounds fun.*

I took my bike up a road with a pretty steep incline. Once I began approaching the apex of the hill, I knew it turned into a long stretch of road. I hit the brakes and came to a dead stop, staring down from the top of the hill.

What better chance to open the throttle . . . fourth gear, anyone?

Then I started going. Perfectly balanced, tires gripping, wind through my helmet, I proceeded to go full throttle through the gears.

First.

A little slow.

Second.

This is nice. Really nice.

Third.

Oh wow, I'm really picking up speed here.

And finally. . .

Fourth!

As I shifted into fourth gear, my front wheel hit a bump and lifted off the ground. I shifted my weight forward to counter the momentum, and *BOOM*. The wheel hit hard, and the handlebars started slapping back and forth like in all those funny viral videos of people crashing bikes. (This was, sadly, before social media was big. That could have been my career!)

The front wheel locked up, and I felt myself suddenly become weightless. I flew over the handlebars and everything slowed down. The bike skidded and flipped on the ground behind me as I began to tumble, *hard*. My helmet hit the ground with such force that it cracked in half, leaving me sliding down the road with a partial helmet and skin ripping gorily off my back and shoulder. I didn't feel a thing except adrenaline and shame. Bloodied, torn-up, layered with asphalt and tar and plastic, I got up quickly, embarrassedly hoping no one saw me. Just when I thought I was in the clear and ready to start assessing the damage, the pain hit. It shot up my back and shoulders, and then this sweet old lady ran outside from her house with a roll of paper towels to stop the bleeding. All wounds were thankfully superficial. Then I saw it—my brand-new bike, my lime-green beauty—completely trashed.

I was so heartbroken and upset that I damn near cried. It was almost like I thought someone owed me a new bike for my misfortune, like breaking a brand-new phone as you walk out of the store before you get the case on. Of course, no one owed me, but I felt that way. All the time and energy, the late nights, the trauma, and I was left with scrap metal. It just wasn't fair. I wanted all the sympathy or pity the universe could give me. I remember thinking that I could only imagine how adults felt with their homes or cars (I wasn't aware at the time of how insurance worked). *How did they sleep at night? What's the point of cool s—t if I can't enjoy it the way it was intended? Why is fourth gear there if I can't use it? They should just remove it if it's too "dangerous!"*

In the moment I couldn't see how my lack of humility allowed me to play the victim. But gradually my self-pity party began to subside, and I began putting the pieces together.

I spent over a year and four hundred hard-earned dollars for a lesson. Sure, I was a kid at the time, but there are countless other decisions I've made in my life that ended up teaching me a similar lesson.

I'd focused my vision of "success" on something material. I sacrificed my already fragile mental health for a physical item. And whether it lasted fifteen minutes or a few years, I had tied my sense of happiness to it, so that when the dirt bike was gone it took my happiness too.

But that's not the way life is supposed to be.

I realized later that, even if I hadn't crashed the bike, I was so blinded by having it that I completely overlooked the fact that I had nowhere to put the dang thing! We didn't have a garage, and I couldn't bring it into the house. The broken heap of scrap ended up sitting in the back of the apartment building so long that it rusted beyond repair and got thrown away.

Not evaluating my priorities led to a quick, uncalculated decision. Was it all worth it?

The truth is, in some ways, yes. Though short, it was a fun fifteen minutes where I experienced an instructive balance between two extremes, which I like to call "min-max."

More importantly, while I made the mistake of not thinking more cautiously about my long-term relationship with my dirt bike, the journey of earning it helped me to overcome negative, unhelpful thoughts. I learned that some items can bring you happiness that reaches even beyond the pleasure their physical properties bring once you've actually acquired them—that, through action, one can experience the real pride that comes with dedication, perseverance, and sacrifice.

Every day we are faced with small choices in our life that determine the quality of our tomorrows. But this is our opportunity to remember that each small choice can move us closer to our goal. The key is that you do not make the same mistake I did—focusing on the material effects. Instead, I want you instead to focus on the *impact* of achieving your goal.

I've said that legacy is not the same as wealth. It's true, and I still want to warn against having a "millionaire mindset." While there are many common challenges you no longer have to endure when you're wealthy, we must remember that wealth itself doesn't solve all our problems. Wealthy people who seem "carefree" often struggle in ways we cannot see on the surface—we're *all* battling something no one knows about. This is something I could not understand as a kid.

Wealth may afford opportunity, but we don't have to be financially rich to make a meaningful impact on each other, so long as we get our priorities straight. If we set our goals strictly on the material object of our desire, we'll find that the joy it brings fades over time; but if we take the time to consider *why* we want a certain thing, we can better assess if our goals align with what we want. In other words, if we take the time to consider the *why*, we can prioritize what is most important. We can make sure our will is to change the world for the better, to set goals on helping other people, on something outside ourselves, thereby leaving a legacy that makes a real and lasting difference.

Just remember: After you get the car, you will want a nicer one. After you get the house, you will want a bigger one. After you get the money, you will want more.

Just be sure to ask yourself: Is what I want worth the sacrifice?

But what if you already made that quick decision? What if you already bought the house, the car, the new fancy gadget?

One word: repurpose. Transform your possessions into vessels for impact. Discover how to use them in ways that help others, that contribute positively to society. Remember this: there is no such thing as self-made success. Anything and everything you consider a success in your life has come in part from the support of others. When I look at my mission, I understand that anything I have gained, either at home or in my businesses, would've been impossible without my teams and customers. I am not self-made; therefore, I like to repurpose my assets for those who brought me success, and you should too.

For example, if you bought a new sports car, you could invite struggling veterans to a track day. You could give terminal kids rides and make their day just a little brighter. You could raffle rides for charity.

Bought that huge home? Dedicate some space for entertaining people you care about or hosting charity events.

Bought the new gadget? Give it away if it ultimately doesn't bring you happiness, or share it with the people around you who could benefit.

These are all things that I do with anything "fancy" that I own; it's my way of giving back and ensuring nothing I own is purely out of selfishness. If I get to enjoy something, I want others to enjoy it as well, because the world we have built together is the only reason I have what I have. So how do I ensure that any major action I take won't leave me in a pool of regret? I review my personal priorities from most to least important:

Priority 1: Does this positively impact my legacy?

Priority 2: Will this make my Fallen brothers proud?

Priority 3: Does this help my family?

Priority 4: Can this be used for positive impact?

Priority 5: Does this improve my wealth?

Priority 6: Does this reduce the noise in my life?

Not all priorities need to be met. However, they should be met in order.

Here are some personal examples of how I can apply my priority set:

Buying a Log Cabin

Priority 1: Does this positively impact my legacy? **Yes**, it will be left for generations to come.

Priority 2: Will this make my Fallen brothers proud? **Yes**, if I use it to help people and not as a bragging right.

Priority 3: Does this improve my family? **Yes**, because time away from electronics and outdoors is healthy.

Priority 4: Can this be used for positive impact? **Yes**, because I can do coaching seminars there and help people improve their lives. I can also use it as an Airbnb and donate the un-booked days to military and first responders.

Priority 5: Does this improve my wealth? **Yes**, if the location is right, it will create a positive financial return on investment.

Priority 6: Does this help reduce the noise in my life? **Yes and no**. It will help me decompress while I'm there, and it will be fully managed by a service when I'm not. However, it will degrade over time, and it will begin to consume my time and energy.

Buying a Luxury Car

Priority 1: Does this positively impact my legacy? **No**, because by the time I die, it will likely be beaten up and worthless; meanwhile it will cost me in insurance and taxes.

Priority 2: Will this make my Fallen brothers proud? **Possibly**, because while my brothers would be proud of my achievement in acquiring the car, they might later tell me that it is a waste if they feel I have not done other good things in my life.

Priority 3: Does this improve my family? **No**, not likely, since it's not something we can enjoy much together.

Priority 4: Can this be used for positive impact? **Yes**, because I can give rides to people in need or even use it for fundraising.

Priority 5: Does this improve my wealth? **No**, because its value will depreciate. Furthermore, while the car can be used to catch the attention of people with whom I may do business, that's not the type of attention I typically want.

Priority 6: Does this help reduce the noise in my life? **No**, because it adds the noises of registration, insurance, and the logistics of constantly parking far away from others, as I would fear the car being damaged.

As you can see, one of these situations is more aligned with my values than the other. Hopefully, the right answer is obvious.

Consistently applying my priorities to my life ensures that my decisions serve my legacy: they will be financially smart, good for my family, and will keep my moral compass pointing in the right direction.

Let me be clear, you don't have to give away the things you own or feel bad for having success; but in many cases, sharing your possessions can assign a more meaningful value to them and redefine what they mean to you. Just keep in mind that at the end of the day, the only things you truly own are your memories. Don't waste your time trying to buy things that only give the illusion of ownership. Instead, focus on building memories with the people you care about. Memories are the one thing no one can take from you.

Summary:
- Material possessions and wealth, while valuable, should be prioritized behind character and choices made in the pursuit of a meaningful legacy.
- During goal setting, it's important to examine WHY certain things are valuable to us and what we are willing to give or sacrifice to obtain them.
- Embrace a legacy mindset by making it a point to serve others and give back. Doing so enriches your life and those around you more sustainably than material wealth alone.
- Prioritize actions and goals based on their potential to create lasting, positive impacts rather than focusing on instant-gratification status symbols.

Chapter 5 Exercise

Take a moment to think about one of your biggest material goals you hope to achieve in your lifetime, then write it down. Next, ask yourself if anyone else in your life would obtain pleasure from your possession. Then, ask yourself if you would still want to pursue your goal if you couldn't share it with those you care about most. Finally, explain how you came to your conclusion and set a rule or a guideline that gives you permission to chase this goal while still keeping your priorities and legacy in mind.

Example:

Possession: I want to own a 20,000-square-foot mansion in the Hollywood Hills.

Vision: I envision all my friends flying out to see my mansion and my mom moving into one of the house's wings, and we're all smiling together. My family comes to visit often, and I'm able to let my brother and sister move in rent-free because there's so much room.

Risk: If I were in a position to achieve this goal and could not share it with my family, friends, wife, or kids, I would pass on the opportunity and choose a more modest home close to them.

Why? Because gaining a possession is only worth the memories it brings; otherwise, it's a burden.

Guideline: It's okay to chase this goal as long as I don't lose my family and friends in the process.

LEGACY MINDSET

CHAPTER 6

LAW OF ATTRITION

We always have the option to avoid the pain of discipline—but what we often don't understand is that the pain of guilt for having not tried can be much greater.

There are two laws you hear about fairly often in business and entrepreneurial circles: the law of attrition and the law of attraction. Let's start with the former.

The law of attrition is essentially the rate at which an object or person will deteriorate over time. Everything wears out and decays eventually. Bread gets stale or moldy, cars get too many miles on them, and as much as we don't like it, we get older. The crucial part of the law of attrition is that it considers the additive effects of smaller causes. If bread is left out, it gets stale more quickly. If it's left in a humid environment, it gets moldy faster. Tons of things can wear on a car over the years, from how you drive it to how you maintain it—and our bodies and mental health are the same. What are we eating? How are we sleeping? What do we consume daily? What are our good habits? What are our bad ones?

Some employers try to be aware of the law of attrition to avoid burnout in employees; some motivational speakers try to be conscientious of this law to avoid burnout as well. But I want to take it a step further, because what I discovered about the law of attrition isn't simply that we decay but that our choices can compound. The negatives in our lives that we try to endure and accept can spread outward, webbing to those around us like a parasite. Sometimes the decay and rust we exude can spread so far that we can't even see the extent to which it travels. As these negatives get past our sight, any hope of remedying them gets well past our control.

And that, as you might expect, is a dangerous thing.

As I started my first year of high school in Rhode Island, I looked for validation in people notorious for their "don't look at me or I'll knock your lights out" mentality. In hindsight, I'm sure it gave me a sense of security and attention that I longed for at home but couldn't get because of my parents' situation.

The truth is, I just wanted to belong somewhere.

I didn't fit in with the smart kids because everyone knew I was in remedial classes; I hated the concept of sports, so I had no place with the jocks; and even things I took an interest in, like robotics or science, were all taught in a way that couldn't keep my attention for long. Even if I told my teachers I wanted to be an astronaut or send a rocket to space, my grades, attendance, and work ethic sure didn't reflect those desires. I felt like there was no one to believe in me. So, where did I belong? It's sad to say, but I fit in well with the outcasts.

Within the first few months of my first year of high school and hanging with these new friends, my mom also got a first: her first phone call from the police station, saying she needed to pick me up.

I was out with a "friend" of mine, and our intention was to go to the park and hang out. It was a ragged little park set between two very old apartment complexes with old park benches with rotted wood, small patches of dead grass, and a chain-link fence that had clearly been cut through and patched several times due to vandalism. The park was meant for the residents, but we thought the rules didn't apply to us. I brought my girlfriend at the time, and we were enjoying the unsupervised freedom of being young teens.

We sat at the park just joking around, jumping on tables, reading the graffiti that littered the gazebo area, and all around acting like fools. Suddenly, as I stood atop one of the tables, my foot cracked through the rotted wood. Stunned and worried, I made eye contact with my friend, and he just laughed.

Andrew was fifteen years old but was much bigger than me, around 6'2", maybe 230 lb.; he could pass for his early thirties any day of the week. When people asked his age, it always made us laugh to hear "Wait, you're *how* old?". It was like someone put growth hormone in his Wheaties as a kid. He had a thick, full black beard shaved into a goatee—the kind of beard you have to shave twice a day to keep in check.

Meanwhile, I was this 5'7" baby-faced kid who was fourteen and looked ten. I hadn't started shaving because the peach fuzz on my mustache still didn't demand it. So, from an outside perspective, it always looked like there was an adult with the group. But mind you, Andrew was still just a kid.

After my foot went through the table, Andrew walked over to the bench of another table, lifted his leg, and just axe-kicked it, breaking the whole bench in half. My girlfriend and I both erupted in laughter. This encouraged him to walk over to another bench and do it again, then again on another. Within thirty seconds, this "kid" had stomped through and broken all the benches in the park, and we just laughed like it wasn't a problem. But we all knew it was vandalism, so I said, "We should probably go."

And we just started walking down the road, remarking how strong Andrew was for his age, cracking jokes while fake drunk-walking in a line. Then I heard a car speeding up behind us, almost as if it were going to hit us, and I turned my head to see a police car with no sirens on. Another car trailed the cop car, and the driver rolled down their window and said:

"That's them, officer."

We knew we were in trouble as both officers exited the car.

"Were you three at the park?"

Andrew and my girlfriend stayed silent, frozen in place.

"Yeah," I said, "we were."

"The other driver said you were in there breaking benches. Is that true?"

"I broke one on accident," I said, hoping they would think the person was overreacting. "Those benches are junk. I about gashed my leg falling through it."

The officer eyed me up and down.

"You *accidentally* broke all the benches in the park?"

That's when Andrew came clean and told them he broke the benches, but by then the officer wanted him and I to go to the station. My adrenaline was pumping. *My mom is going to kill me when she finds out,* I thought. Then they put us in the back of the cruiser and drove us to the station up the road. The ride was probably just a few minutes, but it felt like an eternity. I remember how hard the seat was and how aggressively the officer drove, making me slide around in the backseat. *This is it,* I thought. *It's really happening. My life is over.*

I maintained hope that, somehow, they would just let us go and never get the message to my mom—allowing me to keep the deep, dark secret long enough for the dust to settle. That was just wishful thinking. The officer sat me alone in a room and slammed the door.

"Shit, I really messed up," I said under my breath.

I took note of the cold, hard metal chair; the beige color of the room—the lack of, well . . . anything. I immediately felt out of place. This room was for criminals, guys and gals who did terrible things to people.

I don't feel like a criminal. I hope the officer sees that and lets us go. Somehow, in my mind I saw the police officer empathizing with us, almost like a father figure. I could imagine the conversation going more like, "You know you kids messed up right?"

"Yes, sir," we would respond in unison.

"Alright, get out of here, and don't let me see y'all doing this again."

Yeah, that's what going to happen, I thought to myself while waiting in the world's most uncomfortable chair.

The officer barged back into the room after what seemed to be an eternity.

"Your mom is on the way, kid. She doesn't seem too happy," he blurted out and shut the door before I could even get a word out.

My heart dropped. For one of the first times, I felt terrible for my mom's misfortune of having a son as lost as I was.

"She's going to hate me," I thought to myself.

Just by trying to fit in, I ended up in a room at the police station. But she couldn't be there all the time to hold my hand.

What I didn't realize then was that my choices were having a cascading effect. My mom was a single mother with three kids trying to keep the bills paid. Every time she missed work, I saw the fear in her eyes, as she knew it meant asking for forgiveness on the rent or collections when bills came due. I didn't want my mom to pay for my lack of value, and I didn't intend for her to get hurt over it. And at that time, to be honest, I was simply embarrassed—not enough embarrassment to stop the mischief altogether, mind you, but to not give her attitude and accept whatever consequences with humility.

I knew instantly that the news of my arrest would quickly find its way to my relatives because when my mom had something to say, she would call the entire family to share the news, as she didn't want to go through these things alone. That would spark phone calls to me from all my family members, where they would provide their own version of a scolding.

"You know your mom works very hard to provide for you and your siblings. Why would you add this stress to her?"

"If you keep this up, you will be in juvie before you leave high school."

"Do you want to end up like . . ."

I didn't get put in cuffs, so I might have harped on that particular caveat and technicality, but as I said before, perception is reality.

After I got home, I could see the stress in my mom's eyes, and it didn't feel good. We briefly discussed what happened, and I put it all on Andrew to make it seem like I was the good guy—anything to minimize my involvement.

And, to my surprise, everyone took the bait. I was banned from hanging out with Andrew, even though we weren't that close to begin with. Not a huge loss. And thankfully, the conversations of my would-be criminality died out faster than I would have thought.

To the law of attrition, that's fuel—because, unfortunately, so too did my lessons of humility and empathy for my mother's circumstance begin to fade. Like an answered prayer that you soon forget.

After Andrew was out of my life, I befriended someone else my age, a guy named Joe. Though Joe was a decent kid, we went from setting small fires in his backyard to stealing money from his parents' "secret stash."

At the time my only care was what was good for me, and why the hell should I care about anyone else? Even Joe. In a shoe box in his parent's closet, they hid away thousands of dollars, and we used that money to live the high life. BB guns, knives, expensive RC cars, anything we wanted. We even got the idea that we could build a man cave in one of the abandoned factories just beyond the train tracks and fill it with all the crazy stuff we wanted. It felt like some *Wolf of Wall Street* stuff and came with the feeling of being unstoppable.

It was addictive—so much so that we began getting complacent in our newfound "wealth."

As young teens, we felt deserving and lived like kings, getting whatever we wanted whenever we wanted. We had both essentially moved into this building except to check in at home and go to school. Other than that, we would roam the backstreets and abandoned buildings like they were ours. We broke windows, set things on fire, made makeshift beds, and stole more money. It was our own little version of *Mad Max*.

But it wasn't good enough. I always wanted to keep pushing the limits.

So I considered the next thing to try while we had this freedom.

The answer? Smoking.

I knew that the bus driver (whom I'm sure you remember) would buy cigarettes for the other kids, so if we wanted to try more adult things, we just needed to have him get it. The next day Joe and I got on the bus and told our bus driver what we wanted, which he didn't even question. Joe and I agreed that smoking would be the easiest sin to get away with because our parents were smokers and wouldn't notice the smell. Alcohol, on the other hand, would have been much harder to hide. *Something for later.* And after two days, we secured two packs of Marlboro Reds from our driver, and we could not have been more excited to get out of school so we could go to our hangout and start becoming grown-ups.

"You ready?" Joe said as we walked off the bus.

"F—k yeah," I responded as we made our way to the woods next to my house.

Joe took the first one out and lit it up. He passed the pack to me, and I tapped the bottom of it like I knew what I was doing. But in reality, I had just seen my mom do it every time she smoked.

"How is it?" I asked, bringing one to my mouth and looking for reassurance before I committed.

"Not bad, kinda minty," he said.

I lit mine up and forgot that smoking wasn't for show. I blew smoke in the air like I had been doing it for years. Feeling like I'm finally an adult.

"Are you inhaling it?"

Right . . . duh. I forgot you're supposed to hold it in your lungs, not your mouth.

I geared up for a deep breath and the second smoke hit my lungs, I started old-man coughing uncontrollably, making Joe laugh mid-breath and choke on his as well. We both just laughed and awkwardly continued trying until it got smoother, not knowing when it was the right time to take another breath.

I remember thinking, *Man, I can't wait to tell some of the kids at school.*

But as we sat there smoking our first cigarettes, coughing up a lung and feeling a little queasy, I realized I finally felt like I fit in somewhere with Joe. Even if that meant living in an abandoned building outside the real world, I felt I was in the place I belonged. My mistake, however, was confusing fantasy with real life. Worse than that, it was a fantasy that was dependent on stealing, causing misery to others—yet a misery I still managed to keep far enough away that I didn't think about it.

But sometimes, the law of attrition demands more decay. Like cancer, it grows stronger and deadlier the more it spreads.

Joe shared a lot of the same interests as I did, especially when it came to cars. We would talk about and plan for these awesome cars we would own one day, and we would keep any parts we found on the road, our "spares," in our little hideout for when we finally got our licenses.

One day, I had the idea to go up to the local used car dealership that was closed for the weekend and look at the cars they had for sale and their prices. This was a ragged dealership with some tuners likely to break down before you left the lot—if not two days later. But they were still cars—cars with price tags that didn't make me immediately cringe. And so I thought, *If only I could get my hands on one.* But after some elementary arithmetic on what job I needed, how much I needed to make per hour, and how many hours I needed to work to acquire it, even a clunker seemed like a pipedream. But that day was different. That day, I *needed* to get my hands on one to visualize my future.

It was Sunday after 6 p.m., and the dealership had closed. The lot was chained off so no one could get in. But it was still light outside, and Joe and I had already ridden our bikes for over an hour to get up there, so simply turning around was not an option.

With a bit of encouragement from me, we hopped over the chain like it wasn't even there. Then, just like our hideout, we started to treat this dealership on a main road like our little hangout—playing around like we owned the place.

We tried stupid feats of strength, like seeing if we had enough power to lift the back end of small cars (we didn't) or checking door handles to see which were unlocked so that we could sit in them. I set my eyes on a mid '90s Mitsubishi Eclipse GSX that was all green and had peeling paint and a cracked windshield. "I want this one," I said like it meant something.

I pulled the handle on the driver's side door, and to my surprise, it was unlocked just for me. I hopped into the driver's seat, pretending to drive, envisioning myself taking this car to school in the next few years when I got my license. Joe was getting a little nervous by this point, scanning around, worried someone was coming.

"Let's see what's under the hood," I said, pulling the latch.

It was utterly filthy and poorly taken care of. I checked for leaks and loose parts, getting my hands dirty.

"What are you doing, Korey?" Joe asked.

"I can fix it up, and we could cruise around town!" I said as I closed the hood.

"What? Right now?"

"Nah, man. Next year for high school. We can go wherever we want."

He offered a friendly laugh, but his hands were shoved in his pockets, and he was already heading back to our bikes. I think he noticed my disappointment in him because he spotted a little Honda Civic as we walked and said, "This one is nice too."

"Not as nice as my GSX."

"I bet it's faster," Joe said, almost as if he were looking for my approval.

"I actually like the hubcaps on it," I conceded. "I would want those for my car."

Joe agreed with me. He liked them, and they would probably be the ones he chose for his hypothetical future car.

Then I asked, "How well are they on there?"

Suddenly, he reached down and started ripping the hubcaps off.

"One less thing to buy," I said. We figured they wouldn't miss them.

Joe and I walked over to our bikes and prepared to make the long trek home when we heard distant sirens approaching. *That can't be for us, right?* Joe and I just looked at each other to feel out the situation. The sound grew louder and louder. Before we could say anything, three police cars flew over the hill, approaching fast and cutting off traffic to get to us—so fast that we hardly had time to react.

Joe threw the hubcaps into the lot, hoping they didn't see us do anything. I just stayed put, paralyzed in place on my bike, as the officers pulled up right next to us. They got out and started yelling at us to get off our bikes, with their hands on their guns.

"We didn't take anything!" I shouted, but the officers grabbed both of us, throwing us against the hood to pat us down for weapons.

"If you didn't take anything, why are you covered in grease?"

I had forgotten I got my hands dirty poking around in that GSX. But sure enough, it looked like I spent the day stealing car parts. After patting Joe and me down, they didn't ask any more questions. They just threw our bikes in the trunk and us in the backseat.

It felt like déjà vu. I was scared, I was upset, and I wanted to cry.

Mom is about to get another call within two months for me to get picked up from the station.

What the hell is wrong with me?

At the station, Joe was stoic. They photographed, fingerprinted, and questioned us on our intentions. There was no good excuse, stealing in broad daylight, and hubcaps of all things . . .

After the questioning, the cop looked at me and said, "You can get a pack of hubcaps for $12. Why the hell would you steal them?" I didn't have a good answer. It was just poor judgment from two kids riding a fake high of adulthood after their first queasy cigarette. But this time was different. We were breaking and entering, stealing, and depending on how crazy the charges got, we could have been tried for grand theft since we got in the cars.

We were more than lucky to get a slap on the wrist.

What I dreaded more was the look of disappointment in my mother's eyes when she came walking through the door, because this was not something I could talk myself out of. She trusted me, and I broke that. Furthermore, I knew my dad would be embarrassed of me, and I was especially concerned about how I would explain myself in person when I would go visit him for the upcoming summer. It's one thing to half listen to someone on the phone, but when you're within arm's reach, there's a different vibe. Weak-willed, mischievous people were why he wanted to get out of that state so badly—now his son was becoming one of them. I could feel all the disappointment before it even happened.

The officers walked me to my mom's car, and the yelling ensued as soon as I got in. I just sat in the car with my head down, looking at the fibers in the carpet while my mom's voice faded to incoherent noise. I didn't need her to tell me I was a disappointment. I already knew. I could feel it in the fibers of my being, like dirt on the carpet I couldn't stop staring at. This wasn't life. It was torture trying to be what I thought people wanted me to be. What was I doing wrong?

We arrived home, and my mom said I couldn't hang out with anyone unless it were family. Followed by no leaving the house, and no TV, games, or computer—basically, I could go to school and sleep, and that was it. Which, at that moment, was fair. But what about the next moment? What about when the lesson fades again? That sick feeling in the pit of your stomach when you get caught doing something bad—it doesn't last forever. I could just wait it out.

But I realized all I was waiting for was a phone call that never happened—the one from my dad. I knew I would catch hell for what I had done, but I never got handed the phone.

Instead, my mother spoke to him without me and said, "The police think he's going to be back there again sooner rather than later." Which hurt, but what hurt more was my dad not even wanting to talk to me. After what seemed like an eternity, my mom hung up with my dad and walked over to me with tears in her eyes. "Korey, your dad said you can move in with him if you want. Maybe he can get you straightened out."

Like waking up from a dream, it's hard to see clearly where the law of attrition begins, how far it reaches, and how far you've already decayed. I was still young; I'd still make mistakes, hurt my body in more ways than one, find more ways to deteriorate—but I didn't want to. I wanted to change. I wanted to be better. At the same time, I knew the last thing my mom wanted was for me to leave. I was her little helper, her first child, her baby boy. She wanted us to be happy, and she always took it personally when we became unhappy. So, when the ultimatum was presented, she feared I would accept.

But the truth is, I needed to accept.

The reality was (whether my mom accepted it or not) that I was causing damage to the family, to myself, and to my friends in more ways than one. Negative actions compound, and the law of attrition spreads. News of my small run-ins with the law traveled fast in a state barely thirty miles wide. My being called out of school affected her income and screwed over my siblings. Stealing money from Joe's parents pushed him down a different road than he should have been headed. And vandalizing strangers' property heaped undeserved expenses onto them. All without fear of repercussion—and none of it seemed to be slowing down.

And beneath all these behaviors was my anger. My younger siblings and mom saw it, and it was clear that if I stayed in the picture in Rhode Island, it would result in a more arduous path for everyone—the path of most attrition.

"I'll go," I said.

"What?" my mother asked, tears welling in her eyes.

I gritted my teeth and committed a second time.

"I'm going to go live with Dad and go to school in Florida."

She started to cry, and I almost cried too because I knew that meant abandoning my little brother, Justin, and little sister, Giselle.

But I needed a change. I needed something different. I knew this was going to be hard but necessary. My dad was a no-BS type of man, so when he made that offer, I knew it wasn't to spend quality time. My dad may have left our home when I was five, but he seemed to be building a life of success, with his brand-new house, his brand-new car . . . by all appearances the kind of life I'd always revered.

I wanted all of that too.

My sister was not as close to me then, but my brother was around ten and we were attached at the hip, and I know he didn't want me to go to Florida. He looked up to me in every way, as younger brothers tend to do at that age, and I knew that by doing this I was essentially abandoning him—so leaving him behind was the hardest part. My dad was gone when he was a toddler, and now the only person he related to was leaving too. I still feel guilty about it to this day.

He was my rock, and I was his.

They all took me to the airport, my mom and siblings sobbing. I put on a tough guy facade, dressed in my Affliction tee with long straggly hair, earrings, and baggy pants with a chain, a mix between emo and rapper that I thought was cool. But inside, I was crying like a baby too. I was about to reach a point of no return, and I wondered how they would grow up without me and what they would grow up thinking of me.

They continued sobbing as they walked me to the gate.

We hugged as a family, saying, "I love you" and "Goodbye for now."

But there was something brewing in the background of what felt like one of the hardest days of my life. You see, in the midst of decay, we find the seed of change. The law of attrition reminds us that our choices, like ripples in a pond, affect not only ourselves but also those around us. Being willing to recognize this can lead to an empowering revelation: that we must own the consequences of our actions and accept that our decisions, whether positive or negative, have the potential to compound.

It was time for me to own the situation I got myself in as I gave my last hug and turned around.

Walking away killed me. Every step hurt and my legs felt heavy. It was like walking willingly toward a pain you knew was coming but you knew in your heart was for your own good. And it was, because while living in Florida I had my first introduction to the second law: the law of attraction.

Summary

- Sometimes, significant changes and sacrifices are required to break a negative cycle. Although painful, moving toward a difficult change can be necessary for personal growth.
- It's important to recognize when a change of environment can provide opportunities for growth and success.
- Accepting tough love can be a crucial step toward gaining humility and changing harmful behavior patterns.

Chapter 6 Exercise

Consider a time when you compromised your values or well-being to fit in with a particular group. Write about why you felt the need to fit in, what it cost you, and what you learned from the experience. Structure your response by the following questions:

- Why did you feel the need to fit in?

_____

_____

_____

_____

- What did you learn from this experience?

_____

_____

_____

_____

- What would you change about your behavior if you could go back?

CHAPTER 7

LAW OF ATTRACTION

Passion is more abstract than we make it out to be. You can convince your brain to be passionate about anything that you're doing if it achieves a powerful result.

The law of attraction is not necessarily the opposite of attrition because it doesn't directly relate to decay or deterioration. The law of attraction simply states that you attract into your life whatever it is that you focus on. It's the idea that positive or negative thoughts bring about positive or negative experiences. Now, I'm not going to sit here and explain the "5 BEST Secrets" to incorporate the law of attraction into your own life and business practices—but I will tell you that I believe that practicing certain behaviors help attract positive things into our lives.

I believe we get what we work for and that, if we work hard, our focus is rewarded—because focus, you'll come to find, is its own reward. As Bruce Lee said, "I fear not the man who has practiced 10,000 kicks once, but I fear the man who has practiced one kick 10,000 times." The law of attraction states that positive thoughts bring about positive experiences. If one thing—one kick, one idea, one mission—becomes your focus, that one thing can start to surprise you in ways you never would have expected. Like things that cause attrition, the results of your positive focus can expand and spread out as well, impacting other people, affecting the world. And the people you impact will be motivated to contribute in their own ways, to plant their own positive trees that inspire their own positive changes—changes that build their legacies as you build yours.

At fifteen years old and 30,000 feet in the air, I was reflecting on my life. It had already felt so full of experiences, but confusing and anger-inducing, a war of attrition I didn't even understand that I was fighting. But a new chapter was about to begin: life with my dad in Florida. I was excited, honestly. Although the events that led up to this moment were not all positive, I presented it to myself as a good thing, an opportunity to "focus up."

As the plane's wheels hit the ground, I got the jitters because I realized I was *moving*. This would be the first time in my life that I would live in a home rather than an apartment, in a state that takes more than an hour to drive through, a state with sunshine, supportive infrastructure, beautiful homes, beautiful beaches, and beautiful people.

You know those movies when someone who has been far removed from society gets to "the city" and is just amazed at every car, house, flower, tree, and store they see? That's how it was for me—it felt like culture shock. Even from the plane window I was able to see big homes, nice cars, crystal-blue pools, and I thought: *Man, they must be so successful. They must be important. They've got it all figured out.* If I had been thinking about the concept of "legacy" back then, I would've thought that theirs were practically guaranteed.

I walked off the plane, felt the humid Florida sunshine, and saw my dad waiting there for me with his iconic half-cracked smile and arms crossed—the look that said, "I'm happy to see you, but I have a lot on my mind." Which was a relief because I honestly didn't know what to expect. For some reason, I thought the molding of the "new me" would be a sprint, not a marathon, and I wasn't sure if he would see me and immediately yell something like a drill instructor: "Shoulders back, stand up straight!"

But no, he waited for me to approach before opening his arms for an obligatory hug. A hug that always felt strange because the years made us distant, and the "tough guy" persona made us more. I felt the side of our faces touch. His stubble felt like sandpaper on my skin, and we immediately pulled away. I have only experienced that closeness with him few times in my life.

But a scratchy, stubbled hug meant one thing: *I made it.*

And I was taking *it* all in.

My dad had a long-term girlfriend with four kids of her own at the time. I hadn't spent much time with them in length yet, but I was about to live with two of the children—and the girlfriend. On the drive home, it quickly became apparent that I was in for a rude awakening. As we drove from the airport toward our new subdivision, I noticed kids playing outside, tan-skinned, happy, throwing a football around and having a blast. I thought, *Wow, that takes guts to hang out in the open like that,* because I was so used to the little rivalries that would happen back up north. I was also amazed at how many people were outside and happy, just walking around and enjoying the weather and the people around them. It felt like I was on another planet. But one thing was for sure; I didn't see anyone who looked like a troubled goth kid like me. This was about to hurt!

As we approached our subdivision, the greenery, the cleanliness, and the people all took me by surprise. People were washing their boats and kids were playing in the yard. There were new basketball hoops in many yards, and the houses looked beautiful, yet I saw no one that looked like we could be friends. The kids were all so different; they were in shape, playing sports, wearing bright-colored clothes. They were my polar opposite. As I sat in the back seat looking out the window, my dad spewed out information to me about the area while periodically looking back in the rear-view mirror and locking eyes with me, as if I were on a paid tour.

"Are you paying attention?" he would interrupt his tour.

"Yes sir," I responded.

"Good . . ."

"So, you now live in Middleburg/Fleming Island, Florida. In a subdivision. Our house is currently being built, and it has four bedrooms, two baths, and one of those will be your room. Your school will be Ridgeview High School, where you will start your sophomore year in August. They have a great sports program. You will pick whatever sport you want, and we will arrange—"

"Sports?" I interrupted. "Dad, I don't do sports."

He didn't even look back at me or lock eyes in the rear-view mirror. "You do now."

I knew the objective of coming to Florida with my dad was to get straightened out, but this caused my first feeling of disdain toward him on my path to getting corrected. I hated sports, and for someone who never fit in, I was scared I would get bullied into submission. But it was nonnegotiable. I wasn't in control anymore—he was.

High school began after a summer of what felt like strict structure compared to how I was living before, consisting of only eating at the dinner table, helping Dad with tasks around the house, having limited screen time and clothing options, bed times, curfew, etc. Overall, I hated doing these things, but I was looking at my role model in real time, thinking if he was telling me to do these tasks, then there must be a bigger reason, even if I didn't know what it was. I trusted the process. So, I just put my head down and did what he asked, until it came to one thing. My dad still tasked me with that one objective: find a sports team. Well, two objectives: don't fail classes, and find a sports team. "I don't care which one," he said, "but you're joining a team. No exceptions."

I was furious with him for that. I was doing everything he asked, with minimal complaints, so I figured he would drop the sports topic, as I was clearly developing positively and growing already. I think this was one of my biggest motivators, showing him that I could change. But I still felt blindsided by the topic and reminded him how much I didn't want to do sports.

"Listen," he said, "there are good opportunities and respectable people on sports teams that you're not going to find just sitting around doing small tasks. They're driven people and great to be around. You don't have to pick one now, but you *will* pick one."

I didn't even respond. Being on a sports team was a concept that was beyond my understanding, but I just absorbed the lesson while trying to maintain my frustration mentally and physically. One thing I *did* appreciate was that he told me *why* he was forcing me instead of delivering the tired "because I said so" response. It was like when you give someone the illusion of choices to make them feel in control: "You're taking this step, but it's up to you how."

A little desperate to find something and not end up hating it, I picked my poison: wrestling. Since I was short, had a decent build, and typically harbored a lot of anger—especially toward other people—I figured it was a good call. Then again, a goth-looking kid on the wrestling team was an unfamiliar sight to most. It wasn't long after that conversation that I found myself walking to the gymnasium on my first day of training, realizing I was staying *after* school while everyone else went home.

I got a lot of looks during those first days of training, and it wasn't long before I got the "you don't belong here" vibes from the other kids, especially when they would huddle together and keep me out of the loop, or I would see a group of kids looking at me only to turn away quickly when I made eye contact.

Little did they know, I agreed with them.

But, at my dad's insistence, I stuck with it, trusting the process once again. And over time, something odd happened—I discovered how I react in the face of adversity, of forced discipline, and how others in the same or similar situations band together for support. When we did stair runs or drills, I would get so winded and beat down from years of no cardio; I felt defeated, like an outcast, unworthy, overcome with a sense of not belonging as I got passed up by all the other kids my age.

. . . But somehow, amidst my negative thoughts, hands on my knees, leaning over and struggling to find my breath, I would feel a hand on the small of my back, followed by:

"Come on, brother. You can do it."

That would pull me out of whatever mental spiral I was having, enough for me to think to myself, *What the hell? This guy doesn't even know me. What gives?*

Motivating someone you didn't know to *keep going, keep climbing, keep moving forward*, that was such a foreign concept to me—but it kept happening. Someone always came back for me, believed in me. That's brotherhood, and it was a change I could get used to.

And the more it happened, the more I found myself reciprocating it to others as I got better, stronger, faster, more driven. When I had the extra energy to give, I would turn around, run to the people falling behind, and tell them, "Let's go, only a few more rounds, we can do it together," while putting my hand on the small of their back. And after a few months, I was amazed to see that some of the people I was helping were the same kids that helped me in the beginning. I was amazed by how something so small as words of encouragement brought the light back into their eyes. "I've been there before. Keep going." And they kept going.

I did that.

It made me want to do more, to help more, and to lift more people up.

Now, I didn't particularly like wrestling and wasn't very good, as I didn't take the mechanics seriously, but I did like the attitude change I was experiencing. The team mentality centered around quantifiable success. There were measures of strength, weight classes, and points for movements. When you got better, you noticed because you compared it to your prior week's self. When you broke personal bests, you felt it. It was good for my analytical mind.

And perhaps the most impactful change was starting to form in my choice circle of friends.

The more I hung out with people who were driven, people that were pushing each other to be better and do more, the less I tolerated and talked to my "emo" friends. In that group, we were always the victims of adversity and looked down on the "preppy" kids, even when I tried to be the voice of reason. But then I would get back from some serious training, losing what felt like gallons of sweat, feeling the brotherhood, and they would mope around, talking about some depressing situation and complaining how no one was there for us and how we were alone in the world. When I arrived with that ever-developing alternative philosophy of "it's not all that bad" and "overcoming adversity can help you grow and get stronger," it didn't go over well with them. And meanwhile, these "preppy" kids were out fighting for something and inspiring each other to improve daily. They welcomed me with open arms once I began training; all I had to do was show up. I began spending more and more time with the wrestling team and even got to know their parents.

My attitude completely changed within the first year as I realized the adults I was interacting with were the very people I envisioned from the plane that took me to Florida—these educated, professional, and successful parents I continually saw at wrestling meets or celebrating at teammates' houses. In their driveways I'd see muscle cars worth hundreds of thousands of dollars, realizing that many of these people shared the same love and appreciation for things that I did. I would hold conversations with parents at length about the engines, maintenance, and horsepower, which surprised me because my teammates couldn't care less about what made a car tick. This showed me that even people who have seemingly dissimilar interests can have a common goal. I was also gaining more confidence and learning about success by becoming ingratiated with people who had it. And I was meeting attractive girls because I wasn't dressed like a '90s identity crisis and was getting in remarkable shape, which helped me feel more comfortable in my skin (something I had never felt before). All because I was forced to communicate with people I didn't initially fit in with.

I'm still thankful to my dad for that.

I wasn't the only one noticing this change in me, and I found the appreciation from others addictive. My dad would show up to the matches telling me how proud he was of the effort I put in, and I would also hear from his friends, "You know he's super proud of you, right?" My mom began to say I was unrecognizable in photos she saw and how I talked "different" on the phone. On my family phone calls every few weeks, I would hear my brother or sister asking me how I liked sports, and my aunts and uncles would tell me I was changing fast and "looking good." My family would make good-hearted fun of me because I was developing a slight southern drawl that was noticeable to them as northerners. Most of all, the people I initially hung out with began to push me away for my positivity. And for some reason that felt great, because it seemed like I had permission to change.

Over the next two years I evolved into someone addicted to self-development, because I saw firsthand how fast things could change when you put in the work. I observed other parents who were smart, so I wanted to be smart. These parents were physically active, so I wanted to be active. These parents and their kids dressed nicely, so I tried to dress nicely. I learned that if I wanted success, I needed to emulate it. And that's precisely what I did—I dropped my initial circle of friends, keeping only the music I couldn't let go of, and moved into a more positive environment.

But senior year was coming fast, and it was time to think about the real world—and, more importantly, my place in it. I could see how much of a 180 I was making and hoped that my family, including my brother and sister, could learn that changing the "norms" of their environment—that is, refusing to engage in drama, improving one's financial status (and thereby changing its impact on others)—was possible.

With graduation around the corner, it was time to figure out what I wanted to do in life, but it felt impossible to pick a permanent path I was passionate about. I wanted to be all these different things, but there was not enough time in the world to give each of them the time they deserved. The job I had always wanted was to be a car mechanic like my dad, but he pleaded with me every chance he had not to follow in his footsteps. The more he worked on cars, the more he hated them, saying things like, "Don't become a grease monkey like me."

But what were my options? I felt like there wasn't much else I was qualified for.

When I looked at my new friend group, it felt like they had their lives and futures laid out. One would go into banking, the other accounting, another realty, the rest medicine or law or whatever their parent excelled at. But none of those things appealed to me, let alone applied to me. They were confused why I didn't have a set goal—and I realized that, although they were now my closest friends, in some ways we were as distant in likeness as the emo kids.

Who I was with them was decidedly better, but it still wasn't me. And with school ending, it seemed like it was finally time to figure out who I was. Any profession that sounded like it could help me achieve my dreams of unshakable success was on the table, but most professions I could think of required *passion* if one was to build a legacy there. My only problem was that I had no idea what I was passionate about.

I liked cars, but Dad said no to being a mechanic, and I had to trust his word.

I enjoyed helping people run up stadium steps, but I didn't want to coach.

I was addicted to self-development—but . . . *Where does that leave me?*

It was 2010, and, in a year, I was about to graduate at 18 years old. I knew that changing my environment helped. I knew growth was essential. I knew forced discipline, like my father offered, helped me. And that became a word I focused on: *discipline*. Where could I gain discipline? I knew I wasn't mature enough for college yet, but I wanted to be, so how could I keep this train rolling and learn the most discipline I could *right now?*

We lived in a town that was 95% Navy; even ROTC in high school was Navy. Many people, even some on the wrestling team, decided that this was a path for them—at least in the interim.

Then one day, as I wrestled with my choice of a future, I got a call from a recruiter for the Marines. She said something like, "Are you looking for personal development?"

"What?"

"Are you looking to grow?"

"Is this a recording?"

"Are you looking for discipline?"

"*Discipline,* you say?"

"How would you like to be part of the most elite fighting force in the world?"

Most elite? That sounded bold.

I think the recruiter only asked the last question, but the energy of the conversation makes me remember it like that. If anything, she was very good at her job, but I still barely knew anything about the Marine Corps. *Then again,* I thought to myself, *there's only one way to find out.*

When I started to tell people that the Marines were calling me, they would say, "Screw that! That's brutal work," or, "Those guys are beasts." Many people would make fun of them, calling them "grunts" and "jar-headed trigger pullers," but no one denied that they were ruthless warriors that got the job done, even if it meant sacrificing their lives.

So, I called the recruiting office back and asked where I could find the *most* discipline and serve the *most*. They responded almost immediately with "infantry" or "Special Forces." I didn't think highly enough of myself to believe I could do Special Forces right off the bat, so I signed on the dotted line for the Delayed Entry Program and went home to tell my dad that I had joined the Marines.

The entire ride home, I was jittery with excitement and nerves. It felt good to make such a big decision in life, and I knew it was going to blow everyone's minds. When I pulled into the driveway, I resolved to telling Dad in passing, nonchalantly, maintaining the element of surprise, but the second I walked in the door and saw my dad standing at the kitchen counter, I smiled uncontrollably, giving myself away.

"Hey, Dad! Guess what?"

He looked at me concerned, with one eyebrow raised, as if I was going to lift my shirt and show him a giant "thug life" tattoo or crazy new piercing I got on a whim. To be fair, when a visibly proud teenager suddenly appears, it does merit some concern, so I understood.

"What . . . ?" he said timidly. Almost like he was going to regret asking.

"I joined the Marines!"

He turned his whole body toward me and gave me his full attention.

"What? That's great son!"

He seemed relieved of whatever nightmare he thought was coming for him. But it wasn't the jump for joy I had envisioned in my head when telling him. So, I just stayed quiet, waiting for the "but" that I could see coming a mile away.

"But. . . why the Marines? That skill set doesn't transfer well back to society."

He could see me becoming less excited, and he quickly digressed. "Never mind. Congratulations, kid, I'm proud of you! Have you told your mom yet?"

My excitement came back. "Not yet, but I'm going to call her now!" I said as I walked away to my bedroom, looking forward to telling everyone, "See, I'm actually doing something important with my life." But I couldn't shake off my dad's initial reaction.

He was proud, yet upset that I didn't choose something more beneficial to my future. He saw that I was doing better overall with grades and finally digging myself out of the rut I had put myself in all these years, but to him becoming a "jar-head" and getting deployed to the frontlines as a rifleman to go toe-to-toe with the enemy was not "using my head" to elevate my life. I saw a level of disappointment, if not concern, but he was still quick to go out and tell friends and family, buying T-shirts that said his son was going to be a Marine.

And he was also right about one thing: I was looking for a change in mentality—one that reduced my fear and helped me take ownership of my life. *If I don't gain the discipline I need, I could die out there.* Becoming a Marine sounded like the ultimate test of fortitude. In the Marines I would gain a brotherhood, learn discipline, and if I was lucky enough, I could die for something important. As a Hero, maybe . . . If I didn't belong there, they would make me belong, and I was open to that.

Square peg in a round hole.

At that time in my life, I began to learn that it's crucial to take moments for self-reflection as often as you can. Passion, as I've come to understand, is not some concept confined to any specific interest; passion is a force we can channel into any endeavor that aligns with our mental or physical goals. Passion and the law of attraction go hand in hand. The law of attraction reminds us that our thoughts directly manifest and shape our reality. Meanwhile, approaching our positive goals with passion ensures that we attract positive opportunities, prompting more doors to open for us.

The law of attraction has played a huge role in my own journey, particularly in joining the Marines. My decision wasn't about conforming to societal expectations but manifesting the discipline, personal growth, and courage needed to tackle my life's goals and finally be happy. As you stand at the crossroads of your own life, think of what could happen if you changed one thing, made one major decision, or did just one thing that you know is good for you, and push away the fear that it might not work out.

Whether it's a skill, an idea, or a mission, directing your energy toward one positive thing can yield unexpected, transformative results. Like a tree with deep roots, your efforts can impact not only your own life but the lives of those around you, as well.

Try to also understand the power of perspective. Embrace challenges as opportunities for growth and learn from the adversity you encounter. Just as I found unexpected brotherhood and support in the wrestling team, you too can find strength in unexpected places.

Lastly, acknowledge the role of discipline in positively shaping your path. Life will throw unexpected curveballs, but facing them head-on with discipline and a positive mindset can lead to profound personal success that extends into society. Remember that change is a constant, and every challenge is a building block to a stronger, more resilient version of yourself. And once you make those changes, no one can take that away from you. People are going to be confused and disheartened by your drive—it makes them feel inferior. They may start to push you away, but that's okay. Don't slow down. One day (if not already) *you* will be the one placing your hand on a newfound brother's or sister's back reminding them to "keep moving forward."

Summary:

- Just like joining a sport, when faced with a new environment, embracing the change as an opportunity for growth can be transformational.
- Spending time around successful and ambitious individuals can inspire and motivate personal development and growth.
- Being forced out of your comfort zone, like moving out of state or deciding to serve others at a larger level than you're accustomed to, can help you grow and find inspiration.
- By observing and emulating the positive traits and habits of successful individuals, you can better foster your own personal development.
- Self-reflection can be a critical tool in uncovering what is holding you back, such as a lack of personal maturity.

Chapter 7 Exercise

Below are five sources of discipline that are often available to people as they mature. Reflect on your life and write these down in the order you think they influenced your growth. Number them 1 to 5. Then take a moment and analyze those choices, writing down what the order means to you.

- Parental guidance
- Educational system and teachers
- Extracurricular activities and sports
- Peer influence and social environment
- Self-discipline and personal goals

_____

_____

_____

_____

_____

_____

_____

_____

_____

_____

CHAPTER 8

MENTAL DISCOMFORT VS. MENTAL ANGUISH

> There is a big difference between mental discomfort and mental anguish. One is pointless pain. The other is personal growth disguised as pain.

After I joined the Marine Corps, quite a few of my fellow classmates questioned my decision. But I'll be honest, I liked how fast the word was getting around by going the path less traveled.

"Aren't you scared or nervous?" they'd say. "You're going to get you're a— kicked!" "You'll regret signing on that dotted line."

My replies were: Yes, I am scared. Yes, I know I will get my a— kicked, in more ways than one. No, I don't regret signing on that dotted line.

I was well aware of the risks associated with joining the Marine Corps, but regretting my decision was never part of that. On the contrary, *not* signing certainly would have been a risk. I have never been the person to quit or regret something simply because it got hard. I knew that on the other side of that Herculean feat there was going to be a big reward, one that would allow me to grow into the person I knew I could be, wanted to be, and deserved to be.

Becoming a Marine was going to challenge me in every sense of the word, but I embraced all that came with it because it helped me build mental fortitude. You see, the people who questioned my choice were scared I would experience mental anguish, which is very different from mental discomfort. Mental anguish is pain without recompense; mental discomfort is pain with the biggest reward: personal growth.

Understanding the difference between these two and learning to recognize opportunities that will lead you to one and not the other is one of the most important lessons life will teach you—if you're willing to pay attention and follow through.

A few years before I began writing this book, a friend randomly texted me to tell me he wanted to buy a dog. He was a single guy with a stable job who didn't have much going on in his life besides work, so I thought getting a dog was a good idea for him.

"A dog will encourage me to get out of bed in the morning, and he'll be my new companion who will help me stick to a healthy lifestyle and structure," he wrote.

"Awesome!" I said, "I'm all for it. Congratulations!"

Fast forward three days, and he texted me again:

"I'm thinking of returning the dog."

"Why?"

"He's just up all night, peeing all over the floor, and throws up after he chews on the couch and my shoes. I'm exhausted."

"He's a puppy!"

Then he asked me my opinion on whether he should return it. I responded by saying that he should keep the dog because he made a commitment to himself and another living thing.

"It's okay if it makes you a little uncomfortable," I said.

"I'm very uncomfortable."

"It's good mental growth, and you'll both figure it out together. Just stick it out!"

A few more days passed, and he sent me another message telling me he returned the dog. In his message, he cited my being an "advocate for mental health" and said the dog was "negatively impacting" his state of mind. He was right. Not about the dog negatively impacting his mental health, of course, but about my being a mental health advocate. By the time this conversation took place, I had been through many adversities. After Dunston's death, I chose to turn my traumatic experiences into fuel to help me advocate for positive mental health in the hopes of helping even just one person struggling with their inner battles.

But with this conversation in particular, I had to set my phone down because I wanted to type back in all caps, "THAT'S NOT AN EXCUSE!!!!!"

Honestly, I wanted to use even more exclamations than that.

However, I held my tongue as best I could and tried to calmly explain that mental discomfort cannot and should not be used to discourage positive personal growth. A cute puppy that's a little rowdy because it hasn't yet been trained isn't the end of the world. Is it annoying? Yes. Is it uncomfortable? Sure. However, you both need to learn and fail forward, together. That's what builds the strongest bonds between pain and a desired outcome. You get up each day, you grow with the new part of your life that you chose, you learn how to live together, and over time you develop a strong relationship with "man's best friend."

None of this should have come as a surprise to my friend. I am the type of friend who will not allow you to choose the easy route, especially if the hard route leads you to personal growth. I want you to win in life, period. And when the going gets tough, you bet I will be there, cheering you on and reminding you not to give up until you get there, and then some. If you're in my circle, I'm here to watch you grow, and I expect the same treatment if you see me looking for the easy path. Do whatever you need to keep me on track, tighten me up, tell me I'm being lazy. My feelings don't matter to me nearly as much as growth does. That's what I knew I would get out of the Marines: brothers that would not allow me to fail based on the premise that I would reciprocate the same to them. One team, one fight.

The cost is mental discomfort that pushes you to your limits—but it can break the very mold that you only *think* makes you who you are.

As an advocate for mental health, I encourage people to open up about their struggles so we can erase, once and for all, the stigma associated with it. Being open and honest about our inner battles is crucial to our healing process, not only because it leads us to the betterment of our mental health but also because it can be another person's survival guide.

However, it's crucial to understand the difference between using the phrase "mental health" to perpetuate a healthy narrative and excuse one's own laziness. Setting boundaries to protect yourself against toxic behavior is perpetuating a healthy mental health narrative; giving up a dog after three days because it's inconvenient to you is excusing your own lack of discipline. Such behavior makes me want to say, "I am sorry you're going through a rough time. But that's not an excuse to give up." In my experience, the most successful way to understand whether you're using mental health for growth and not as an excuse is to ask yourself two questions that will help you classify your emotional responses:

1. Am I going through mental discomfort or true mental anguish?
2. Is the potential future lesson of my mental state constructive or destructive?

A pebble in your shoe is annoying and can distract you from what's important, but it's a simple fix (most of the time) and will not impact you long-term—and if you are particularly driven, you might find yourself keeping it in there to establish discipline. That situation is vastly different from experiencing and reliving a traumatic moment every day until you feel you cannot live a normal life, or even feel that you must end it to escape your anguish.

In the latter example, you need help, period. You need to talk to someone who can help you break down your experiences, help you find value in yourself, then rewire your brain to turn that anguish into fuel and power to keep you moving forward. But not every sign of discomfort is a severe mental health issue. The storms falling over our "mental health umbrella" at any given time might be vastly different in nature and strength.

If my mental health is suffering because I'm struggling under the pressures of Marine boot camp, I need to ask whether it is destructive or constructive pain. Foresight might tell me that these moments of discomfort will benefit me in ways I can't yet see, but in the present moment, my desperation in the face of getting screamed at, beat up, and having sand kicked in my face can convince me that the entire process is destructive to my psyche overall. From personal experience, I can tell you Marine boot camp offers innumerable lessons on the other side of true and grueling challenges. You must decide if the lessons coming to you, whether from adopting a shelter dog or having sand kicked in your face, are worth it. I've spoken about my friend's challenge with the dog through my lens because I have a fairly good understanding of where he is and where he has been mentally—but I'm still not in his head. He could have gone through those two questions and decided the dog was destructive to his mental health. I believe that keeping the dog might have been constructive if he held out, pushed through, and carried on, but I concede that feeling may be from my own bias.

At any moment, in almost any situation, we can find ways to justify the narrative, so we must always ask those two questions: Am I experiencing discomfort, or is it anguish? And is the lesson to be learned worth it? Just remember: nothing is worth mental anguish without a valuable lesson on the other side. If you find yourself in this situation, act by seeking help or taking the first steps to cutting off the source of your pain. Leave your destructive pain long enough and it can make good things seem dull, and make even the most minor of inconveniences seem like a perfectly logical excuse to give up entirely.

Mental health is not black and white; there are so many different shades, and we handle them all differently. You must navigate the dichotomy between discomfort and anguish yourself. But I hope you pick the path that allows growth and cut out the situations that are destructive to you, and if you find that everyday tasks or situations are destructive—please, I implore you to seek help. You *deserve* help.

You should prioritize your mental health, but never make it an excuse to cheat yourself of an opportunity that makes you slightly uncomfortable. My dad always seemed to understand this. His work had destructive pain, but he continued to push through because he developed a constructive plan to get out (moving to Florida) and knew that there was a light at the end of his tunnel.

I'll be the first to say that some negative thoughts are simply intrusive and harmful, only providing true mental anguish, and I would *never* tell you to "push through" those. There are moments when you need to raise your hand and get professional help to offer guidance on developing the tools you need to overcome destructive mindsets and situations in your life.

When it comes to your mental health, you also need to make it a goal to *own the outcome* of your decisions. In some of the most difficult moments of my life, I had to put myself in the mindset of, "There are certain things no one can do for me but myself." No one is going to pay my bills, no one is going to hand me the things I want, no one is going to give me happiness if I don't go out and create it myself. We can take the easier paths, but we don't reserve the right to complain about them. Growth happens on the opposite side of adversity, so if you constantly shy away from anything difficult, don't expect to have more going for you than the average joe. But I don't suspect that you're looking for the easy way; if so, then you would have stopped reading a while ago.

So, remember those two questions during your next moment of adversity:
1. Am I going through mental discomfort or mental anguish?
2. Is the potential future lesson constructive or destructive?

When I decided to take the big step toward becoming a Marine, I faced those two questions daily.

Let's see where I landed.

Summary:

- Oftentimes, personal growth can be uncomfortable. It's essential to recognize that not all discomfort is bad—it can be a sign that there's a new opportunity to learn and develop positively.
- Mental anguish is pain without purpose, while mental discomfort has the potential to lead to personal growth. Understanding the difference can help in making decisions about when to persevere through a challenging situation or when to seek help. There is no shame in seeking professional help for destructive mental health issues.
- Recognize that everyone's mental health and personal battles are different. It's key to empathize with others, understand your own issues in perspective, and not overshadow the struggles of those suffering in silence.
- Opening up about personal experiences with mental health struggles could help someone else in a similar situation. Sharing stories can be a powerful tool for connection and healing.

Chapter 8 Exercise

Step 1: Annotate three areas of your life where you have identified **mental discomfort**. What are some ways you can push through these mental discomforts, and what are the first steps toward accomplishing this?

_____

_____

_____

_____

_____

_____

_____

_____

_____

_____

_____

_____

_____

Step 2: Annotate three areas of your life where you have identified **mental anguish**. How can you eliminate this mental anguish from your life in a healthy and nonaggressive way?

___

___

___

___

___

___

___

___

___

___

___

___

___

CHAPTER 9

FORCED DISCIPLINE

Your fulfillment in life is always directly related to the standard of excellence you apply to any task you set for yourself.

On July 17th, 2011, just a few months after walking across my high school's graduation stage, I was in the back of a van shaking in my boots. Why was I nervous? Because I was a "fresh recruit," and my destination was the Marine Corps Recruit Depot on Parris Island, South Carolina.

I was headed to boot camp. It was a one-way trip to a brand-new life because I knew, for me at least, there was no turning back to my old life. The only option was to succeed, because I would be damned if I came back to my family a failure after all the support that got me here. About a dozen of us were along for the journey, sitting on a bus, guessing and imagining what the next three months of training would be like. We had heard every type of horror story about drill instructors who would beat you when you made mistakes, curse you up and down when you set one toe out of line, and even how some young Marines had died from the extraneous, grueling work they'd very soon be putting all of us through. Nothing was scarier than daydreams of what might happen when we arrived at those gates. But it was going to be for the better—I could feel it.

The nerves eventually ran me ragged, and I fell asleep on the drive. I woke up to the driver yelling, "Get ready! We're fifteen minutes out!" Every single pair of eyes was glued to the window. Then we pulled up to a massive set of double doors that said:

> *Through these portals pass prospects
> for America's finest fighting force,
> United States Marines.*

I felt this overwhelming sense of pride wash over me. I was proud that I was there, reading a sign so many others had read before. All the young Marines who came before me and all their experiences. Great men and women who had lived and died by these words, fighting for something they believed in. I was on this natural high that felt surreal, like I could sense the souls of these warriors looking over me, so much so that I forgot where I was for a second.

That is, until we heard the drill instructor:

SLAM, SLAM, SLAM!

The van doors were thrown open.

"GET OUT, MOVE. MOOOOVEEEEE!" the drill instructor yelled at the top of his lungs. "GET ON THE YELLOW FOOTPRINTS, LETS F——ING GO!"

We all yelled back, "AYE SIR," and began tripping over each other as we ran to the back row of the iconic yellow footprints on the pavement, symbolizing the many generations of Marines who stood before us. Something about me wanted to stand out, so I jumped on the closest row, right in front of the drill instructor. I figured the faster I got in place and didn't hide in the masses, the quicker they would look past me, as it made the other recruits easy targets as they scrambled. It worked. The drill instructor pushed passed me to bring order to the swarm.

"MOVE YOUR A——ES! LET'S GO!"

Standing there, I thought, *This is it. No way out now.*

Over the next four years, I will learn discipline whether I like it or not.

Boot camp went on for three months, and I learned a lot about who I was during that time. Being in wrestling and having that brotherhood beforehand set me up perfectly as a motivator for those who had trouble keeping up. The only difference was the methods of coaching. "Acts of good," like volunteering for a difficult task or carrying someone else's gear so they don't fall, might endear you to a coach, but there was no getting on a drill instructor's good side—they "hated" us all equally. You would never get commended for noble deeds or going above and beyond, because everything was always wrong in their eyes. Someone could frame that in a destructive way, but it taught us a hard lesson about integrity: Would you still do the right thing if no one was watching? If no one is there to pat you on the back after a job well done, will you do the job? And will you do it *well*?

I would be lying if I said I never tried to cut a corner on an obstacle course or get away with something to avoid pain. We all did. But I can say that, even to this day, the lesson stuck. I make it a point to always practice good integrity because there is always someone over my shoulder watching—the friends, Afghan National Army (ANA) soldiers, and Marine brothers I would go on to lose after Afghanistan. They became my moral compass, as did my dad.

Marines have this reminder baked into their core values from the beginning. Now, I fear the results of poor integrity more than I do the fear of honesty.

The drill instructors also taught me the value of positive recognition. There were only a few (well, maybe not even that many) times I received positive recognition from the drill instructors, which made me truly feel I was doing something right. I'm not saying their methodology is something to incorporate in life or business, but there is something valuable about knowing we earned the recognition we receive.

The first time I received this kind of recognition was during "The Scare." The entire base of drill instructors and leaders got in on this elaborate hoax where they woke us all up, screaming, "The Russians just bombed the US! Our nation is under attack! This is NOT a drill."

It was a drill.

However, it didn't feel like one in the moment because of the daily ritual and routine of boot camp. Every day, on the dot, we would wake up, brush our teeth, shave, and train. That day, it was all pushed off. To add to that, the drill instructors showed us their acting chops. They weren't mean. If anything, they seemed nervous. They spoke to us as humans rather than insulting us as the grime under the "boots" that we were.

"Let's go, guys," they said. "We need to meet in the arena."

Everyone was on edge, in shock, focusing on one thought.

Holy hell. We're at war.

They sat the entire company in a big auditorium and gave us an extensive fake briefing. They told us something like:

"At 5 a.m. this morning, a Russian submarine launched three missiles that struck the US, killing thousands of Americans. President Obama has declared war on Russia, and we can no longer continue training. We need to get ready to go. Now. Today. Those of you with non-infantry contracts will be moved to infantry. It doesn't matter if you are a cook or an admin. You will get a rifle in your hand and fight. We are expecting many casualties."

Many recruits began crying right then and there. Some because they were scared, some because we weren't sure if our families were okay. Seeing how we had zero contact with the outside world, we could never have guessed that this was all BS.

I took it completely seriously. I thought we were on the precipice of a Russian invasion, and we would all probably die.

But here is what these crafty drill instructors did next. In their friendly, humanizing tone, they went on to say something like: "We know this can be scary, especially for those who didn't sign up to go to war. Therefore, we are allowing anyone who does not want to go and fight to terminate their enlistment early with zero repercussions."

A quiet fell over the room. You could hear a pin drop.

"Everyone, right now, put your head down and close your eyes. This vote will remain anonymous. If you want to go home, raise your hand over your head, and we will take your name to get you out of here to be with your families."

I won't lie to you, their acting was Oscar-worthy, and I thought by not raising my hand I was effectively signing my death warrant. I was shaking, but I kept my hand down, as firm as I could, pressed on my lap, thinking about how no one else would raise their hand because this is what we were here to do. But . . .

Man, we're going to die.

I tucked my hands between my legs, squeezing them to resist a constant urge to raise either.

After what felt like an eternity, we were all told to lift our heads to see all the people with their hands up, accompanied by the drill instructors smiling with sinister looks. To my surprise, a sea of hands was raised, almost ninety percent of my entire batch of recruits.

The instructors paused for a moment, then burst out with:

"ARE YOU KIDDING ME? COWARDS!"

And just like that, we were greeted by our normal drill instructors. They marched us back to our barracks angrily, reminding us the entire way how weak and pathetic we all were for quitting on our nation. On the way back, our senior drill instructor stood before my platoon and called out my name alongside two others.

"SHAFFER!"

"AYE, SIR!" I yelled.

Then he called on the other two.

"AYE, SIR!" they echoed.

"I don't see your names on this list to go home. What are your contracts?"

"INFANTRY, SIR!" I shouted back. My fellows said the same.

The senior instructor looked at us, up and down, in front of the platoon.

"At least you know why you're here."

It was a compliment I will never forget. Over fifty percent of our class was infantry as well, so he was singling me and my other two fellows out for our commitment to our nation.

"You three," he said. "Stay with me." Then he turned to the other drill instructors. "Drill Instructors? Go remind the rest of this platoon *why* they are here."

The entire platoon looked defeated as they got marched out the door to spend time in the sand pits for the next few grueling hours.

"Good on you guys," the senior drill instructor said when they were out of sight. "Go relax until they're done. Then fall back in line."

"AYE, SIR!" we shouted and headed quietly to our racks.

It was the first time I had been singled out for doing something commendable. Something right. I was so used to being the bad kid or the failure that I couldn't help but smile uncontrollably. I made sure no one saw it.

Maybe I am meant for something better, I thought. *Maybe I belong here.*

Outside of that tiny glimpse of appreciation, we returned to being ordinary dirtbag recruits in their eyes, so the feeling didn't last long. However, something that did stay was the feeling of being in the right place. I chose to be there, but everything that happened to me once there, every struggle and challenge I encountered, was mandatory—forced.

There was no highway option. Well, I suppose there was, but after that day, when I kept my hands tucked firmly between my legs, I felt like I had removed it. In those early days, I was already uncovering a part of myself I wasn't sure was there before—a part of myself that for years I was told never existed.

The truth is, in those days I kept hearing the universe telling me, "Korey, you're a failure."

But there, during training, for brief moments, I wasn't a failure. We often tiptoe around the right way of doing something, especially after we make a mistake (or a lot of mistakes), to avoid the pain or responsibility of disciplining ourselves. We do this as a means of protecting ourselves from pain and change. But sometimes, when discipline is forced upon us—or we force it upon ourselves because the alternative, we know, is nothing but destructive—true and powerful growth is waiting on the other end.

Sometimes we need a blank canvas. Sometimes we need a reset. When we crumple up the paper after we realize what we're writing isn't what we want it to be, we create a path of no return, forcing our brain to forget about it and start over. There have been times while building plaques, after hours of work, that I would make a small nick in the finishing while attaching the final piece. Upset, I would start to think of ways to cover it up to avoid having to rebuild with a new piece of wood. In some instances, that little cover-up might be okay, but before I got too caught up in the thought of covering up my error, I would put a big scratch across the whole thing to FORCE me to get up and do the right thing for these Heroes I was Honoring. When it came to the plaques, these Heroes deserved my best, and my best was there, ready to emerge if I was willing to put in the work.

Most of who we are today is a direct reflection of small amounts of discipline that have crept into our everyday lives. Do you brush your teeth in the morning? That's a small habit backed by discipline because, at some point, you assigned a value to brushing your teeth and a cost associated with what will happen if you don't. My wife would run away from me all day if I ever forgot to brush my teeth, making it known every five seconds that my breath stinks! This is the type of situation we try to avoid through applying micro-discipline. But fall off these "micro" things for good and watch how your life changes. Your teeth will fall out, and you might lose the respect of others who decide that you have poor hygiene. Such people might continue to make wild assumptions about you that impact your experience in the world, affecting your opportunities.

Things like toothbrushing are normally nonnegotiables for us; that's how our brains are wired. The risk does not outweigh the reward, so we do such things routinely. But if small things can make a massive difference, imagine what big changes can do. What happens when you don't give yourself the option to quit? What happens when your *best* is your only option?

Unstoppable growth, that's what.

Forced discipline isn't about forcing yourself to do something you despise or framing pain that's plainly destructive as constructive; it's about proving to yourself that you have something to offer. It's not about cutting wood, writing a paper, or brushing your teeth, but being willing to put everything on the line, to give your all to something because that's how much you believe in it. It's the discipline you need to start a business, to forgive yourself, to reconnect with someone you love—to learn that you have something good and worthwhile to offer the world.

Your small behaviors add up. When you have the humility and fortitude to utilize forced discipline as a tool in your daily life, you will notice the world starting to open up to you, perhaps at first in small ways, then bigger and bigger.

Find a way or create a way, but don't create an excuse.

In truth, I hadn't yet grasped the impact of boot camp and the concept of forced discipline while I was there. To be sure, most of our life's lessons arrive with reflection.

. . . But there *was* one way I stood out.

Rifle qualifications.

I took all the shooting instructions my superiors offered me to heart: anticipating my gun's blast so it wouldn't scare me, using careful and considered breathing techniques, and keeping both eyes open and on the target. The result? I ended up in the top three shooters for the company, shooting two consecutive "possibles," which means I hit all my rounds at distance in the bullseye, twice. Such an achievement was an honor we all received proudly, and another opportunity for micro-discipline to take center stage—or hit the bullseye.

For hitting such high scores, we were given something rare—a phone call home. After two months of zero contact with the outside world, it was one hell of a privilege. There was only one person I wanted to call—my dad. I wanted to tell him about what I'd been learning, how this sense of forced discipline was uncovering something in me, how I wasn't a failure here, how I felt like I belonged—but unfortunately the phone rang, and my dad didn't pick up, and there was no voicemail. That was okay, though, I realized.

We keep doing the right thing, even when no one is there to pat us on the back.

And I was finding a place where I belonged.

As I reflect on the transformative journey through boot camp and the Marine Corps, the essence of discipline and its role in personal growth becomes even clearer. It's not merely about enduring challenges; it's about embracing micro-disciplines that pave the way for substantial transformations.

Boot camp was not just a rigorous training ground; it was a crucible of self-discovery. The lessons learned in that environment continue to shape my character, including the micro- and macro-decisions I make today, reminding me that discipline is not confined to any single moment but a guiding force in everyday life.

In navigating the desire for a disciplined life, it's crucial to recognize that small habits, like brushing your teeth or making your bed, are the bedrock of greater disciplines. These seemingly trivial actions instill a sense of routine and responsibility that extend to more significant aspects of our lives. Think of it like Mr. Miyagi's lessons from *The Karate Kid*: just when it seems like "wax on, wax off" is a mundane task, it shows up in the future as a fighting tactic to save the day. You never know when a past tool will solve a future problem.

Whether it's hitting the bullseye in rifle qualifications or making the choice to do the right thing when no one is watching, discipline remains a necessary companion on the road to personal and collective success. So, I pose the question, what is your version of boot camp that can instill a greater sense of purpose, discipline, and value in you?

Summary:

- Maintaining integrity, even when no one is watching or there is no immediate reward, is an essential character trait. It begins to define who you are and gradually guides all your actions and decisions.
- Build forced discipline by starting small. Maintaining essential habits like going to the gym or making your bed helps develop the muscles of routine, which carries over into more significant aspects of life.
- Facing and overcoming challenges will reveal a side of yourself that you didn't know existed. The more you learn about what you can accomplish, the greater your opportunity for growth.

Chapter 9 Exercise

Put a check next to any of these daily micro-disciplines that you do currently (you might be surprised how much discipline is already present in your life!). If there is a micro-discipline that you do but is not listed here, add it to this list and check it off.

- [ ] Waking up on time in the morning
- [ ] Making your bed
- [ ] Brushing your teeth
- [ ] Flossing
- [ ] Taking a shower or bath
- [ ] Getting to work/school on time
- [ ] Exercising
- [ ] Reading
- [ ] Packing a lunch or snacks
- [ ] Making dinner
- [ ] Tidying up your living space
- [ ] Journaling or reflecting on the day
- [ ] Setting out clothes for the next day
- [ ] Going to bed at night
- [ ] _____
- [ ] _____
- [ ] _____
- [ ] _____

CHAPTER 10

ADAPT AND THRIVE

It's one thing to make a commitment to yourself, but when that commitment is shared as a common goal within a group of people, it becomes ironclad.

Boot camp went by quickly, as did SOI (School of Infantry) afterward. There, I learned all sorts of infantry tactics and did some pretty cool things like shooting rockets or throwing hand grenades. Everything was meant to prepare you for what you would likely see overseas. And from the beginning of signing the paperwork, I knew deployment was in my future.

However, before that happened, something else occurred at the end of SOI that changed my life forever. You see, when you complete SOI, waiting for you is a list of bases where you might prefer to be stationed, but most of the time you almost never get the base you want, even though you usually at least end up on your desired coast. My entire family was on the East Coast, so I wanted to be stationed there. But come graduation day, they came out with a change of plans for our class. There was no sugarcoating it, either.

"Things changed, and we need replacements in several areas of the nation. If your last name starts with A-Q, you stay on the East Coast. If you're R-Z, you're headed to the West Coast."

Simply because of my last name, all my plans of getting a car and spending time with family disappeared in an instant. I was getting sent to 29 Palms, California, notorious for being a "hot-as-hell hellhole" in the Mojave Desert. To say the least, I was disappointed. More than that, I was nervous to be so far away from family and friends for the first time in my life.

But this is what I signed up for—I didn't have a choice.

Within a week, I was on a plane to California, learning about 29 Palms, the history of my new "hellhole", and the "treat" I was in for on the way. I was assigned to 2/7 Echo Company, a Marine Infantry unit that saw some intense combat in 2008. And on that plane ride, as I learned more about 29 Palms, the more nervous I was to get there. It was essentially a barren wasteland in the middle of the desert that more closely resembled a war zone like Afghanistan than any place you might want to live stateside—or, at least, a place I'd like to live. It was miles away from civilization, the days could hit the 120-degree mark, sand covered everything, and the whole base smelled awful because they had a massive sewage lake called "Lake Bandini," where it was common to joke about going fishing to catch things with names like "brown trout."

The place was an uncomfortable dump—in other words, a fantastic mountain warfare training ground. All I could focus on was the luck of my other buddies stationed in Pendleton, right next to all the fun of California—rather than the heat. They'd see sandy beaches, LA, great bars, and clubs. Those guys had it made. Meanwhile, if you blindfolded a "boot" and flew them around in a circle long enough only to land in 29 Palms, you could probably convince them they had been deployed to Afghanistan already.

I can say that because I've been to both. But let's not jump ahead.

Now that I had officially earned the title Marine, I was ready to meet my new brothers-in-arms and all the fellow Marines I envisioned going to battle with. My new unit would welcome me with open arms, right? After all, I'm a Marine! I got through boot camp, passed my tests, and did very well in rifle quals. Well, I was in for a rude awakening.

You see, when you hit the fleet and don't have a combat deployment, that derogatory word "boot" is always present, reminding you that you are nothing until you have done some real Marine stuff. As

I walked up to my brand-new barracks for the first time, a bunch of Marines shouted "boot!" and "fresh meat!" from the balconies.

I was regularly told in passing by the taxi-drivers who dropped off boots to their new base not to look the "senior Marines" in the eyes and stay indoors whenever I could.

"What the hell?" I asked. "Seriously?"

I thought boot camp was my chance to prove myself, but the next six months of our work-up to get to Afghanistan would be a different kind of hell.

On day one, I remember myself and a handful of new Marines making our first stop in the admin building to get checked into our new unit, hoping to avoid any of our seniors, only to arrive at the glass doors as two sergeants came walking out. We stepped to the side to get out of their way, which screamed, "I'm new here!" in their eyes.

"*What?!* No good morning or nothing?" one of them barked at me.

"GOOD MORNING, SERGEANT!" I shouted back like I was in boot camp.

"What unit are y'all with?" he said glancing at the group of us who were now all at the position of parade rest, a submissive position you go to when talking to leadership.

"2/7 Sergeant," we all said back in unison.

"Oh yeah?" he said with a smirk and looked right at me.

"You, let me see your paperwork."

"No, Sergeant," I said timidly, expecting this moment to be a test as we were told as soon as we got off the bus not to let anyone have our paperwork and go straight to the admin building.

"What the f—k do you mean, no?" he said, stepping right up to my face while flexing his entire body.

Before I could even respond, he snatched my paperwork from my hands and threw it over his shoulder.

"Go f—ing get it, BOOT!"

As I scrambled to go get my papers before they blew away in the wind, he turned to the rest of the guys and said, "*Never* let someone get your paperwork. Now get the f—k out of my face."

"Yes, Sergeant!" they all said while they scurried inside.

I wasn't embarrassed or anything in that moment; we were all about to experience much worse than that daily and we knew it. I was just the unlucky SOB that was first in line to take the heat and be made an example of.

For six months, this constant hazing only got worse. All the new guys, including me, were not allowed to have hair on our heads until after our first deployment. We had to "earn our right" to a full head of hair. So, every day, we would all help each other shave our heads to avoid getting our butts kicked by our "seniors" the next day. This was a constant, legitimate fear we all dealt with—they were the predators, and we were the prey being hunted like animals.

The scent? Anyone who didn't have a perfectly shaved head would be terrorized and made to do whatever the "seniors" demanded. "Seniors," looking back, is a loaded term. It was just a bunch of power-hungry kids that ran the barracks like a fraternity. They made us mop rocks, disciplined us whenever they felt like it, "counseled" us in whatever way they felt, and assaulted us, even if it meant drawing blood.

It built a culture of "tough skin," but not in a controlled or arguably constructive way. These guys were passing down the beatings they got as initiation into the Marine culture. Not lessons, not because they wanted us to be strong, but because it had been done to them. Some of us saw it as mental discomfort, but others deemed it mental anguish and actively tried to report it to command so it would stop. I felt like it made the future brotherhood that much stronger. When the guy hazing you became your future friend, it felt full circle. I could just be trying to justify poor behavior, but again, perspective is a powerful thing. They had "boot be good" sticks they would go around whipping us with when we did something wrong. The lessons they taught us were "valuable" in different ways, though, and we always wanted to earn their respect. Not only because it meant fewer butt whooping's but because it meant you were doing something right and might have a place in this brotherhood.

And that brotherhood, in a war zone, became invaluable. Only a few seniors stood out from the crowd as ones who wanted to lead with their hearts rather than those trained by pain.

That's when I met Dunston.

Out of all the guys running around screaming at boots, he was calm, cool, and collected, and he was trying to make sure we knew our infantry knowledge like the back of our hands. Could he snap and get angry like anyone else? Of course, but he led with kindness first. I didn't get to link up with him much initially, but he would soon grow into a senior I respected.

When I got to my unit, it was disorganized, which is abnormal. Usually, when you get to a unit, you get assigned to a platoon and meet who you will grow to know and love as your brothers. But because we were all fooled into thinking that we would be the last unit in Afghanistan to finally end the war, I got moved around constantly, and my direct leadership was always changing before I could build a bond or rapport with anyone.

This changed two months before I deployed.

During cold-weather training in Bridgeport, California, I suffered a major back injury that fractured one of my vertebras. I slipped and fell on some ice, causing my legs to fly over my head, and the impact caused immediate excruciating pain alongside a daily, dull ache. When we got back from the training, I immediately linked up with my doctors back in 29 Palms. When I finally got called into the room I said, "Hey, Doc, this s—t hurts," while lifting the back of my uniform to show my hunched, bruised, and swollen back.

"Jesus Christ, Shaffer," he said with a laugh. "What the hell happened to you?"

"My dumba–s fell in Bridgeport. I think I'm f——ed."

We both found it appropriate to laugh over my jacked-up back; then he decided to remind me that it was serious.

"Well Shaffer, we're definitely going to have to do some X-rays, get you an MRI, and start you on physical therapy . . ."

"Doc, I'm deploying soon," I cut him off. "There's no way I can fit that all in time before I go," I said, hoping he would have a better solution.

"Well, you can go untreated and tough it out, but I don't recommend it. If you make it back in one piece, you could still end up needing surgery or at best intense physical therapy."

"Thanks, Doc, I'll get with the team and let you know the plan," I said as I began to hobble out the medical bay.

I went on with the go-ahead to tell my team the news. Then, right as I went to tell my platoon sergeant that I had to go to at least a few appointments to see how bad it was, we all got called into a meeting to talk about a new "A-team and B-team."

None of us knew what that meant.

Essentially, we got word that we were no longer deploying to Afghanistan as a single unit, which at the time, was a very foreign concept. Our unit would be cut down the middle and divided into two tiers, the A-team and the B-team. The A-team would deploy first as combat replacements to ensure the areas of operations were cleared of the enemy and fortified suitably before the B-team would come in and start deconstructing the Forward Operating Bases (FOBs) since we were "leaving" Afghanistan. This was in 2012. We now know that we wouldn't pull out of Afghanistan until 2021, resulting in the loss of thirteen Marines killed upon exit.

The question was, what determined if we were on the A-team or B-team?

The answer: our performance evals and mission-essential roles.

Through those, they determined who was a necessity, and as an IAR gunner (infantry automatic rifleman, previously known as a SAW, or "squad automatic weapon" gunner) with a few accolades going for me, I was selected for the A-team. That also meant everything was about to change because every platoon got reconstructed, and every Marine got reorganized for the last time before deploying to a war zone with whichever guys were around you. It was a scary feeling.

Who am I going to war with?

We had been passed around so much that we didn't know who we might be sitting in the proverbial foxhole with. Historically, the goal before deployment was to be blood-brothers with your team before any blood was expended. The goal was to know each other's strengths and weaknesses like the back of your hand at least six months before deploying. You would do everything together. You would go to the chow hall (cafeteria) together; you would work out together; you would train in gunfire together; hell, you would even go to the bathroom and shower together sometimes. You needed to know how they shot, when they tended to give up on the run, who was the fastest, who was the slowest. This helped the leaders identify key roles that would serve us best as a team. And there, less than sixty days before deployment, I was going to be introduced to my final deployment team for the first time. I was going to leave all the guys I had learned to love behind, like Dunston.

The thought was untenable to me. In just two months we would be hopping on a plane and going to war, and here they were, mixing up teams in a big open field and starting to call out names for our final deployment squad. I need you to remember something: none of us was having some "Aw, man! I want to be close to my friends" teenage emotion. We're not on a dodgeball team. This could be life or death for us, our futures. Instead, it's more like, "I'm about to put my life in the hands of someone I never met?" It was a genuine concern, because the worst time to find out who you're working with is when you're being shot at or rendering first aid. We wanted to come home in one piece, and mixing teams seemed almost like sabotage to ensure we didn't. My new team could have a bunch of "skaters," or people who did the minimum to get by. They could be cheaters, thieves, or cowards. But I had no idea until I got to work with them. Everyone looked around, confused, and you could see the sadness in their eyes as they got stripped away from the brothers they had been training with for so long.

Then I heard it.

"For A-team, second platoon: Shaffer, Catterlin, Jackson, Switzer, Moralez, Fernando, Repreza, Alvarez..."

I recognized none of the names after mine. I knew none of those Marines. They could have been names of Vietnam vets, and I wouldn't have known the difference. I never talked to them once, and now I was their IAR gunner. *Great . . .* What makes Marines so lethal is their shared connection and desire to bring their brothers home. We all accepted each other as brothers but required a personal connection for maximum effectiveness.

After shouting off all the names, we shifted out of the pack to go meet one another. Faces that I had seen passively around base but were now my new battle buddies.

The first person to stand out as we meandered into a small circle was Corporal Switzer, another senior, this perfect specimen of a man that everyone talked about. Coming from security forces as security to President Obama, he stood 6'3" and was 240 lb. of lean muscle. He was tan, looked like a damn Greek god, and we all knew he was on the "juice," (aka steroids), though, honestly, no one cared. He was pure leadership material.

"Shaffer?" he said as I walked out of the crowd toward him.

"Yes, Corporal?" I responded quickly.

"Are you my IAR Gunner?"

"Yes Corporal," I responded quickly again.

Then came Lance Corporal Catterlin, a senior who was now my new team leader. He was a tall, skinny guy who was a little older than the rest of us because he joined in his early twenties, whereas most of us did at eighteen.

"This is bulls—t," he said as he began walking away from the team he trained with.

I didn't say anything, just kept quiet and waited for the rest of the team to show.

Lance Corporal Jackson began walking toward us; he was someone I had seen more than others around the base, but never spoke to. We shared the occasional head nod as we walked past one another. He was a machine gunner in my peer group, short and stocky like me except with blond hair and always with what seemed like a full can of dip, making his bottom lip stick out a few inches.

"What's up dude?" he said as he walked over.

"Nothing, man. This is bulls—t, isn't it?" I said, echoing Catterlin's sentiment.

"Yeah man, for sure," he replied, then spit his dip out and waited with the rest of us.

Then one by one, the Marines all emerged from the crowd.

Lance Corporal Moralez approached.

"What's up?" he said as Jackson and I both responded with a simple head nod, and he joined the back. Moralez was a shorter Spanish kid who seemed to wear his uniform more like baggy civilian clothes than a uniform, but he was in my peer group as a mortarman.

Corporal Alverez showed up and went straight to the leaders and stood with them. He was my senior as a machine gunner.

And Staff Seargent (SSgt) Repreza and Lieutenant (Lt) Fernando were our leaders that I wouldn't come to meet until later in the day.

Very quickly, I learned who Catterlin and Switzer were as leaders. Switzer earned everyone's respect because of his sheer size and looks. Coupled with the humility of someone who wasn't arrogant, he was an even more likable person. He was tough but fair in everything he did and became like the "dad" of our group. We all wanted to make him proud. Catterlin, however, was my direct leader and made sure I knew my place, just as a good leader should. Anytime I slipped up, Catterlin ensured I learned something from it.

So, as we boarded that plane two months after meeting, I already felt like we would be a good team when things went sideways.

And I was right.

Looking back, I couldn't be more thankful to have served with each of them.

After a few brief stops and exchanges, we landed in Sangin, Afghanistan ("Bangin' Sangin")—a notorious place for improvised explosive devices (IEDs)—in mid-September, not knowing what to expect.

Would we land under fire?

Is it like in the movies where we come out guns blazing?

Nope.

Our helicopter hit the ground, the hatch dropped, and they yelled at us to get off quickly—we were in a "hot zone." You could see in the new team's eyes that we were all running on pure adrenaline. Do we get right into it with the enemy?

Are we about to walk into a brief on our first target?

We all ran off the helicopter fully equipped with our gear, taking in this new terrain quickly and ready to do the work of our nation.

Even now, I still find myself reflecting on how the hell I got there in the first place. Sure, getting to the deployment was a crap show, but only four years before I was rolling around in a cop car after stealing hubcaps. And there I was, four years later, in a desert I never expected to see, an expert marksman, respected for commitment to my role as a Marine, and despite growing up as a heavyset kid, I was in the top percentile of the physical fitness standards. I searched for discipline via ironclad commitments, and I was finally finding it.

And there, after just turning twenty years old, I found myself in a war zone, ready to lay it all on the line, to prove to the world and myself that I was capable and willing. I don't say any of this to aggrandize myself by any means. I have come to terms with the fact that I am just an average guy—if not below average by most standards. I'm shorter than average, weigh more than average, hold a sub-average grade point average, and I could go on—but I was making choices, calls, and commitments that were drastically changing the outcome of my life and how others perceived me.

I still didn't feel like I belonged completely, because I was not someone who had wanted to be a Marine all his life like some of my fellow brothers had, but I was still proving something to myself. I was proving that change is possible if you take the necessary steps.

If you make the small choices.

If you accept the ironclad commitments.

So, what does that mean for you?

Well, let's review: I got a 47 out of 100 on my Military Aptitude Testing. I grew up in special education classes and sucked at every sport I tried. I got held back in 3rd grade and maintained a 1.7 GPA through high school. By those standards, it is an irrefutable fact that I am nothing special—but I can tell you I am ecstatic with my progress and growth as a person. If I was able to make those small changes, to make those ironclad commitments to something more than myself, to build up my mental fortitude, imagine what *you* can do.

I'm willing to bet that no matter where you are in life right now, if you acted upon opportunities for growth just as I did, you would walk circles around me. So don't wait. Start taking them. Make the small choices and the commitments that build you up rather than keep you down. I'm not saying you have to do something extreme like join the military or search for added hardship—but you can write a book, join a running group, take up art, do volunteer work, see a counselor, take a walk, turn off social media, attend a masterclass, do something great for yourself! And even if you don't get the lesson you were aiming for, you will almost certainly still walk away with valuable and positive mental development.

Because even there, fresh off the plane, sitting on a base in Afghanistan, I thought I had already learned a lot about life. I had made small choices and big commitments, but compared to what I was in for, my growth and development had barely begun.

Summary:

- Sometimes small, seemingly insignificant choices can lead to big changes in your life.
- When you make a commitment, especially to something bigger than yourself, make it ironclad. Stick to it, and let it drive you forward.
- Regardless of past failures or challenges, there's potential for growth in everyone. Your past does not have to dictate your future.
- If one person can make changes and commitments that lead to growth and development, so can you. Don't underestimate your potential.
- You don't have to take extreme measures to grow. Engage in activities that build you up, no matter how insignificant they seem.

Chapter 10 Exercise

Reflect on an instance where you were placed in an unfamiliar or uncomfortable situation. How did you manage your feelings, and what strategies did you use to overcome the adversity? Make the answer as simple or complex as you'd like.

LEGACY MINDSET

CHAPTER 11

SPEAK UP

When our fear renders us silent, we might later hear echoes of regret. Speak up for yourself, for your voice can unveil the truth and reshape destinies, even if criticism awaits you.

"This is it?" I asked.

"What were you expecting?" Catterlin replied.

Our helicopter lifted off while we provided security, kicking up "moon dust" and clearing enough in our path to plainly see what was right in front of us. Other Marines who arrived earlier sat idly on their packs, eating MREs, laughing and joking around, and throwing rocks at each other in sheer boredom. They were relaxed. Unbothered.

Not an ounce of perceived danger was in the air.

I didn't know how to answer Catterlin because I didn't know exactly what I expected, but I can tell you it wasn't to get off the helicopter only to hurry up and wait as we did back in the States. I was so disoriented by my vague expectations that I felt I was back in 29 Palms, getting ready for another field operation. Where was the danger? The explosions? The firefights? Where was the war? Were we too late? Did we miss it?

A staff sergeant walked by and snapped us out of our reveries by telling us to grab our gear and "line it up single file" to wait for instructions from our senior leadership.

"Yes, Staff Sergeant," we all said and followed suit with the other Marines.

And following suit meant to sit on our packs, hurry up, and wait. Corporal Switzer looked at us and repeated the order:

"Come on, gents, let's move our bags over here. Stay together."

"Yes, Corporal," we all said.

The sound of brass and belt-fed linkage from the wars fought before us crunched beneath our feet as we walked. Then, on high alert, with adrenaline still spiking and our brains confused about why we weren't running, fighting, or shooting, we sat down on our packs for the first time and took in our surroundings. As we learned, especially as Marines, no matter where you are in life, everything you observe tells a story. From your home to your school to your town to your country, to the detail of the walls in front of you, the solidity of the floors under your feet, the language you hear people speaking, it all paints a picture and sets your mind racing with either positive or negative preconceptions that influence your level of awareness.

In a war zone, nearly all those preconceptions are going to be negative.

And the story that Afghanistan told us, as we sat in a line and pointed toward different telltale signs of combat in a war-torn country, was tragic and sad. Each iota of detail you grabbed from the environment told stories of lives lost and dreams shattered, in detail so extreme you could hardly miss it—even if you wanted to.

The barriers surrounding our forward operating base (FOB) were littered with bullet holes and shrapnel. The glass that surrounded our observance posts had been shattered from incoming fire. The vehicles parked on the base were blackened from blast exposure to IEDs. The walls of the Afghani houses were chipped and broken from an ongoing exchange of gunfire and rockets. The craters, bullet holes, and gashes in the architecture were everywhere; all of it was a reminder that someone had stood or taken cover in this exact spot and fought for their life. And many of them did not make it out—and if they did, they might not have emerged unscathed.

It was like standing on the yellow footprints again, feeling the millions of others who had stood in the same spot over the past one hundred years, except this was different. It wasn't the eager beginning to a new journey at boot camp. I wondered if the Marine who fired those rounds was still alive or if the Afghanis who lived in the littered houses still lived there. I wondered how many of them were killed, how recently it happened, and whether their families, standing at their graves, still carried on with the understanding that they themselves may not wake up the next morning. I could feel the souls of the lost weighing heavily on the sand. It wasn't eerie or distant or ephemeral. It was real. It was close. It stayed.

And it was just plain sad.

Even if no combat ensued for the rest of the deployment, being able to see where people had lost their lives while fighting or fleeing several times over, and knowing there was no blanket or force protecting us from the same fate, was enough to change the way I looked at the world. At everything. Right now, we were also the force, the blanket. Our experience was not a walk in the museum. We were there to survive the exhibit and, if called for, become another story of loss and warning for the next set of Marines.

That was the thought none of us could shake.

What if, in six months, the rest of my team goes home with a flag draped over my casket?

But then, I snapped back into reality and thought, *All of this is past—we must have missed the boat for combat.* We sat on our backpacks in the carnage that came before, not wearing our vests or helmets, as fellow Marines kicked rocks beside us. No one was shooting at us, and we were there gearing up for a winter deployment. A season in which the enemy didn't want to fight because they didn't have modern clothing and equipment like us to protect them against the elements. And suddenly, with those thoughts, complacency began settling in almost as fast as the somber feeling of generations of loss and fighting had come.

We missed the boat, I thought. *This is no longer a war zone.*

Then something happened to remind me that we weren't in Kansas anymore . . .

As I sat there against the bullet-riddled barrier, sipping some water from my Camelback with my team gearing up for what seemed like an easy deployment, I started thinking of other things. Looking over the HESCO barriers (defensive walls), I took in all the history and sat in awe that just a year before I was sitting in a high school classroom, wondering about this exact moment as if it were manifested (go figure). I gazed up toward a group of compounds on a hill straight ahead, and it was silent outside of the light chatter of Marines and the sound of departing helicopters.

Then, while staring at the compounds nearly 700 yards away, a plume of black smoke erupted, followed by fire and debris. Before I could understand what happened, a shockwave raced toward us, rattling our chests and eardrums.

If you haven't already experienced it, watching something explode is a surreal experience, because there is a lag from the compression of the sound waves that shake the core of your body. Before you can even comprehend the situation or raise a concern, it's too late.

As my eardrums rattled, you could hear about thirty Marines in unison, all yelling out in surprise. Once again, we were as fresh to deployment as we could be, and we had no idea what was planned, what wasn't, or what was a big deal. So, after ping-ponging between each other, we looked to those who had been there the longest for visual cues and confirmation on how to act.

My first instinct was to turn toward the staff sergeant, who had instructed us off the helicopter. He navigated and organized the backpacks, looking unfazed and sleepy.

"Staff Sergeant," I said. "What the heck just happened?"

He barely looked up from the bags. "Was that you in the compound?" he said calmly.

"No, Staff Sergeant."

"Good. Then don't f——ing worry about it."

"Yes, Staff Seargent."

The war wasn't over, I realized. It had just gone on for so long (eleven years at that point) that explosions and death were commonplace. For some, it wasn't even worth turning their head. We weren't sitting there without gear because we were safe, but because comfort and downtime were worth the increased risk of death if a lucky mortar shot from a Taliban fighter landed at our feet. And yet, as I looked at the staff sergeant so desensitized to the sounds and sights, I won't lie, it got me worried.

This place is going to be hell, I thought. *And it's going to change me.* Then, almost as a mantra, I repeated: *Learn from it, channel the lessons, and become a better person.*

After a few days, we were settled into our sleeping bags trying to ignore the sounds of explosions and gunfire that littered the night. We were called early in the morning to a small part of the base for an announcement from our unit commander. We all knew this was "The Talk" that all leadership gives their unit before they start patrolling and going off on missions. Something to the order of: "You guys are supposed to be one of the last units to control this AO (area of operation), and the Taliban will hit you with all they've got. You won't all make it home, but this is what we are here for."

This is a standard "moto" speech that every infantry leader gives, designed to desensitize you to the things you are likely to encounter: death, destruction, guilt, and fatigue. Many of these speeches include stories of great infantrymen who came before us, like Carlos Hathcock, or other men known for valor and "kill streaks."

These speeches would always start the same. Something on the order of "Listen up, warriors! I've got a legendary tale of Carlos Hathcock, a true American hero!" And so they would continue:

> Vietnam, a jungle hell where danger lurked at every turn. In the midst of chaos, there was a Marine sniper, a silent and deadly force to be reckoned with—Carlos Hathcock! This man wasn't just a marksman; he was a phantom in the shadows, a nightmare for the enemy!
>
> Hathcock didn't just face the enemy; he hunted them down with an unmatched determination. Crawling through the mud, concealed by the unforgiving foliage, he became the stuff of legend. "One shot, one kill—" his mantra echoed through the trees, striking fear into the hearts of those who dared to oppose him.
>
> But the legend doesn't end there, oh no! In the scorching heat of battle, Hathcock faced a ruthless North Vietnamese sniper known as "Cobra." This was a showdown of epic proportions, a duel between two masters of the craft. And guess what? Our man Hathcock, he emerged victorious, sending a

powerful message to all who doubted the indomitable spirit of the American warrior!

So, warriors, let the spirit of Hathcock fuel your determination! Face your enemy head-on and be the relentless force in the chaos.

Upon the conclusion of the speech, we would shout back "Kill!" or "Rah!"

At that time, "kill streaks" were something almost every young Marine was interested in. The more kills someone had, the more we looked at them with awe. In hindsight, it's wild how we measured our success as infantrymen by the number of kills or firefights we had been in. However, that was the infantry in a nutshell:

Have you ever seen combat? If not, you're a boot.

They didn't care when you joined or what circumstances led to your not firing at the enemy. If you hadn't done it at least once, you hadn't earned your stripes—in truth, a pathetic mentality that no real leader would ever hold against a warrior. Having employed several hundred people in the past few years, I am glad I learned this lesson upfront. Authentic leadership identifies tenacity and courage through close monitoring of traits and personality, not whether a person was "lucky" enough to get caught in a bad situation and have to fight their way out. That type of leadership, which was more common than not, started a bloodthirsty and toxic culture where there were only two ways to measure a Marine: by their combat record or accolades (aka the ribbons on their chest).

The damage this would do came during and after deployment.

Our senior enlisted would tell us about about room-clearings in Fallujah, Iraq, where Marines cleared dozens of enemies from a room, taking fire from all sides, we all thought: *Yeah, that's going to be me, clearing out bad guys for my country.* We put stories like that on a pedestal because those warriors were American Heroes to us, doing God's work and keeping our nation safe. Their stories would circulate through our barracks, going from one boot to the next until that Marine had total respect in our eyes. Each of us wanted that respect for ourselves one day when we earned it, just like they did. That's all that mattered to us, getting over there and doing our job to the fullest, even if it meant laying down our life in the process.

This is also the point in the story where I must remind you of two major things:

This was 2012, and though there was less 2010-style action going on, it was still the fourth deadliest year of our war in Afghanistan. Essentially, ever since 2010, the level of fighting and loss of allied forces declined each year with the initiative of earning the "hearts and minds" of the locals. A good thing for our families, but for the warrior trying to prove he's capable, not so much.

Every year that passed, Afghanistan seemed to get less and less chaotic. Or so we thought. My initial reaction upon landing wasn't uncommon, because there was a legitimate fear that we had "missed the boat," especially being in a majority winter deployment. The other reminder was that our only measurable success metric (against someone else's scale) was combat experience and kills. Many of us just wanted to live up to the title of Combat Veteran and be well-respected like those before us. We longed for it. We craved it. We needed it.

So, if the goal was to give it all for our country, the declining violence and season were not playing into our unit's favor, and we wondered: *Are we going to be that unit? The one that's just one deployment late to a twelve-year war?*

Of course, now we know the war lasted over twenty years, but at the time, we believed this was our last chance to shine. And after about one month into this deployment, we learned more about what Afghanistan was actually like, and the stories of the detritus we saw upon landing all started to add up—the war was still here.

Yet one month into our deployment in Sangin Valley, Afghanistan, the desensitization was already taking root. The sounds of mortars landing close by didn't even make us look up from what we were doing, whether it was working out, cleaning our weapons, getting ready for another patrol, or sleeping. Machine-gun fire and potshots were a natural ambiance, and most of the time, none of us could shoot back without putting the villagers at risk. It was mostly observing a war zone while feeling almost powerless. Uninvolved. A lot like watching a movie that we wished to be part of.

We learned quickly that IEDs would be ninety percent of our encounters with the enemy. Not daily firefights, which none of us had experienced yet, just a lot of explosions going off around our area of operation: those IEDs being stepped on by allied forces and local nationals (LN), incoming mortars from the Taliban, or even farmers being forced by the enemy to engage us for fear of losing their family or crops. Thankfully, our unit casualties were virtually nonexistent, but local nationals, kids, and the Afghan National Army were not as lucky.

But I wanted the "excitement." I wanted to be part of something. *Let me go toe-to-toe, put pressure on a bleeding wound, and make the call to decide if I go home a Hero or not at all.* I wanted to be challenged. As a wise man once said about seasoned veterans:

"You want to become like us until you become like us."

So, at twenty-years-old, fresh out of high school, hot and sweating and a little hungry, I stood post waiting for "excitement," staying on high alert for my chance to see the infamous Taliban tribe coming to attack and failing to overrun our base.

But alas, nothing.

I observed local nationals and their strange customs and culture through the scope of a rifle pointed at them, often making fun of or commenting on them for being different—like a bunch of children watching older people. Catterlin and I talked about how we couldn't wait to start patrolling more and getting into fights with the enemy.

But the enemy was nowhere to be seen.

Catterlin and I were chosen on this day to provide security on a road that came to a T-shaped intersection. We were at the bottom of the T, staring down the road to the intersection at the top, all lined by mud buildings.

And we were BORED.

Time on post was spent doing whatever you could to stay entertained for eight hours while staring down your scopes in consistent intervals to call out anything that seemed suspicious through the radio. About an hour into our post, Catterlin walked up to a bullet-riddled chunk of glass procured from a retired High Mobility Multipurpose Wheeled Vehicle (Humvee) that sat placed on some raggedy sandbags that were supposed to protect us. The sound of distant gunfire was present, but nothing we were worried about. The sun was high in the sky, and the day was just perfect, which meant a lot of the locals came out of their homes to shop in the bazaar. Catterlin walked up to the glass to take an obligatory peek, while I was just leaning back watching him. Suddenly, I see him freeze for a second and duck his head.

"Oh s—t! Is that a sniper?" he said, now crouching behind the glass.

"Wait. What?" I said as I cracked a smile in disbelief, crouched low and walked over.

"Right there!" He pointed to a dark spot on top of an adjacent roof.

My adrenaline started flowing. *This might be our chance to engage!* I slowly peeked my head up for a better look, gun in hand. I scanned the area for a second through my scope, being careful not to expose too much of my head just in case. And then I saw it . . .

"Dude. That's just a smokestack." I burst out laughing in mockery.

A confused Catterlin looked up at me, still crouched. "What? Are you sure?"

I was now standing up, full-on belly laughing with tears in my eyes.

"Keep laughing," he said. "But I gotta be here to pick up the pieces if you get your head blown off."

Which, for whatever reason, caused us both to break out simultaneously in tear-filled laughter.

"Man, what if we just started lighting up that smokestack while screaming SNIPER! Could you imagine what the command would say?" I said through laughter.

"They would absolutely crucify us!"

The rule of combat, in a nutshell, was if you were not getting shot at from three feet away by a guy standing out in the open holding a Taliban flag and screaming "Death to America!," they threatened to have you tried for murder. Okay, that's hyperbole, but it felt that way! This was passed down from our leadership to convey that we were not there to hurt innocent people, which I agreed with, but shouldn't be scared to defend ourselves from the enemy either. As eager young Marines, the strict rules of engagement made us feel like we had enemies both outside and inside the wire. Like they cared more about protecting their image than appreciating the complicated situations we Marines could find ourselves in.

After Catterlin and I settled back down, we took a visual inventory of anyone in our line of sight. The sporadic sound of gunfire reminded us that, just because the smokestack was a fluke, it didn't mean the next time couldn't be real. I got behind the machine gun on post and used the scope to set eyes on a group of local nationals on the right-hand corner of the intersection.

"Shaffer, what do you see?" Catterlin asked me passively, while looking down and fixing his gear that had shifted in his panic.

"Not s—t. Just some local nationals on the corner d——ing around."

I pulled my eye from the scope to get a better view of the road, but before I could stand up straight and blink . . .

Flash . . .

BOOOOOOM!

Shockwave.

A massive cloud of dust erupted from the same corner, right at the end of the road where the local nationals were. The shockwave rattled our chests, teeth, and ear drums.

"Holy s—t!" we both yelled, putting our hands up like we were going to block debris from hitting us. "What was that?!" we screamed as we watched the blue sky start to darken from the moon dust.

Of course, we knew it was an IED. *But so close?* The area was under watch 24/7, 365 days a year, because it was an area that was commonly foot patrolled. Heck, I had just patrolled it the week prior. Our tech allowed us to see the heat signature through thermals of any freshly dug dirt, and beyond our standing post, we had overhead imagery watching everything on that street. But this was different and went against our experience up to that point. An explosion went off, and people were caught in it.

Without hesitation, we got on the radio. We called up to central command and told them a group of local nationals may have just stepped on an IED right in front of us, but we couldn't confirm because the area was completely cloaked in dust obstructing our view.

As Catterlin came off the call, our weapons had already come off safe, because the enemy was close enough to engage in broad daylight. And from our unit's experience so far, IEDs could be accompanied by sporadic gunfire.

At this point, you may think we would run over to help the downed LNs, but that's not how this works—especially when on post. Your objective is to watch and wait for orders or for someone else to send a team to investigate.

We were to never leave our post unless as a squad on patrol.

Still trying to process exactly how the enemy got so close to us, we sat there waiting anxiously for orders and for the dust to clear to see if there were any live bodies on the ground. As the dust settled, I still hoped it was a fluke—that a goat had set it off—but we weren't so lucky. I saw remnants of clothing and debris through the dust, enough to know that the people on the corner were not okay. However, my view wasn't clear, and it was tough to see the whole picture. It looked like the explosion went off on one side of them, pushing them all in the same direction and out of view. All I could think about was the size of this explosion.

A bomb that big is not easy to hide or bury. More than that, it would leave a massive crater for everyone to see. But as the dust began to settle, I saw nothing that tracked with traditional logic. Without saying a word, I was stumped for an answer.

IEDs don't do that. This must be a suicide bomber.

Then something else appeared within the fading of the dust: a motorcycle, in perfect shape, idling, sitting upright on its kickstand at the top of the road's "T," dead center.

That wasn't there before. What happened?

"Is that a bomber's bike?" I asked Catterlin.

"I don't know," he said.

"Did he jump off and detonate?"

"I don't know."

"It's right side up and in good shape with nobody next to it," I said, staring at it through my scope. "Do you think it was a LN's that just died?"

"Shaffer, I don't know, dude," he said while scanning the area via his rifle's scope.

Mind you, as much as we got along, Catterlin was still superior to me, so when I started to get on his nerves by asking too many questions, I shut up because there was a line between friendship and leadership that needed to be kept. So, I shut my mouth and took in the sight of what seemed to be a group of people who had just died in front of me, and possibly because of me not being on the rifle the way I should have.

We met a part of the Afghan National Army whose commander seemed like the epitome of a good man. He always led his men no matter how dangerous the situation was, and was especially quick to make calls that neutralized the risk of any Taliban member getting to our doors. You could pick him out from a distance because he walked with his hands behind his back, slightly hunched over. The oldest man among the crowd, constantly inspecting situations, like the Sherlock Holmes of Afghanistan.

We sent the commander and his team of two soldiers over to assess the explosion's damage and do the ANA's version of an AAR (After Action Report). Catterlin and I stayed there at post, waiting for an answer, hoping for something positive to come through the radio.

After reviewing the area with an aerial camera, the news came back through the radio: "We're tracking remnants of a suicide bomber," the Command Operation Center (COC) said, followed by indistinct chatter.

Right in front of us, a suicide bomber wearing a vest, just barely out of our vision, detonated on the street, killing himself and several local nationals. I couldn't believe it. *That close to us?* It's an unexplainably chilling feeling to know that the enemy was right next to you and chose to let you live. Like sitting next to someone and finding out they were a serial killer. We had the enemy in our rifle sights and didn't even know it.

Perspective came flooding in, and I felt a weight on my shoulders grow . . .

This was right in front of us, and none of us saw it coming. People died.

The bomber could have came toward Catterlin and me and taken more people with him, but instead, he just detonated in an open and relatively uncrowded area. That's when I learned a little more about who we were fighting. It wasn't about how many people they killed but how many they scared. How many they sent home that day thinking it could happen on their street—to their family and friends. They wanted their enemies to live in terror.

Terrorism is a mind game, and they had Catterlin and me shaking in our boots, knowing we were spared. But we weren't done yet. We were still providing security, and when something like that happens, you stay on extra high alert because you never know if it will be followed up with an attack. Meanwhile, the ANA continued to "pick up the pieces" so to speak, and everyone navigated around the bike, ignoring it. As the ANA finished, however, they began to huddle around the bike, seemingly intrigued by it.

My heart began physically pumping harder because I could see, for the first time, that no one knew where this bike came from or what part it played in the attack. These guys had lived there for their entire lives, and I was sure they had seen it all, but I was invested. I couldn't look away.

Whose bike was it?

One second, everything was fine, then the suicide bomber.

Now the dust settles, and there's a random bike.

What's going on?

After the ANA commander and two of his men concluded their huddle and deemed the bike safe, they grabbed it by the handlebars and started walking toward Catterlin and myself. My mind was racing because it just didn't make sense. I trusted the ANA leaders and their judgment because of how long they had been at war, while I was just a boot from a first-world country on his first tour. At only a month in, we quickly realized that half the stuff they told you in training that were "red flags" or "dos and don'ts" get thrown out the window as soon as we land. And even though the IED 101 rule is "If you didn't put it there, you don't pick it up," they were violating that rule and bringing the bike right toward us.

I wanted to yell "*Wadarega*!," which meant "Stop!" in their language, but I didn't because of a fear that sat inside me saying, *Don't make your team look stupid, they know better than you.* If it was nothing, I'd be setting myself up to get chewed out for overstepping by the seasoned veterans in my unit.

So, I just sat there beside Catterlin, clenching my jaw.

About halfway down the road, the three guys stopped and turned to their left into what was an office for the commander, or at least a building they were familiar with. I was expecting them to leave the bike outside, as you would expect, but in Afghanistan, the mud-hut city homes treated small vehicles the same inside or out.

A home could be a garage.

The commander entered and the two guys followed, bringing the idling bike inside. There was a sigh of relief because once you made it off the "X," the area of incident or combat, you were usually safe.

And everything was good for about ten seconds.

Then . . .

Flash.

BOOOOOOM!

A shockwave of dust and debris flew out of the building as the roof caved in. The sound was deafening to Catterlin and myself, rattling our teeth.

"What the f—k!" I yelled. "Are you kidding me?!"

It turned out my intuition was correct. The bike was packed with explosives and set up as a secondary by the suicide bomber, rigged to explode when someone turned it off.

We both panicked at this point as Catterlin swiped the radio off the sandbags, almost dropping it because our gloves were bulky, and hands were shaking from adrenaline.

"COC. COC. This is post three."

"Go for COC," they immediately responded, knowing that there was an enemy in the area.

"We have a secondary IED that has just detonated in the commander's office. They need medics ASAP," Catterlin said quickly but clearly. "I repeat, they need medical assistance ASAP." The ANA may not have been American troops, but they were still our allies, and I cared for them even though it was an unpopular opinion. We were supposed to be there fighting as one team. I embraced that and befriended as many as I could—like the commander.

Then I found myself sitting there again, ears ringing, staring at a cloud of smoke and moon dust, trying to see if anyone would come out of the rubble alive.

Nothing.

Every second that passed, I got more and more angry.

"Where the f—k are the medics!?"

"I'm so f——ing stupid, I should have said something while I had the chance!"

"How did I miss the suicide bomber?"

It felt like time itself froze in place, and the only people not affected by this dilated time were the wounded ANA soldiers and me. I was frustrated with Catterlin for shutting me down, and even more pissed at myself for not having the balls to say, "Listen, something doesn't add up. Tell COC that the bike is likely a secondary. Better safe than sorry." But as I stared at the dust with regret for sending these guys out, I felt no response speed would have been fast enough to serve as an apology to those wounded. If they were even alive.

After about ten minutes, with the dust settled, they spun up a team of Marines, a Navy Corpsman (a medical specialist commonly nicknamed "doc"), and another team of ANA to render first aid to the survivors. You would expect them to sprint to the rescue, but that was a humbling moment when I understood why they weren't running and just taking their time.

Complacency kills.

This guy just detonated two bombs and successfully hit his targets (except he hoped it would be Catterlin and me who grabbed the bike during our report). It only takes about forty seconds for someone to pass away from blood loss, so as I counted the seconds, my anger grew, and I felt like no one cared.

The team arrived at the bombed-out building and spent about five minutes inside—what felt like an eternity. Then the doc came over to Catterlin and me and said:

"No survivors."

"This is all my fault," I said. My chest began to tighten as if I were being crushed inward, and a lump in my throat began to form.

I sat and thought of a hundred scenarios in which grabbing the radio and voicing my suspicions got me chewed out and made fun of, but the one scenario that could go wrong did, and three men died because of it. I have lived with that guilt for years, and it will never go away, no matter how often people tell me it's not my fault. It's okay. I get it. How could I have known? But nothing will ever change the fact that I didn't *speak up* when I had the power to, and these men paid that price while the ANA lost a great leader.

I wanted to share this extreme example of how I learned an important lesson: *Speak up, even when there is a fear of criticism.*

My hope is that you can empathize with this lesson at a safe and nontraumatic level. My situation is not exactly relatable to most people, and that's okay. Reality is perception, and often perception determines impact. It's so natural for us to believe that what we have to say is not valuable or that, compared to the people around us, we're not important enough to bring any ideas to the table.

At that moment, I thought I was the most novice in situational awareness, but it turns out that if I had spoken my mind or engaged in conversation, those men could be here today, and this chapter wouldn't exist. But this chapter is here because these events are real, even when they don't feel like it. So ask yourself: *How often do you hold back?*

How often do we not raise our hand, speak up, volunteer, ask questions, or ask for help for fear of being criticized or judged?

Every. Single. Day.

And I get it, finding someone to talk to about your struggles or ideas often isn't the problem; finding someone who won't judge you is a different story. But that's not the sad part. The sad part is that you have no idea how many amazing stories and alternate paths might have manifested in your life, had you not let fear close the doors of opportunity in your face. While being involved in a suicide bombing is not something I would have actively sought as an opportunity for growth, I believe that my traumatic experience can serve a positive purpose, even just as a cautionary tale: speak up, or face the drastic consequences of your silence.

There is a proverb from Cormac McCarthy's novel *No Country for Old Men* that goes, "Anyway, you never know what worse luck your bad luck has saved you from."

I'd argue the flip side. You never know what opportunity your misfortune has brought upon you. What are you afraid of? Looking dumb? Looking weak? Looking poor?

Join the club! Almost all of us fear how others perceive us. If you don't confront those fears, they will force you to stay where you are, paralyzing you from getting to where you want to be—because growth is on the other side of those fears.

I'll be the first to tell you that I have asked some dumb questions that made everyone turn and look back at me. Even laugh. I'll also be the first to tell you that when I started dealing with PTSD and suicidal tendencies, I would wipe my tears away before anyone could see them, especially my wife. I would lie about "feeling great," posting on social media so everyone thought I was on top of the world. I didn't want anyone to see me as anything other than a resilient man who had his stuff together.

Change happened when I confronted the fear of looking weak and made it a point to *speak up* when things were wrong—not just with me or my mental health, but in the situations I face daily.

If I experience a PTSD episode triggered by a certain situation, I communicate to those around me—especially if I anticipate an awkward or negative atmosphere due to my delayed responses or thousand-yard stare—asking for some time and understanding until the distressing thoughts subside and I can get myself back to normal.

If I'm looking at some work someone did for me and it's not to my standards, I will tell them to do it again.

If I don't feel in the right mental state, I say, "Hey, I'm going to reach out to a therapist. I don't feel myself."

That is the standard of people with which I surround myself, and I hope you can do the same. My friends and family know to never, ever pass judgment on anyone for speaking up. They would be booted from my circle so fast, it's not even funny. Value your voice and make yourself heard. This is your life and mind you're caring for. It's not worth us starting every day of our lives wishing they were better.

So please, for your sake, set a standard around not bottling up your emotions and speaking your mind. Absorb the people who support you and push away those who violate that standard. Because you never know when one of those people will be the reason you shut the door of opportunity on yourself. There is:

No Professor

No Family Member
No Orator
No Politician
No Boss
No Friend

There is *no one* worth you feeling like you must withhold your voice.

I'd rather look stupid asking a question and risk rejection or take the chance on a therapist despite the outcome than not try. People will see that you don't have the same fears that govern everyone else, and that will naturally inspire an unstoppable confidence that propels your personal growth.

Don't stay quiet. Speak up. You don't want to live with the regret of missing an opportunity to change lives or, in my case, save them.

Summary:

- It's crucial to voice your concerns or ideas even if you're afraid of criticism or rejection.
- Your insights and instincts have value; never assume you're too inexperienced or ignorant to contribute.
- Rejection and setbacks can sometimes be stepping stones to something bigger. Don't be afraid of rejection; learn from it and move forward.
- Create an environment where everyone feels safe to speak up. Encourage open communication and support among peers and eliminate judgment for expressing concerns.
- By confronting fears and speaking up, you can inspire others and contribute to your personal growth and the growth of those around you.
- You have no idea what life may have in store for you, so long as you do not let fear close the doors of opportunity in your face. The consequences of our actions can ripple out and influence the future in ways we cannot foresee.

Chapter 11 Exercise

Affirm your confidence in sharing your opinion without fear of rejection! Write "I have a voice and I'm not afraid to use it!" below. Then circle or highlight it.

Next, think of something in your life that you have felt hesitant to speak up about. Make a list of reasons you're afraid to speak up. Then, list out all the positive things that could happen if you spoke up. Review your lists and consider your next steps.

CHAPTER 12

EMPATHY IS A TOOL

The thing about having a heart of gold, it's always heavy.

In November 2012, my unit needed replacements in Kajaki, Afghanistan. I had recently heard of the place from a buddy who returned from Kajaki one year prior. His stories of engagements, rocket-propelled grenades (RPGs), and mortars excited me (I had a lot to learn), so I was ecstatic when the word got out that they were sending our squad over there.

"This is going to be our chance to go toe-to-toe!" we would say.

As a unit, we wanted to do our job: to rid the land of the Taliban. But it always seemed like some red tape at the senior leadership level stopped us from doing what we came there to do. The units before us were able to "kick the hornet's nest" so to speak, while we were left fortifying a more defensive position.

This felt more like cowardice, affecting the mentality of many of the Marines on base. Once again, that "missed the boat" feeling settled in. However, since we had just been selected to go to a more active area, one known to have firefights and the enemy at our door, we knew that it would also come with some opportunities for valor and "excitement" for once. We all want to be the seasoned, war-torn veteran until we get what comes with it.

On a cold day, we loaded up the helicopter to take a trip over to the Kajaki Sofla, a giant hydro dam that fed raw power to the land. The Taliban ultimately wanted control over the dam because it would give them more influence over the people than just the crops and roads. So naturally, the Marines built patrol bases around the dam because that's where the fight was.

At this point in the deployment, we had experienced the dangers of IEDs firsthand and watched good people perish. But getting into a firefight like in the olden days excited us. It's hard to describe, but what started with swords, then muskets, then repeaters, and now the modern rifle in my hand, it just felt like an honor to experience what countless warriors had faced before, an opportunity to pay homage to their bravery. For some service members, the reality of never getting that opportunity led to their taking their own lives out of embarrassment for not being able to live up to their greatest ideals.

The thought of never firing our rifles overseas weighed heavy on our minds, because we knew we wouldn't be able to share our stories with the other Marines back in the States. This was a sad way of thinking, but the military is like a cult, and several unspoken judgments are shared before and after signing on the dotted line.

We were welcomed by the other unit that had yet to be RIPed (relief in place), and we immediately asked them about the hot spots, common IED areas, and, of course, the firefights. The day was spent going around and identifying the dos and don'ts. In particular, they pointed out the Shrine, a patrol base all the enemies seemed to have dialed into their weapon systems.

"Rockets, mortars, small arms, IEDs. You name it; it's been hit with it."

And we were right next to it.

The more questions we asked, the more we seemed like noobs looking for a fantasy, while they had just lost their Navy Corpsman to an IED right outside the base. That humbled us quickly, but the humility didn't last long. They had a wooden cross right in the middle of their compound with the collar devices (ranks) of all the Marines and Sailors who had died defending the area. We all stopped, struck by the reality of our situation.

Then, I'd imagine one of two thoughts popped into all our minds:
That's not going to be me.
Or:
We might not make it home the way we came.

Catterlin tapped me on the shoulder as I stared at the collars.

"Let's bed down and rack out so we can get a fresh start with them tomorrow."

"Roger that, Lance Corporal."

Except that night started much differently. It was much louder, and much closer than we were used to. As soon as the sun crossed below the horizon and we lay down in our sleeping bags, gunfire started erupting near the Shrine. You could see tracers going both ways from the enemy to the ANA shooting back. It looked like lasers from a freaking Star Wars battle.

It was impossible to sleep, and we all got up and went outside to see if we needed to engage—Lord knows we wanted to. But we couldn't get a positive ID on the people shooting, so we just sat back and took it so that we didn't risk unnecessary casualties.

And then, something even more unexpected happened.

After about thirty minutes of firing, it all stopped.

We laid back in our sleeping bags like kids giddy with excitement, talking about the spectacular light show we had just witnessed.

After only a few months in Kajaki, the splendor of the nightly light show started to dim, and the effects of deployment started getting to me. On the physical side, I still had terrible back pain from the fractured vertebra after my fall that occurred right before deployment. PT and medication helped, but the pain was consistent and would come back worse later in life. To add stress to that injury, one of my consistent jobs was moving the dead and wounded to get medevaced in Kajaki. This, unfortunately, was a much more frequent occurrence than we initially expected, and it started to impact my mental health as I would see the faces of those people whenever I went to sleep.

One night, Catterlin and I had an experience that amplified both.

Whenever you return from post, patrolling, or another mission that takes you off-base, you are what's called QRF (a quick reaction force). Essentially, this means you are "on call" if anything happens, like IEDs, mortars, a firefight, or dead or wounded showing up. We slept with radios on for any incoming distress calls and kept the volume high to alert us to any sounds they made. The hope is that you don't get a call and can sleep through the night. As my team and I were settling in to rest, we heard a loud explosion.

S—t, I thought as I rubbed my eyes.

We all knew that if something exploded off-base, there was a sizeable chance someone was injured, and we just sat there glued to our radio afterward, hoping it wasn't Americans or Allied forces. In hindsight, it's awful to think of the sigh of relief we all had if we discovered a local national had been killed versus one of our own. It shows the cold mentality we started to develop—a mentality that didn't take long to settle in. So, at this point, we were all more frustrated at the interrupted sleep than the potential loss of life.

The radio chatter started. "QRF, QRF," we heard the COC shout over the radio.

All our ears perked up. It's never good news. Furthermore, whenever that call comes in, we have no idea if it's our own who has been hit, so the room gets dead quiet as we hold our breath and wait for instructions to come from the radio static.

"We have an ANA casualty en route to VCP (vehicle control point) East. I repeat, we have an ANA casualty en route to VPC East." That information is all we need to get our gear on and take action.

"F—k. Let's go," Catterlin said.

While we were throwing on our gear as fast as we could, like we trained for in boot camp, the radio continued to keep us updated, like a podcast playing in the background as you work.

I was looking down, getting my last boot on, when we heard: "We have extreme trauma to several limbs from a direct IED blast, significant blood loss, and . . . ." From there the adrenaline started kicking in, and my ears calibrated to only receive direct commands from my team. To me, the radio went silent; all that mattered was that we got there ASAP.

Catterlin and I were the first ones out of our sleeping bags and geared up, ready to get this man help. We started sprinting to the VCP where we saw an ANA Humvee speeding toward us with one of our docs in the back. I couldn't see the injured soldier yet because the Humvee bed was too deep. Our training kicked in for both of us, and I jumped in the bed of the Humvee only to be brutally reminded of the horror these bombs could do up close.

"I'll get his head," I said.

"I'll get his . . ." Catterlin paused at the sight.

You see it in the movies—explosions and extreme gore. But there are so many things they miss. My mind had a hard time processing it all.

The first thing we noticed when lifting this man was obvious: he had no legs. One was shredded from the knee down and looked like rags tied together. His other was at the hip, barely hanging on. The doc had slapped a tourniquet on him, but it looked more for show because there wasn't much to tighten against. And as we searched for a way to grab him, a handhold on his gear with blood draining from him, I finally saw his face less than a foot from mine.

A face that would haunt me for a lifetime.

The explosion hadn't shredded his face, but it was covered in sand. Sand filled his mouth completely, like a mummy, and the blast forced what looked like entire handfuls of dirt under his eyelids, making them swollen, protruding out with the skin stretched to its limits, and muddy from his tears. His nose looked like he had no nostrils, just packed tight with sand from the brute force of the IED.

This man is dead, I thought to myself. *What are we even doing here?*

But we don't get to make that call—that's for the docs to decide. We continued our hustle from the Humvee to the stretcher, me running backward while Catterlin ran forward, telling me where to go. He hardly weighed anything at all as I kept his head upright, and Catterlin kept what used to be his legs balanced. And I just kept staring into his sand-filled eyes while running him to medics, thinking:

He's dead. There's nothing we can do.

About three-quarters of the way to the medical tent, I glanced behind me to ensure we were headed to the right place. The second I looked back, I heard severe coughing, almost choking, followed by: "Allah!"

A plume of dust flew out of the man's mouth.

Holy s—t! This guy is alive.

That was the expression Catterlin and I shared as we doubled our hustle toward the medics. We couldn't believe it. We went from "We're transporting another dead body" to "Hurry up, let's get this guy some help!" Adrenaline kicked into overdrive, and everything else blurred. The man mumbled and groaned to himself between screams of "Allah!" over and over and over as we carried him, but I didn't look at his face again before passing him off to medical. When he was out of our hands, I stood outside the tent with Catterlin, both of us covered in the soldier's blood and sand.

My hands looked the same, covered.

Adrenaline settled, and we looked at one another as if to say, "Job well done," when we heard the soldier's screams weaken and fade behind the flap.

Did he die? I asked myself.

A barrage of thoughts followed that question.

He was alive when we found him. I should have moved faster. I jogged, assuming he was dead. With bleeding like that, every second counts—and I wasted seconds.

But our job was done. It was in their hands now, and I was sure he wouldn't make it. Another lesson at the expense of someone else—*move with a sense of urgency with everything you do.* We believe the man died on the helicopter shortly after, but we never confirmed it.

Why would we? To stack guilt?

There are no clear answers, but he wasn't returning to the war.

Catterlin and I just sat down after that, both soaked in the soldier's blood.

"Well, I'm going to have nightmares about that."

"Yeah," I said. "Me too."

But that's the thing I realized about hearts of gold, they're always heavy.

Every IED that went off, whether during the day or QRF at night, became a soul stripper. Every mangled body we saw, every face or set of eyes. One thought kept pushing in more than the rest: *That's going to be me soon.*

I hoped they'd move faster than I did if I was in the bed of that truck. Because if it were me on that stretcher and a foreign allied force was carrying me, how would I want to be treated? The answer: better than I treated that man. I had a family to get home to, and so did he. He had people that cared, and I still wasted seconds as if he weren't worth that precious time. The soldier wasn't even one of our own, but the pain he felt was real, and I felt it as if he were one of ours. The place just kept getting more and more real each day. *Hell.* There was no better way to express it. And I was waiting for the fires to swallow me up.

But after that night, a lesson was driven home about the ANA warriors. They were fighting for their home, their God, and their lives. They'd lay their lives down on the line if it meant they were free from the "enemy," oppression and terror. And yet, after that night, I also learned about the people we were fighting together. I saw them as *more* than targets. You might think that's obvious, but when you're brought through training to only see an "enemy," humanizing them can become dangerous for a Marine. You're given a mission, and if something like empathy interferes with that mission, the assumption is that you might be less effective in what you were sent there to do. But that didn't change the fact that they were humans.

I met more ANA soldiers and carried more bodies like that sand-filled soldier. I met other locals trying to get back to the way things were—or some vision of what they could be in an idyllic future. The people who still went about their days and stuck to their daily schedules in a war-torn country. These feelings of empathy, pain, and pity for what their home had become and how it affected them didn't stop me from doing my job, but they let me set my heart closer to my head when making decisions.

Then again, I was still a Marine, and orders were orders.

Back in Sangin we mostly did mounted patrols, which meant we were in a Humvee's relative (or at least the feeling of) safety. In Kajaki we often patrolled on foot, and walking outside the wire for hours on end toward known enemy outposts or to meet with the village elders was a constant adrenaline rush. But one day, we needed to get a little further than a foot patrol would allow, so the mission was a simple mounted patrol. Our machine gunner was Jackson, who was in the turret on the 240 Bravo, a belt-fed machine gun that chambers in 7.62 × 51 NATO.

Something to realize is that when I was in Afghanistan, automatic weapons were legal without concealed-carry permits. Local nationals wore them daily while farming or going about their day. So, when on patrol, it's not as simple as yelling, "He has a gun!"

Potshots were always taken at random intervals while on patrol—some malicious, and some not. As we walked or rode around, we essentially had no idea who was shooting at us unless they wanted to make themselves known.

You wouldn't go more than a few minutes without hearing a brief string of gunfire; at some point, it just became background noise.

As our truck left the wire, we began a short convoy down the road from the base, scanning for bombs, people, weapons, and anything that stood out. Jackson and I were chatting and surveying when gunfire suddenly went off, and it sounded too close. But the difference between the ambient sound of gunfire and being shot at is obvious.

Rounds that are meant for you break the sound barrier and snap like the sound of a cracking whip. You hear that before you hear the bang of the gun that created it. Every one of these Marines on the convoy knew that, but it never seemed to stop many of them from instantly pointing their weapons toward the noise and firing.

These fellow Marines we were swapping places with were cowboys, meaning they wanted a fight, whether right or wrong. I can't blame them; it was exhilarating to be in dangerous situations, but that also meant innocent people got their homes damaged, animals slaughtered, or even a loved one killed. To me, a ribbon or a story wasn't worth creating more enemies over.

If I fired a round and it killed an innocent father, then that man's son might grow up to be a suicide bomber and kill several Marines, much like the situation a month prior. Those deaths would be on me. Why would I blame someone for avenging their father's death? It seems fitting to me.

There is a perspective that I always kept in the back of my mind: if I were able to take a terrorist from a place of discord and send them back in time to raise them in Florida, they would not likely develop into such a violent person. It's their situation and environment that failed them. But the same perspective goes for me: if you went back in time and took my childhood self, with his passion for engineering and taking things apart, and raised me in Afghanistan in a time of war, who knows what these hands would do to the people I love today. It was important for me to recognize that, in another life, these guys are likely great people. Hell, they could even be our friends. But that perspective was only allowed as an afterthought to action. In the moment, there is no daydreaming of "what could have been." Act first, empathize later.

About an hour into this mounted patrol Jackson and I heard some close gunfire, but no rounds snapping. *Farmers shooting at birds or in the water*, I thought. But we couldn't tell. We rotated our turrets and saw nothing but fields, tiny mud houses, and tree lines. Sometimes you wished the enemy wouldn't show such cowardice—but I started to understand. We have planes, tanks, and drones, and some of us don't even have to get out of a chair or spill our morning coffee to send you to your god—so I get why "toe-to-toe" wasn't their strategy.

The shots could have been the Taliban testing the waters to see our tolerance level, which was typical. Nonetheless, we didn't have PID (positive identification), and I wasn't going to shoot. The other Marines inside the truck were at my feet, excitedly yelling for us to shoot back.

"At what?" I asked in panic.

"No," Jackson said timidly.

"Come on!" they yelled. "Crack some rounds off!"

"I see nothing or no one that needs to be shot," I said. "I'm not f——ing shooting."

They kept on goading us, but Jackson and I kept steady.

"No," Jackson repeated as they got hyped up on the potential of firing into a tree line. Passing the burden to us, just so they could watch it, whatever chaos ensued. So they could experience it and feel close to it.

When the convoy started up again and the sounds faded, the other Marines quieted down or moved on to something else. Something felt wrong to me, though, about the whole encounter. When we got back from the patrol, Jackson and I stood an eight-hour post together and we talked for hours over what was probably the most eye-opening conversation I have had to date.

"I can't believe they wanted us to sling rounds into the trees, man," Jackson started.

"You were reading my mind, dude. I'm not just going to risk killing people for the hell of it," I said, raising my hands in anger.

"Don't get me wrong, I will do my job when the time comes. But I also don't think a lot of these guys are as bad as we make them out to be," I continued. "Most are just farmers being forced by the enemy."

"One hundred percent, man. They're ground-level fighters, just like us. I don't want to give the locals a reason to turn on us and the units to come," he said.

"Exactly! That's what I'm trying to tell them," I shouted.

We went on for the entirety of the eight-hour shift, talking about right from wrong and deciphering where our boundaries were. One thing we both agreed on, there was no time for empathy; if we see an immediate threat, we would act first and ask for forgiveness later. It's not that we weren't damn well willing and ready to kill, we just knew that our conscience would be the enemy when we got home and did our best to preserve it. We knew that if we did anything we didn't truly agree with in our hearts, no matter how justified it seemed or didn't seem on paper, the dissonance would haunt us. Kill for a ribbon or a story—how do you tell that to your wife, your kids, your grandkids? You don't. You lie. And if you didn't lie, would they love you the same way, knowing the monster you once were?

Would you be able to love them the same way?

Through the second half of this deployment, I felt sad celebrating any death that occurred on our behalf. Knowing each one of those people was a friend, a father, a brother, a lover. Empathy is a tool, skill, and muscle that must be utilized often to stay sharp. Once again, these situations are a bit extreme, but I always think back to every person I am judging and think of them as a kid. *My kid. Your kid.* I don't get mad at people who lack empathy; I feel sad for them. Life wakes us all up eventually, just hopefully before the damage is done.

We think we have all the answers until we don't. It's those of us who have realized we're not in total control who are able to feel empathy. Lack of life experience makes people so candid about laughing at other people's misfortune. If you want to see a lack of empathy firsthand, look at YouTube comments or social media posts.

It's easy to yell your opinions when you're not the one holding the gun, so to speak.

There's a condition known as "sentience syndrome" where people cannot look at another person and see them as anything other than an NPC or a vessel brought into their life for them to experience. The way in which we ingest news stories today surely nurtures this syndrome—we cannot really see the actual people on the other side. This is why we must use empathy to help us understand those whom we don't understand, or who challenge our own perspectives.

How many judgments do we make on any given day? To the person who cut us off in traffic? To the person sleeping by the gutter? To the person sleeping in the penthouse? To the person across the political aisle? Who worships a different god? Who leads a different lifestyle? To the person who is nothing like us?

If Catterlin and I saw something horrible and he laughed about it while I cried, it is incumbent upon me to work my empathy muscles and try to contemplate how he copes differently than I do. Practicing this type of empathy has completely changed my life.

Friend. Family. Enemy. Everyone struggles. Do not judge. When you can give a compliment, not for your personal gain but simply to bring a smile to someone's face, you have truly understood the meaning of empathy.

Your next challenge: Look deep into others, and do your best to understand their own struggle and how they find their own way through it.

Summary:
- Just because an action is justified on paper doesn't mean it aligns with your personal morals or ethical code.
- Recognizing humanity in others, including that of opponents or enemies, is crucial for maintaining perspective and building your empathy.
- Building our empathy also builds our emotional maturity.

Chapter 12 Exercise

Write about a time when you had to exercise empathy in a challenging or uncomfortable situation. How did it change your perspective?

_____

_____

_____

_____

_____

_____

_____

_____

_____

_____

_____

_____

_____

LEGACY MINDSET

CHAPTER 13

THE FORGE OF ADVERSITY

We always look to idolize and emulate those we witness as Heroes, wishing to share a similar blessing, until we realize that blessing is a curse.

It would be impossible for me to explore all the effects of war and what many of us saw while deployed; and to be honest, many of our experiences didn't seem to have a lesson attached to them of any value.

A vast majority of our experience was defined by unaddressed sadness and long stretches of routine boredom.

Over the next three months, we made countless casualty runs, patrols, mortar attacks, control detonations, offensive attacks, and the occasional firefight. It was now getting close to the end of our deployment, and who we were when we showed up and who we were getting ready to leave were two different people.

My empathy put me in a near-constant state of dissonance. I empathized with the locals and beat myself up whenever we got excited about the chance of bringing the fight to the enemy. And the reality was that the tactics of the enemy were cowardly. Bombs hidden in garbage and potshots taken from cover, threatening the lives of farmers and their families to engage the allied patrols. It was guerilla warfare, hit-and-run, and all too often, the casualties of war were the people that wanted no part in it. And to us and our orders, there was no separation of the "true enemy" and the "forced enemy." As a unit, we would locate, close in, and destroy them all the same.

They got some sympathy afterward if they were lucky.

As a point man, most of our engagements were special offensive attacks I had little use in. They would fire javelins, tow missiles, and high-mobility artillery rocket systems (HIMARS), or shoot sniper missions from a distance, where I had an opportunity several times to call or identify targets but not pull the trigger. There were a few minor engagements where some of us shot back, but nothing lasted long. I still hadn't fired my rifle at a real target yet, and that was getting to me and several other guys who just wanted to do their jobs. It was not lost on any of us that most units before us were dealing with firefights daily. So for us to only see a few a month, many being small TIC's (troops in contact) with unseen targets, we all felt let down. We were fighting ghosts.

That changed two weeks before I was set to go home.

But before I tell you what happened, I feel obligated to say that this experience is difficult to recall for reasons that will be apparent soon. Timelines are a big blur, but to the best of my knowledge, this is how it all happened.

It began as another day providing security on an eight-plus-hour shift. The word in the air was that we were next in line, slated, and starting to get ready to go back to the States. I tried to put that out of my mind until I was on the plane, but it's hard when working security. Security feels demeaning to any infantryman who wants to do their job. You sit there the entire time hoping for something that would allow you to shoot back while simultaneously hating that you are within a safe zone and not finding trouble to get into with the insurgents.

We all hated it. We felt worthless.

As Catterlin and I stood there, we scanned the area and reported any anomalies in the baseline, waiting for our shift to end around two or so in the morning. Hooray . . .

But this day was different.

Usually, you would get off the shift late at night, maybe muster up the energy to go work out, or go to sleep in your sleeping bag and hope nothing happens in the middle of the night that makes you have to spin up as QRF and handle a casualty; or that incoming mortars don't screw everything up, because then you'd have to seek cover and stay put until leadership gave the all clear. But tonight, leadership greeted us on our way back to our sleeping bags and told us that our squad needed to meet with our captain in the COC.

"That's weird," I said.

"What the heck does he want with us at this hour?" Catterlin replied.

We grabbed our gear, passed off the post to the next Marines on duty, and headed to the COC, walking side by side. We had been through a lot together, so now the relationship between Catterlin and me was less leadership and more friendship, as we earned that of each other. Never freezing in situations, helping each other out, and watching each other's back, we became closer than we expected.

We sat at the table, and the rest of our squad was waiting around a map. Our captain walked in and gave us the briefing. He said something like, "In two days' time, we're going to lead the ANA into a Taliban stronghold to begin clearing Nawzad. You guys will be patrolling with them and establishing QRF. We expect to take casualties."

This blindsided every member of my squad for several reasons. While we were used to patrolling, the kicker on this particular patrol was that seventy-five freaking ANA guys were coming. A twelve-man patrol? No problem. But seventy-five?

What the hell? That's a big target, and a lot of muzzles to account for.

So, my first "oh s—t" moment was thinking: *We're going to have the entire village after us.* My second "oh s—t" moment occurred when I realized we were headed to the Shrine, a location smack-dab in the center of enemy trajectory, where the nightly light show erupted. My third "oh, s—t" moment: *I'm going to be walking as lead point man toward a Taliban stronghold.* And, for my fourth and final "oh s—t" moment: *We're less than thirty days from going home.*

What a time to schedule an impromptu deadly mission. I'd be lying if I said my stomach wasn't in knots, twisting and turning while simultaneously engaging and paying extra close attention to the plan of attack. I was also trying to silence the nagging voice that said, "Don't be the guy who gets killed days before going home."

And to end the meeting, a staff sergeant said, "Get your guns cleaned up and ready, top off your ammo, and check your gear. We're going to get lit up out there."

He was right.

My entire squad immediately went to our area and started getting our gear ready for hell. Because I was a point man, I had to stay back to collaborate on the route we would take so that I knew where to lead my guys. We decided to move out at night so the enemy wouldn't see us coming. That was the plan, at least.

For what little time I could that night, I slept under one of the Humvees for warmth, and then at first light the ANA started their push for Nawzad as we pushed toward the village to establish QRF. And just like that, the mission began: I walked through the poppy fields with no one in sight, and only the enemy stronghold directly ahead.

This was the most scared I have ever been on patrol.

We walked through the poppy fields because I decided my team wouldn't take the roads we knew were littered with IEDs that had been buried for a while, meaning they would be very hard to spot. As we approached the village, I saw a freshly dug hole in the ground with a shovel, knowing they were planting new IEDs in just the past hour. Just for us. And all the while, I had an interpreter behind me relaying messages he heard on the radio from the intercepted Taliban radio signals.

With every step, the thought rolled through my mind: *Everyone here wants us dead. We shouldn't be here.*

Then, over the radio, a man said in Pashto, "We have the front man in our sights. Get the women and children, praise God, and prepare for victory." I don't care who you are; when you know there are dozens of muzzles pointed directly at *you* from a village, from people you can't see, who would *love* to die for their cause—you are going to s—t bricks.

I wanted to throw up, but I kept us moving through the field.

There was a surrealness to the situation, almost like a high. I kept thinking the next round fired in Afghanistan would be meant for me. Every *pop!* of a stick breaking from my steps felt like it was my time. I waited for my vision to go black and my consciousness to be stripped forever because the Taliban landed a lucky shot right in my forehead, before I could even hear the crack of the bullet. With a message like that coming directly from the enemy who has everything to gain from killing me, I felt like I knew I was going to die.

But there's no turning back.

For the three longest minutes of my life, I crept through the poppy field until we all heard a *pop! pop! pop!* from the village. I froze. They were taunting us.

As I started walking again, another set of rounds popped off, except this time they were much closer and more on target, because I could hear the distant snapping through the air. Not directly at us, but much closer to us.

F—k, I thought as we all ducked down.

They were playing with us, seeing what we would do and finding our standard operating protocol. Usually, when you are on patrol and get shot at, you turn to the direction of the incoming fire and just let loose to suppress the enemy. But this wasn't one of those times—the shots were coming from the village, and we could not under any circumstance let loose in that direction or we were sure to kill civilians. The problem is that our response, or lack of response for that matter, proved to the enemy that we weren't going to fire. They now knew we would not shoot unless they hit one of us or made their position obvious.

With no snipers in overwatch to eliminate a target, we just had to suck it up and keep walking until something more direct happened. A call came in from the higher authorities (well above my pay grade) to push closer to the village, grab some biometrics on the local nationals, then head back and move the QRF position to the PB (patrol base) Shrine.

I timidly shifted course toward the village, and one of the gunnies patrolling with us decided to take the lead so he could get the biometrics, as us grunts "didn't know how to use all that fancy equipment." And as we patrolled closer to the village, more and more chatter was happening on the radio from the Taliban.

Hearing the voice of an enemy that you are actively playing cat and mouse with can haunt you for a lifetime. They are never more real than they are in that moment—you identify them as a person, not some

NPC you have to kill to get to the next level. Someone who is there, formulating a plan to make sure you don't go home alive.

It was bone-chilling, and I felt even more sick.

As we approached the village, things got quiet. The pot shots stopped.

"That's not good," I said to Catterlin.

"Push out and hold security while they get their DNA enrolled in the SEEK (secure electronic enrollment kit)."

"Yes, Lance Corporal."

I crouched a few paces away, scanning for whoever the jerk was talking on the radio. *He's watching me clear as day*, I thought, but I couldn't see or hear him, other than over the radio. He was the cat, I was the mouse; and I wanted to get out of there—fast. Unless they were going to let us go in and start going door-to-door and clearing the place out as a team, we needed to get out of there because they were ready, and with our rules of engagement (and dare I say leadership), we were not in a position to fight. Our leadership was known for double standards; they could cause insurmountable damage and take lives, and if they were wrong, they would just fudge the paperwork and make it go away. But we were always told, "If we find that you engaged someone without having one hundred percent certainty that they are the enemy, we will crucify you."

It made us scared to protect ourselves appropriately. This was obviously the enemy, but one "Oops" shot and, even if we made it home, we were going to jail.

Unless the person on the other end of that shot had a high rank.

Let Marines loose, and they will destroy everything with a smile. Tie their hands and put them in a box—just like anyone else, they become helpless. No one wanted to be there at that moment, and in a moment, our prayers were answered—sort of. We started the long patrol back to the Shrine to evaluate and get an angle on the apparent situation that was about to ensue. We turned our back to the enemy, and, taking point once more—I started walking.

Almost immediately, you could hear them on the radio plotting to attack when our backs were turned, and once there was enough distance, they would commence. The countdown started in my head. They were going to fire.

"We have two machine gun teams moving in," they said.

Remember, we were in the middle of a poppy field. If we started taking fire, there would be no micro-terrain, rocks, buildings, or anything to hide behind.

"Our team is almost in position," they said.

I started to pick up the pace so we could get back to cover sooner. The road might have been faster, but the IEDs meant certain death for us all.

"Get ready, gents," I heard from the gunny in the back.

My skin felt like it was getting tight, like I was shrinking to make myself a smaller target with my back toward the growing enemy. I could hear my heartbeat louder than the radio or the commands coming down the line.

I kept moving forward, one foot in front of the other, looking down often to ensure I didn't hit a pressure plate. I kept thinking, *This is it. This is when its fades to black.* I just kept my head down while the adrenaline coursed through my veins. But alas, nothing but silence as I marched through the field, which is arguably even more scary than gunfire at times; it means everyone is watching you. I walked at a fast pace for what felt like hours, but was only a few minutes. When I looked up, I would lose all motivation; it was like I wasn't even moving. The Shrine felt like it was further away than the last time I looked. A nightmare. I finally decided to just keep my head down, and say to myself, *we will get there when we get there*, throwing my analytical mind out the window and letting the universe take the lead. I treaded ground for what felt like an impossible amount of distance, and just when I was ready to snap emotionally, I lifted my head at a road crossing and I saw it. Like an answered prayer.

The Shrine was now within a few hundred meters, and I felt a sigh of relief, starting to slow down the whole patrol because my adrenaline and the pure weight of my gear and extra ammo had drained my body. I didn't want us to get burned out for no reason if we were safe.

We're good, I thought. *We made it.*

I got complacent.

Then we heard a sound I will never forget—the sound of seventy-plus rifles firing all at once from countless directions, and rounds cracking through the air.

The sound was deafening.

You couldn't tell where one shot was fired and the other began.

"Holy s—t!" We started running (which looked like a fast-paced walk because of how drained we were). The Taliban had started engaging the ANA right behind us at the same time, and all those ANA troops let loose with a wall of lead, slinging rounds wherever they felt like, even if that meant hitting villages or local nationals while standing in absolutely zero cover. I couldn't tell what sounds were incoming and what was outgoing gunfire.

Our Marines and ANA back at the Shrine started suppressing and engaging the village area, shooting over us to keep us safe. We had hundreds of rounds flying over our heads from the Marines on top of the hill, shooting over us and the Taliban on the other side. We were caught in the middle. Explosions started ringing out behind us from RPGs, mortars, grenades, and 203s.

I had no idea what was friendly or enemy-fire.

I just kept pushing toward cover.

Rounds were coming from both directions, and the adrenaline was hitting too hard. One second you're thinking of how proud you are that you have your brothers there to defend you. The next, you just think how amazing it is that you're still breathing.

We got to the base hill of the Shrine under covering fire, rather than dropping and fighting where we were.

The Shrine is a big hill in Kajaki that overlooks the valley. It makes an excellent observation post for a visit and great cover from direct fire if you're in a war. We scurried up the hill, and it felt like running away from a monster that was right behind us.

Once up the hill, we took cover near the original spots that we slept the night prior. I got behind some HESCO barriers and analyzed what I could from the muzzles flashing and rounds popping off. We couldn't fire blindly into the village because the ANA and other Marines were down there. The last thing you want to do is hurt one of your own.

So as bad as it hurt, we just had to sit there and watch.

(If I told you that it was all serious, by the book, and we all executed our jobs perfectly, that would be a lie. When adrenaline peaks, sometimes moments turn to uncalled-for laughter and crude humor, even when lives are on the line.)

I looked around and saw some Marines planning attacks while others waited for an opportunity to fire and find areas to suppress. I decided I was going to get down and face the village to scan for targets or anyone to engage—hoping to find that one f—k who was watching me.

When I hit the dirt, a scout sniper and machine gunner let loose at the same time, just off to my right. *They must see where these guys are*, I thought to myself. With a sniper who takes a controlled and calculated shot and a machine gunner who suppresses, the IAR I carried was intended to be the middleman, because it was accurate and had full auto if needed.

I consider myself a pretty good and intuitive shot, adjusting well to round feedback. So even though these guys were good to go, I sprinted toward them to see if I could help. Before I could ask a question, I heard, "I need a spotter," from the sniper. He heard me approach and said, "Get down and tell me where my rounds are going. I got a guy in this building 800 meters out." That was about the maximum target area for my rifle, but for a Barrett .50 caliber like he was shooting, it was a walk in the park.

If you don't know what a Barret .50 caliber is, it's essentially a semiautomatic anti-material rifle that shoots a round that is the length of the average thumb. The concussive force of this gun's sound when something is near its muzzle explodes watermelons, destroys water jugs, throws rocks, you name it. Forget the bullet for a second. The beast is like a semiautomatic cannon that weighs a ton. It's great at tearing down enemy cover, and even though it's not necessarily antipersonnel, anything that can take down a wall does not shy away from harming the person behind it. And at this point, I wish I could say I did a good job and that I was a big help to my new sniper sergeant—but the truth is, I wasn't.

I only had a 3.5X magnification on my rifle, while he had some serious glass on top.

"Do you see that building?" he asked, pointing at what seemed like a sea of buildings in my scope.

"Yes, Sergeant," I said without humility, trying not to piss him off in a firefight.

The truth is, I had no idea. There were dozens of buildings at that mark, so I had no idea which one he meant. *I'll figure out which one he's talking about when the round hits.*

Our hearing was all screwed up from the gunfire and explosions, so I got closer to him in a prone position to communicate. We both peered down our scopes, waiting for an opportunity to pop up in the window. I surveyed as many windows as possible, searching for muzzle flashes in the sniper's target area or any unlucky heads popping up over walls.

He saw someone and engaged.

BOOM!

I was *not* ready for the type of concussive forces that came from being too close to a .50 cal. My brain felt like it was bouncing inside my skull like a super ball and my vision faded to black, while the blast almost completely deafened me on my right side.

"Did you see it?" he asked.

In a liminal state of consciousness, I barely put together what he asked.

"No impact, no idea, Sergeant," I said.

He could have drilled the target, and I would have had no clue. I was too embarrassed to say, "I got rocked by your rifle." Lives were on the line here, and this seasoned veteran was asking me to participate in helping him kill some insurgents. *Get it together.*

So, I let that one slide and said to myself: *Ok, now I know what it's like. Tough it out this time, and let's take this guy out and move onto the next.* You could see people ducking and running around in the village. Muzzle flashes and kicked-up dust would appear in windows all around. But I couldn't do anything until this main guy was taken care of.

He fired another round, and this time, I fought through the fading vision to wait for an impact via my scope—but, once again, I didn't see anything.

"No impact," I said again. "No idea."

"S—t. I think I'm shooting high."

Before he got another round out, I saw two RPGs shoot into the air, and the gunfire started to get even heavier. One looked like it came from the ANA side, and the other from the middle of the village. Both shot up into the sky, appearing to cross streams, and I felt lost on what was happening, imagining they were trying to shoot someone off a roof with an RPG but missed. It all just added to the fog of war.

Immediately after, an officer yelled down at us (which we could barely hear).

"You two are taking accurate fire! Get behind cover!"

I know that seems like something that would be obvious, but I was almost completely deaf at this point, and I'm sure my sniper was too. We couldn't hear incoming rounds unless they were snapping by our ears. But apparently one of the Marines next to us almost got hit, and rounds were hitting the HESCO barriers around us. I was so out of it that I didn't even notice.

After our officer barked his command, we shifted back and ended up closer together. At this point, it was clear that it wasn't the time for slow communication and that he would choose accuracy by volume and be his own spotter. Within a few seconds after shifting back, we both saw dust kicking out of a building, and I realized where he was engaging.

He fired another round, and I fired simultaneously while trying to account for the distance aiming with the bottom of my rifle scope. This time, however, the concussion from his rifle knocked me completely unconscious.

I went to sleep.

I couldn't open my eyes or talk; it was all black, but my unconscious body could feel his subsequent shots rattle my brain.

Was I hit?

What's going on?

I feel drunk . . . I can't move.

Every time I would start to come to, he would engage again, and I would slip back into blackness. It wasn't until he went for a magazine change that it gave me enough time to recover, roll over, and get the hell away from that Barrett. He didn't even know, and likely doesn't even know to this day, that I would go on to later need hearing aids and be diagnosed with a traumatic brain injury resulting from that engagement.

When I finally came to, the battle was just starting, so I was fighting my spinning vision and spitting the taste of pennies from my mouth. I got back in the fight and knew where the target was. The sniper began engaging again; this time, I was at a much safer distance, where it wasn't messing with my vision anymore. When I saw the dust again, I started firing into the building to get my rounds through the window.

However, there was a new problem: my vision and hearing were screwed, my equilibrium was all jacked up, and I felt like I had just drunk a full bottle of Jack Daniels. I started firing away at any promising areas to keep heads down and hopefully get one of them—windows of buildings, murder holes, any flash of a muzzle or RPG trail. I only remembered firing three rounds from my rifle before getting knocked out and waking up to the adrenaline surge. But it turns out, when I got out of my haze, I only had half a mag left and had more than three hot casings around me. I was "awake" and shooting at things, but I had no recollection of those subsequent shots. Then, we were told to assault another building with a Taliban flag sticking up from it. As the ANA came to take our spots, they laid down and started shooting wildly.

I have no idea what or whom I was shooting at. I might have panicked in the chaos, but until those synapses in my brain connect again (if they ever do), I must hope I was making a positive impact.

With the Taliban flag ahead of us, we started taking sporadic fire, and our gunny told us to "take it down," even if it meant the building going with it. Everyone turned their guns toward the building only a few hundred yards away and started firing, including me. The objective was to get whoever was inside to come out, or bring the place down on top. We didn't even really know if the enemy was in there. I remembered thinking about the enemy on the radio who had me in his sights and found myself squeezing the trigger faster and faster, wanting to scream at the same time. Keep in mind, the battle was still going on in full, and there were dozens of rounds being fired every second between us and this valley—but at this point, between my deafness, blurry vision, and the limitation of my rifle, I was in no shape to go for longer-range shooting without putting the people downrange at risk. So, even when we finished the house, I didn't return to the original spot to look for people to engage.

One of our assault-men prepped a javelin and fired it, taking out a building several hundred yards back from the one we were shooting at, and we started cheering like we had just won the lottery. I didn't even know there was gunfire coming from that area. Then another Marine we called "Kush" turned an MK19 (automatic grenade launcher) and started letting loose into the Taliban house where we had unloaded our rifles. We watched in awe with each shot as the moon dust and chunks flew off the building on impact, blocking our view of it completely.

There was only dust.

When the dust settled, I expected to witness a leveled building full of rubble. Funnily enough, the house barely had a scratch, just little dents and dings from our rounds hitting the side and the slightly bigger marks from the grenades. But no one left the building afterward, so we can only hope we did our jobs. We'll never know for sure.

The rest of that fight and that day is a blur for me. After everything was over, the battle lasted around four hours and ended when air support came in. I don't remember anything after firing on that building, outside of more rockets launching and buildings leveled. We must have fired hundreds of thousands of rounds, collectively.

As for me, I held back except for the direct instructions to engage, because the last thing I wanted to hear was that one of my rounds hit someone it wasn't supposed to. Every allied person made it with minimal injuries, and many just shot toward enemy fire to keep their heads down. I have no idea how many insurgents were killed, or if any were. It's one of those things you will go the rest of your life not knowing, because there's no way to see where every round went. At best, your conclusions can take this shape: "There were muzzle flashes, and then there weren't."

But unless you put them in a body bag, you don't know for sure.

Ultimately, the story of that firefight is one I've hesitated to tell, but I wanted to relate my experience of walking through that poppy field. I wanted to express the sheer terror of not knowing what's on the other side, of feeling lost in the middle of unknown land with unknown fire on all sides. On any given day, we can all feel the way

I did in that poppy field. When bad things happen in life, they tend to happen all at once. I don't know the science behind that experience, but I know the feeling of it.

Sometimes life throws us into the deep end, challenging us to just jump and learn to fly on the way down. It's scary, isn't it? Every instinct urges retreat, pulling us away from the most challenging road. That poppy field, a road riddled with bombs, held a profound lesson within its dirt. I realized I couldn't face that level of fear or uncover that inner strength from the safety of home or the comfort of a gym.

With every fiber of my being resisting, every inner voice screaming "Stop!," I pushed forward in that poppy field. Deep down I needed to know what lay beyond that veil of fear, no matter the cost. Life simply presents us with moments where the greatest lessons, the most transformative opportunities, wear the promise of fear and excruciating discomfort. But it's within those moments that we find out what we're truly capable of.

As I write these words, my right ear is ringing so loud that it overshadows my music, set at max volume because I can barely hear. Meanwhile, I need to sleep with white noise so that I don't wake up vomiting from vertigo triggered by that high-pitched ringing. It hasn't stopped even for a second since that day on the poppy field. But since that day, I've had a choice: I can let that experience and its effects on my mind and body become an excuse for why I can't do something, or I can use it as motivation to continue living for others whom I can help, even if I won't live to see it. That's the Legacy Mindset.

Summary:

- Life is unpredictable and can be overwhelming. Understanding and acknowledging this (and knowing you're not alone in feeling this way) helps prepare you for the unexpected.
- In the midst of chaos, it is essential to find clarity and focus to keep moving forward.
- The challenges and adversities faced in life shape who we are. Embracing them propels our personal growth.
- Adverse circumstances can either be seen as excuses to avoid obligations or opportunities.

Chapter 13 Exercise

What is your equivalent to a "walk in the poppy field" moment? What did you do to turn your version of "incoming shots" into something positive? There are no right or wrong answers. Once you've written your response, reflect upon how this moment in time shows how capable you actually are.

_____

_____

_____

_____

_____

_____

_____

_____

_____

_____

_____

_____

_____

CHAPTER 14

THE WAR WITHIN

There is no debt owed to us for amassing difficulties. Hardship today does not guarantee bliss tomorrow, but a resilient mind will ensure you always bounce back.

Sometimes in life, when we go through adversity, we begin to believe that the world, universe, God, or whatever you believe in, owes us a break. Almost as if it were a credit-debit system, where if we have suffered enough mental anguish someone or something is going to look at us and say, "Meh, they've had enough. Give them a break."

I think we can all agree that would be nice, but it's also important to remember that life is not reacting and throwing things at you as punishment or reward. The good and bad will happen either way, but it's your job to navigate the effects and act with your desired outcome in mind.

Easier said than done.

And when I came home from Afghanistan, I wasn't singing that tune. I felt like the world owed me something. I thought I had earned a break. I felt we all deserved one. But it's bittersweet to come home. We all wanted to get home to our families, wives, girlfriends, and partners, but we also half-expected them to have been sitting around waiting for us—that their lives were on "pause" while we were gone, and only when we got back would they hit "play" again.

There was also this sick feeling at the core of our stomachs, knowing that we were leaving a new group of Marines behind to pick up where we had left off. We knew they were about to experience and learn the same lessons we did over there, and it felt wrong not being able to help them through it. They will see death and destruction and may lose people they care about. I'm not sure about all the other Marines, but I just wanted to stay there until the war was done so I could use any of my experiences to improve their survival rate—maybe even help them not look at every Afghani as a target.

None of us at that time would have expected a decade more of it.

But that's when many infantrymen have their hearts torn in two. We knew the longer we stayed, the more we would become a product of our environment and less able to adapt to the civilian world. In our hearts, we wanted to stay.

But our families would never understand why we didn't want to come back.

Overseas, life was dangerous but simple. Most of the time, it was no phones or internet, just makeshift weights, MREs, security detail, patrolling, and keeping each other entertained. I didn't have to worry about the same things I did at home. But we all knew staying or asking to extend the deployment wasn't a realistic option.

So, there is only word that fit the experience of coming back home: bittersweet.

My wife, Tiffany (my girlfriend at the time), was there to welcome me, along with our dog, Koda—a bullmastiff, Saint Bernard, and German shepherd mix—who, of course, I was excited to see. But already, I could tell I was still on high alert the second I walked off the bus, being careful of where I stepped and scanning the sidewalk, the roads, the distant mountains, or tall buildings like it was second nature. I was so excited to see her, but somehow, I knew my smiles weren't as big as before, and I hugged her with less excitement than I expected. Picking up on my own cues, I had a mental battle waging.

What the heck, Korey? Be more excited! She's excited.
She missed you! Show her you missed her. Show her!

But I couldn't. I realized I was running through the events I experienced overseas in the back of my mind constantly, like a virus in my brain's operating system. It's hard to be happy when your mind is tainted with a reality that most people are oblivious to. It's almost as if those smiles you want to share are insulting to those who didn't make it or are stuck in a deadly firefight at that very moment.

I wanted to smile and be excited, but as I hugged Tiffany, all I could think about was the face of the sand-covered ANA soldier Catterlin and I carried. Or the three ANA soldiers that wouldn't get to hug their loved ones again because of me. When I tried to shake those thoughts out of my head, the countless other casualties we carried, dead or alive, in our seven-month stint would start flashing through my mind like an old reel of cinema film on a projector. I realized that situations like that would continue to happen daily, while I stood here safe. It hung over me like a cloud, darkening what should have been one of the brightest moments of my life. I was home. I was finally home, but I couldn't avoid the knowledge of what was still happening in the place I left, and it felt dishonorable to enjoy life while knowing people were fighting and dying. I felt like a walking insult to those who didn't come home.

A feeling I would never truly escape.

So, I pushed through, thinking, *This too shall pass.*

But it didn't.

My first few weeks with my soon-to-be wife were amazing. While I was still deployed, we'd made so many plans for what to do when we hung out that it ended up being hard to think of anything beyond spending as much time together as possible. And keeping busy, really busy, kept me from slipping into darkness. She helped me with that—a lot.

I remember lying in bed with Tiffany watching TV on the first or second night. I was flipping through the channels and saw "Breaking News: Bomb Kills Several and Injured Many in Boston." It was like a bad dream—like the terrorists had followed us home. The news of an attack immediately after coming home did not serve my mind well. I was convinced I was still in a war zone, and my excitement at being home faded in that moment. The next several days were spent taking Tiffany out to nice restaurants, playing with our dog (who would jump around in excitement when he saw me), calling family and friends to let them know I was back, and linking up with other Marines to discuss how their deployment went.

But none of it felt real, and I was scared to sleep because when I had time to think, the guilt of what was happening and what had happened over there took over my mind. But I thought about all those who had it worse and decided, "Don't talk about it, Korey. People don't need to know." So I pushed through silently, acknowledging some minor but increasing night terrors as well as my constant state of high alert, which people noticed but knew it wasn't suitable to address. I felt like that outcast kid again.

After those two weeks they gave us to reacclimate to garrison life, the reality set in: *It's time to start another six-month workup to go back.*

Like many other Marines, I suddenly realized, *Oh right, we're going to do this again. And again. And again.* It wasn't, "Congratulations! You did your tour, and now you can relax forever." It was more like, "Here's two weeks off. Get your s—t together because we're going back until the war is over." I gained a new appreciation for my senior leadership, knowing some had five to eight deployments under their belt. These men were men of war.

A medical evaluation is one of the first things that happen after a post-deployment vacation. This is where doctors check in to see how we are, mentally and physically. Many of us were physically okay, and even some mentally, but then you had a lot of Marines like me who knew a lot was going wrong but weren't going to say much until we were asked directly about it. (You can imagine how often I was asked about an injury I received during training before deployment.) From these evaluations, I gradually learned how important it is to not only engage in conversations with others when you're struggling but to also be attentive to the needs of others to talk about their own struggles, as they might not have been given a chance to yet.

Something that surprised me was that Dunston's team returned home almost the same day as my unit. After we all got off the bus and back stateside, we had to take care of the basics before we could be released to our families: things like doing roll call, storing our gear back in our barracks rooms, turning our weapons into the armory (which felt weird because it's the first time I didn't have a gun attached to my hip for seven months), and of course doing our follow-up medical eval. As a sea of hundreds of Marines, we all navigated toward the armory as we collided with brothers we had not seen in a while, all of us glad they were alive and well. Like a gigantic family reunion, we saw faces we missed, and it was one of the only times where the smiles we shared felt genuine.

Amongst the crowd, I saw Dunston talking to another Marine, and I walked up beside him to give him a one-armed hug while shouting, "Dunston! What's up, brother?! I missed you out there."

I was met with equal excitement, "Shaffer!"—he always pronounced it "Shay-fur"—"I missed you too, brotha!"

There wasn't much time for catching up as we all needed to turn in our weapons, so we parted ways for a bit. "Catch you later, brother," I told Dunston. "We have a lot to catch up on," I spoke loudly so he could hear me over the other sounds of reunion.

"You got it, Shaffer!" he shouted back as we kept moving in different directions. We knew we would separate at the armory but reconvene later. I hadn't seen him overseas, being based in Afghanistan's different areas of operation (AOs). Still, there we were—together again, fresh off deployment. After the armory, we saw each other again in the crowd that was now migrating to the big medical building. Our entire unit, A-team and B-team, were lined up to fill out yes-or-no essay questions on post-deployment paperwork.

Just a few hours prior, our unit had all met up (to talk about timelines and next steps for upcoming operations) and were standing on top of a parking garage for the big company meeting, all lined up in formation. Suddenly, a few floors below us, a motorcycle started up with a loud *bang!* That sent over a hundred Marines scattering for cover like cockroaches, while a slew of profanity littered the air. Then, as if on cue, we all looked up at each other, in the hopes that we weren't the only ones who made an idiot of themselves.

A sigh of relief rang out from all one hundred of us as we burst out in laughter, with our leader sarcastically saying something like, "Sure, none of y'all have PTSD." That made us laugh even harder because it was worn like an earned badge. We were damaged.

Later that day, Dunston and I stood next to each other, not talking much, just filling out our paperwork. Every question, one after the other, made me realize vacation was over, and I needed to face what was going on in my head. I noted severe anxiety in certain situations, like seeing trash on the road, hearing loud noises, or not having a visual of my surroundings. I would go into fight-or-flight mode over a car door shutting, ducking my head and reaching for a rifle that wasn't there. But we were all doing that; we ducked for cover at a motorcycle cranking up. It became so redundant that Dunston and I would make eye contact after overreacting to various environmental circumstances to see if either of us would judge. Then we would burst out laughing.

It was "normal."

Some of the yes-or-no questions were painfully basic. *Are you in any pain? Have you ever thought about hurting anyone or yourself? Do you have anxiety?*

They all felt comically rhetorical, but I looked to Dunston seriously on how to answer.

"Are you going to tell them the truth?" I asked.

"Hell no," he said. "They would crucify us if we told them."

I just nodded, but knew I was struggling. We all were. From the sharp pain and swelling in my back, to the "Huh?" I had to respond to everyone with because I couldn't hear, I knew something was wrong, so I didn't follow his advice. I said to myself, *I might as well tell them everything*. When many other Marines like Dunston checked or wrote that they were "A-OK," I answered more honestly.

This led to a path of *absolute honesty* during my exams, where I was surrounded by medical professionals who encouraged me to talk about my pains and struggles. But to Dunston's point, beyond those walls, leadership might not penalize you but would chastise you for getting help and being "weak."

I figured I could take whatever they said on the chin, because my medical record was becoming thicker than a phone book. The more poking and prodding they did, the more damage they found in my mind and body. At twenty-one years old, I . . .

- Required hearing aids for my right ear (from that last engagement)
- Received a diagnosed traumatic brain injury from the .50 caliber blast
- Had a torn rotator cuff
- Received a PTSD diagnosis
- Suffered severe migraines

- Acquired thoracic kyphosis (forward curvature of the upper spine) with fractured vertebrae
- Incurred joint damage to one of my knees
- Had a severely restricted range of motion

. . . And dozens of other issues, including the fact that I could hardly sleep without our dog—in my mind, he was my Taliban alert system.

They immediately submitted me for medical separation from the Marines. I can't even describe the fear that ran through my body for telling these doctors the truth. It felt like I was "ratting out" the Marines because I was going against the grain with my honesty.

And, when it came down to it, only one simple thing set us apart—they chose "No" while I chose "Yes" on a piece of paper. That's it. Hundreds of thousands of Marines with issues worse or equal to mine came before and answered "No," all so they could keep their medical records clean and show their leaders they were not a p——y.

The truth is, I knew I was hurting, and there wasn't anyone's opinion I respected enough to stop seeking treatment to end that ongoing pain. But I was still scared. When I started seeing therapists, it was amazing to meet men of all ranks and deployment theaters reaching out for help. With perspective, my pain felt like a drop in the bucket compared to everyone else.

Just think: one hundred men ducked on top of that parking garage that day, and I saw none of them there with me. It was depressing, because I felt like I was doing something wrong.

It took almost a year and a half to be medically separated from the Marines for my injuries. I was now twenty-two years old, with a plethora of injuries and ailments, and a half-dozen medications to keep me functioning. I hated that I abandoned my brothers who had just deployed, just for being honest. Cowardice—that's all I felt.

The only saving grace I had was Tiffany, and we got married during the very worst of my mental health struggles. I would wake up in the middle of the night, grab a gun and clear the house inside and out, all from a bump of the washer or dryer. I learned that I couldn't wear headphones, because every little sound made me believe an IED just went off outside our house and I would start yelling, "Where is it?!" as if to ask, *Where is the contact?* That and headphones throw off my equilibrium.

My mind was so broken that anytime my brain went idle, I would awkwardly doze off at anything, even a blank TV screen, and start thinking of war. Then, I would be absolutely furious if anyone interrupted my locked-in gaze, because when I was thinking of those lost, I felt I owed it to those who suffered to create that space in my memory for them to live on. I felt like it was no longer my mind; it was a sanctuary for their untold stories.

One *pop!* Or *bang!* would set me on a day full of anxiety and one-thousand-yard stares. I would be almost utterly inoperable if I got behind the wheel of a car, because I felt so disconnected from reality that I would stop in the middle of the road over a piece of trash or drive through red lights like they weren't there. I couldn't tell what reality was anymore. I was a liability and a risk to everyone I encountered, and I was embarrassed that being overseas had affected me that much. I felt insignificant to all my brothers.

But Tiffany stuck by my side, and with my official separation from the Marines, we needed a place to live. At that point, my father was the first to welcome my wife and me to stay in his four-bedroom home in Middleburg, Florida, until I found a job and started college on the GI bill. Before we knew it, we rented a huge truck and drove from California to Florida, over three days.

I felt like I was traveling back in time and hoped it would help me.

On January 3, 2015, we arrived in Florida to my dad answering the door and giving me a hug. Just as before, he still wasn't big on emotional displays. After a quick embrace, he rolled straight into "Let's get all this stuff unloaded!"

I was so happy to see him; I loved living with my dad. He always respected privacy and stayed to himself unless you invited him to do something he enjoyed, like watching a good action movie in the living room or going to the shooting range to test out a new "toy." But then I started to see my mental health's effects on myself and Tiffany (who still *never* held it against me and tried her best to help me through it). Dad would be there to talk and share the stories I didn't want to repress. I felt comfortable justifying all my PTSD-related outbursts to him, and he empathized with my struggle. I remember sitting at our kitchen table once in a state of reflection.

Did I hit anyone? How many people died? Did the first casualty make it?

All these thoughts I spoke silently to myself, while my skin felt like spiders were crawling on it, and every little movement I thought was someone hiding around the corner. I looked around the corner of the kitchen and could swear I saw the Afghani with no legs and sand in his mouth floating out of the corner of my eye, like he was taunting me for being slow to help him. It was like a real-life horror show, and I just wanted to cry—for it to end.

My dad walked up behind me to ask me something, and I grabbed a steel pen off the counter, turning around like I was going to stab him. He looked at me with wide eyes and saw that I was sweating and having an episode. He put his hands up, calmly said "sorry," and walked away. I was so ashamed of myself and desperate for anything to stop the continuous mental anguish. The VA meds were not helping, so I did something I never intended to do again.

I flew my brother Justin down to Florida from Rhode Island and used his presence to justify cracking my first drink in years. Before joining the Marines, I gave up all drinking or experimenting with substances to be at peak performance, plus I had still been underage at that point. But for whatever reason, now seemed like the time to break that four-year streak. I greeted my brother with a case of bottled Bud Light, and as the night drew to a close, I opened up a bottle and had my first sip of alcohol since I joined the Marine Corps.

My first drink since I was legally old enough to drink.

And it only took one beer to knock me on my butt.

I laughed, cracked jokes, and played games with Tiffany and Justin until I passed out after three or four or five more drinks. There were no worries about the Taliban outside our house; I could hear sounds for what they were, and eventually my deployment didn't even seem real. Usually, I was sleeping terribly and waking up with terrors, or simply not sleeping due to thoughts like, *What's wrong with me? Why did they take the bike inside? What happens next?*

I still knew I wanted to accomplish big things in life, and joining the Marines was supposed to give me the discipline to develop a path to success. But ever since I got home, I wondered if these nightmares and guilty feelings would ever stop. My mind raced all night, every night. Then when I slept, I dreamed I was back overseas. I slept lightly in case someone came into the house so I could take them out—protecting my brothers or my family. They made us killers and expected us to simply flip a switch when we got home.

But that one night of drinking let me sleep through the night. I didn't have nightmares. I didn't wake up with terrors. I just had giddy, goofy feelings until I faded into sleep and woke up the following day rested. Amazing! That was the first time in years.

And all it took was a few beers? I thought.

We did the same thing the next day, except we started a little earlier.

Then we did the same the next day.

And the next day.

And the next day . . .

My brother and I drank every day and had a great time until he went home—but the beer was still in the fridge, and I couldn't let that go to waste. My consumption of alcohol went from zero to one hundred over a long weekend visit. I used it as a balm for sleep and a vessel to open up about what I was battling. And I never admitted just how much I was battling.

Fast forward one year, and my alcohol dependence had gotten so bad that we needed *three* recycling bins to house all the cans and liquor bottles I consumed before the weekly bin pickup. You couldn't even see any other items in there; it looked like we had frat house parties every week. Little did the garbage collectors know it was just me, drinking alone because it was ten times more effective than the pills the VA had given me that I was putting down with the drink. I didn't want people around me when I drank. I always wanted to be alone or with my wife or with my dad, to start never-ending conversations with him.

Because when I was drunk, I was vulnerable, and I only wanted people around me that I believed had my back if the "bad guys" came for me.

Both my wife and father expressed concern about my drinking, but in subtle ways. I could read their social cues when I would ask to make another liquor run, or when they would say, "let's hold off for a bit" when I asked if we had anymore. Still, any attempt to help me ease up turned into anger from my side, because I felt it was unsympathetic of them to want me to stop when it was the only relief I had, especially when compared to all the narcotics the doctors fed me that did nothing except make me more depressed—which made me want more drinks.

My VA benefits funded this addiction, a story that is unfortunately too familiar to many of today's veterans—some of whom I've spoken to myself. In my own experience, there is a direct correlation between alcoholism (or drug abuse) and suicide. If someone asked me to stop the only thing that made me feel good, safe, and whole, I felt like they were trying to strip me of my only happiness. I was trying to find a way not to tell them: "If you make me stop before I learn how to handle these demons I'm battling, I won't be here much longer."

In my mind, I knew this wasn't sustainable. I couldn't tell what I was more upset about, the fact that substances now had a hold of me or the fact that I wasn't resilient enough to fight the demons alone. But something needed to change, and I didn't want suicide to be the option. But it was an option nonetheless . . .

Have you ever heard the saying "Fear is not real?" The lesson I had yet to learn at that moment was just how truly remarkable the human brain actually is, and what you can actually do with it at any given time. Allow me to nerd out for a moment and make a tangential connection between physics and biochemistry . . .

Newton's law of energy conservation states, "Energy can neither be created nor destroyed, only converted from one form of energy to another." In the real world, you can't literally run your car on fear, fly a plane with hope, or harness pain to move a boat. However, what I eventually learned is that you can use *whatever* fuel is at your disposal and convert it into drive, into motivation, into positive behavior—whatever you need to get the job done (whatever that job might be). In the moment, the fuel that is at your disposal might not seem like fuel at all but rather a toxic material—for you might see that all the fuel you have to work with is fear, anger, or any other negative emotion or perception. But you must remember Newton's law of energy conservation to realize that *any* of these emotions are not "real," are not actually based in reality, because you can convert them into a totally different form of energy, energy that you can use to solve problems, either those of the world or your own. Isn't that crazy? You have the power to use intangible things like feelings or memories to change your brain chemistry and motivate you into positive physical responses. You are in control of your own mind, but it's so easy for us to forget this and become derailed from our progress, whether it be in relation to substances, health, wealth, the way we show love, how we treat others, empathize, and on and on. In my own case, I quickly went from being alcohol-free to a state of alcoholism because I didn't understand the possibility of converting all my negative emotions into positive action. What I know now is that during this time, I had an opportunity to take all those negative feelings and perceptions that were driving me to drink and use them as fuel to find a different way to deal with my trauma and emotions—but as always, hindsight is 20/20.

Just remember that if there is something in your mind, in your soul, that you truly want to "convert" into something else, it begins with realizing that it is not based in an unchangeable reality, and that the small decisions you make to use your "fuel" in a positive manner—remember those micro-disciplines? They will build on one another to gradually set you back on the right path.

Summary:

- Taking control of your life requires acknowledging the source of your pain and finding ways to convert it into positive energy and action without relying on substance abuse.
- Don't be afraid to go against the grain. Just like the medical eval, you can break the molds of conformity with different thinking.
- Small decisions will get you back to the path of healing if that is what your soul truly wants.
- We are not owed anything for our misfortunes. Life is difficult for most; it's what we make of these adversities that matter.

Chapter 14 Exercise

Think of one good thing that happened today, no matter how small. Write about how this moment felt and how it can be a source of positive energy in your life.

CHAPTER 15

WAKE-UP CALL

Don't wait to build a legacy. We must do whatever we can today to do something we're proud of, because we are not guaranteed tomorrow.

In January 2015, I arrived home from 29 Palms to Florida. From then through 2017, two life-changing events unfolded that began to transform my perception.

It all began when I left the Marine Corps, having completed my service in around three years due to my medical diagnoses. My exit was followed by Dunston's, who completed his full four-year contract. As 2016 rolled around, both of us felt the absence of the camaraderie we had in the Corps, longing for a job that had a sense of purpose.

When Dunston landed a job as a security guard, it seemed like the perfect fit for him, and possibly for me too. The job was not too physically demanding, and it offered decent pay. Dunston shared his insights with me on the industry, guiding me through the process of getting my own license.

Then, on May 19, 2016, tragedy struck: Dunston took his own life. His loss shook me to my core, reshaping my priorities. Suddenly, my future plans seemed insignificant compared to Honoring Dunston's memory, and I founded my project.

But just as Til Valhalla Project began to take shape, another tragedy struck: my father was diagnosed with cancer. My dad was a very fit man in his later years. He found passion and joy from running and biking, which was weird to me because I never saw my dad be active in his life, unless he was working on something with an engine, or yard work, etc. Nonetheless, call it a midlife crisis or an epiphany that woke him up to health and wellness, but he started getting in remarkable shape, running up to thirteen miles a day sometimes and biking double that.

He was drowning out the noise of everyday life and focusing on what he wanted. And to say the least, seeing someone turn their life around in the blink of an eye was impressive. He led by this remarkable example while I struggled with PTSD, drinking, being broke, and trying to find out what I wanted to do with my life. It made me even more acutely aware of my lack of motivation.

Then one day, after completing a half-marathon with his running group and beating an old personal best, my dad came home to celebrate his success with us—which, of course, I saw as an opportunity to start drinking.

"Let's have a shot!" I yelled.

Now, to offer a little background, my dad struggled with alcohol for years after moving to Florida when I was still a kid. I never saw it firsthand, as by the time I moved in he had gotten his drinking under control, but he was more open to talking about it when he saw me under Jack Daniels's spell. As he embarked on his fitness journey, he slowed his consumption from our post-deployment celebrations even more, and likely saw the path I was heading down as a deterrent to his newfound goals.

But that day, after his half-marathon and new personal best, he entertained me and decided to have a few drinks before getting some well-earned rest from his morning run. It wasn't a particularly long night of drinking, but I know by the time I went back into my room with Tiffany I was pretty drunk, and watched TV in a daze until I faded to sleep.

"Korey! KOREY!"

My eyes flew open.

"Who's yelling my name?"

I couldn't tell if it was another bad dream or reality.

"*KOREY!*"

Koda got up and started barking, so I knew it was real.

My brain immediately kicked into overseas alert. Every sound, every shadow, every vibration was something actively trying to kill me (in my mind). So, the only obvious answer was that a Taliban soldier had broken into the house, and my dog Koda and I barreled out of the bedroom, ready for a fight. When I rounded the corner, I saw my dad lying on the ground, barely coherent, mumbling something about "blood" and his "a—."

I kept saying, "What? WHAT?"

"I'm bleeding out of my a—! Call 911!"

I called immediately, and just kneeling there by his side had me ricocheting in and out of flashbacks from treating casualties overseas. I had to physically shake my head to get the visions out and return to reality. Waiting for help wasn't how we did things overseas. We got people on the stretcher, out of the hot zone, and took them to casualty evacuation (casevac) safety.

But I had nothing but a slowly settling-in hangover. I tried to get him to the car but he was resistant, so we just waited for the ambulance. I forgot how close we lived to the hospital, because they were there in what felt like two minutes or less. When adrenaline pumps, moments can trickle slowly, but this was still quick, even in a clear fight or flight mode.

They loaded my dad up in the ambulance and headed to the hospital.

I remember Tiffany and me driving directly behind the ambulance at midnight, thinking how silly this was because I figured my dad just had something like a cut or chafing from the running. He was "wigging himself out." When we arrived at the hospital, they got him off-loaded and into a room for the doctor to see what was up, and after checking in they let us go with him.

After an IV and some meds, Dad seemed to have calmed down.

"Man, what happened?" I asked. I had never seen him like this.

"A lot of blood," he said. "A lot."

Before I could ask a follow-up question, the doctor said he had to check out the source of the bleeding, which meant lubing up a glove.

My wife left the room, but I stayed there and made some smart joke about a finger in the butt to lighten the mood. It worked because we all laughed for a second, then the doctor went to work trying to figure out what caused the bleeding.

"I feel a mass," he said. "We're going to order some tests and see what it is."

We honestly were all calm with the news because that common, overwhelming feeling of "that can't happen to me" gave us peace in the moment. We didn't know what it was, but we just had false confidence and hope that Dad was incapable of being forced into submission.

So, we said, "Sounds good!" and prepared to go home.

A few days later, the tests came back.

We were told that Dad had a cancerous tumor lining the wall of his colon, and that we needed to get him into surgery, cut it out, and then get him on chemo.

What they offered was a problem with a clear solution. So what we all essentially heard was: "Don't worry. Modern medicine sees stuff like this all the time. We've got you covered."

After that, we felt more relief as they explained how the procedure usually works and how it would likely come back in five to ten years, and we would have to do it again, and again the decade after that. *Phew!* I thought to myself. *That was a close call.*

The doctors reassured us that this was a manageable cancer and that it was "extremely common" for people with colon cancer to live long, healthy lives when treated promptly. And again, with my dad running three to five miles a day and eating well, if one guy is going to crush this battle, it would be him. If the average joe is living a long healthy life, then he's going to beat it with ease. *He's literally one of the toughest guys I know.*

So, throughout the family, minor celebrations of "Glad we caught it early!" and "Man, that could have been so much worse!" began. It felt like dodging a bullet, and I felt a massive relief. A couple of weeks later, Dad was brought into surgery to have a part of his colon removed and a colostomy bag placed while he was still healing, and chemo began.

The surgery went off without a hitch, and at the start chemo had minimal side effects. He was still active daily, running with his group, not slowing down, and kept moving forward. We got comfortable with the new routine. Even complacent. They had him go back every month for checkups and MRIs to ensure all was well. A few months later, Dad's colon had almost healed, and things were looking good—until the doctor told him that his last MRI revealed a small mass on his liver.

My heart sank. I don't know what my dad felt, but I can't imagine he could have felt anything different. Still, he would never shed a tear in front of me—him being the old-school, bottle-up-your-emotions type of guy. He handled it like a rock around us, but I had to assume that in solitude, he fell apart just like I would. Of course, the doctors once more told us it would all be okay and that they would immediately take further action.

Except they didn't.

They took months and months to make decisions, pushing his appointments back while I kept thinking, *Isn't getting the mass out sooner imperative to his survival? What's the holdup?* I started getting upset with them, and even with him, whenever he came in and said:

"They pushed it back again."

I would respond, "Dad, charge in there and get it done. Speak up!"

If you aren't already aware, once cancer metastasizes (spreads to other locations in your body), your life expectancy goes from "I can live with this for a long time" to "my time is limited." It was virtually a death sentence. And as my dad put it: "I went from a typical diagnosis to atypical in weeks."

Now it was a race to get the cancer out and prolong his time, while my dad was still working every day as a mechanic to pay the medical bills. He didn't want any of my help with finances, even though my business was bearing fruit. He always wanted to be a provider and an "I did it myself" type of guy—cancer wouldn't change that. Not on his watch. That independence and resilience was something I always admired about my dad, but I still wanted help.

And the situation changed—fast. And it kept changing, but the doctor kept giving us hope for solutions, a longer life for my dad than originally thought. I must have had a broken perception of what doctors were supposed to do with diagnoses like this; I thought they set a low expectation, to later be exceeded, leaving us thankful if and when we made it past the deadline.

But then the hope started hurting, because it felt like lies.

Compounded with that were the struggles my dad faced daily with his insurance provider. Even though he was paying something like $1K a month in health insurance so he could go to the Mayo Clinic (supposed to be the best), they never missed a chance to scare the hell out of him with some bill that was more than he made in a year. Then my dad would have to plead with them and find out why their policy was doing things that contradicted their terms.

It was heartbreaking. And the added stress of the calls to the clinic seemed to be affecting him more than the chemo or treatment or even the diagnosis. A man with some of the worst news you can get had to keep working his a— off, just to break even and contend with the psychological assault of an industry that had the mentality of a loan shark.

No empathy, just a number.

I'd be lying to you if I said I didn't have remarkably violent thoughts on what I wanted to do to those people for treating my dad like that. To me, they felt like insurgents at home. But in my dad's act of humility to the unfortunate news, he surrendered himself to the process that started running him over, and I couldn't understand why he wasn't fighting harder.

"Why aren't you pushing back, Dad? Fight this. Fight them."

"It's just noise, Korey. It's just noise."

Then I realized he didn't have control here.

He couldn't fix this problem or engineer his own solution.

It's important that we try to understand what my dad meant by "noise", which was a term I brought home from the Marines. We can think of noise simply as the perpetual distractions we have day in and day out that prevent us from making real progress with ourselves. Noise is what you get when you conflate movement and "being busy" with actual progress. Noise is, in fact, the killer of progress, only giving you the illusion that you are moving forward, like on a treadmill.

Your definition of noise will change over time as your time becomes more valuable. What might "noise" be? Other people's drama, for one. Or that old pair of pants you're ironing, even though you know you're going to throw them out soon. Or even a task like cleaning your outside windows, when you could afford to hire a cleaning service instead. Ignoring or canceling this noise in our lives can give us the space and time to do the things we actually want or must do, to create a lasting legacy. Whether it's writing a book or starting a business—there are the things that hold real future value for you.

I came to understand the power of noise when I started to realize that I couldn't be in two places at once. Remember when I had to choose between school, work, and starting Til Valhalla Project? I decided that school and work were the noises in my life that had the highest opportunity cost. I needed to be a successful entrepreneur before I could be a successful philanthropist, but that required me to stop the noise. We all have 86,400 seconds in a day; how you spend those seconds determines how tomorrow will look for you.

Stay focused and cut out the noise.

My dad lost his anger but not his will. He was still fighting, but what he was fighting for changed. He lost his concern for the noise, because he knew the noise was not his problem anymore. Noise, like an obnoxious insurance provider, was a problem for people with time—which he knew he did not have. His mind shifted from the minor stuff like those calls, those checkups, those leaky faucets, or squeaky car belts, to his legacy.

How would he spend his time now?

What hadn't he done? What could he undo?

And what could he *still* do?

The problem was that Dad had focused on the noise most of his life.

Now, he wanted to change it. But now, at the end, he didn't have the time to.

Though it was never said word for word, this is where our conversations always ended up. I could see it funneling through his mind and wondered what I could do, if anything, to help. He never quite smiled the same way since he started this battle, and his sideways half smile—the one I adopted—always said, "I'll smile, but I'm not really happy." And I understood. How the hell do you have genuine happiness knowing that you just started to get your life together, and it's getting cut short before you have a chance to build the legacy you wanted for your family?

There are so many instances of noise in life, even for people like me who try to cut out as much noise as possible. It's no wonder many of us live in constant anxiety. Can you go away for three months and feel stress-free? Or does the world we've built around us just not support that scenario?

Think about marketing for a moment, which has built much of the world we see around us. The market not only tries to sell solutions to noise but sells us noise, itself. Thanks to modern marketing, many of us believe we need a nice car, a certain type of home, a certain quality of clothing, until we realize the noise that comes with those things keeps us in a constant state of anxiety over the burden of everything we must do to care for them—not to mention the maintenance involved in preserving our relationships with friends and family. Someone with limited time must look over all that and budget time to where it matters most—family and legacy.

The time you spend now and the impact you will leave behind.

Don't wait to build a legacy. The last thing my dad expected after finishing a half-marathon was a diagnosis of colon cancer. We must do whatever we can *today* to do something we're proud of, because we are not guaranteed tomorrow. "That won't happen to me" is a mentality most of us share, and we try to drown out that mentality with noise. The things that distract us and hold us back from what we want to do and who we want to be. Loss is present in all our lives, and what happened to my dad made me more aware than ever of my own mortality. If I'm anything like him and lucky enough, I have precisely eighteen years left on this earth. That thought drives my every action. That's why, when a cup breaks, I smile.

Because once my dad knew his fate, that's what he did—it was just noise.

Summary:

- Take a moment to appreciate that life is finite and evaluate your priorities. It's crucial to distinguish between what's important and what's merely "noise."
- It's never too early to start building a legacy and do something you are proud of. The uncertainty of life makes it crucial to seize each moment and make the most of it.
- Life is precious. Appreciate every moment, however mundane or routine it might seem.

Chapter 15 Exercise

In our lives, many of us contend with "noise" that exacts a considerable opportunity cost. Write down five examples of noise in your life that cost more than they benefit you—that is, things that occupy your mind and time in ways that keep you from making positive progress. Then, envision and write down what accomplishments you could make if you were able to free yourself from these noises.

LEGACY MINDSET

CHAPTER 16

THE PRICE OF PERFECTION

There is a paradox: even if you know that perfection is just a myth, you can still aim high to achieve it.

Something happened to me when my dad got his cancer diagnosis that changed the lens through which I see the world. In addition to the immeasurable fear and sadness of learning that his cancer was spreading through his body, I became aware of my own mortality in a way I never had before. Sure, I had come to peace with dying before, but that was on my own terms, maybe in battle or even by my own hand—but the fact that something like cancer could happen at any time and any place to anyone was like having a ticking time bomb in your chest that you never knew when or if would go off. This realization felt overwhelming—like Afghanistan times ten. You can plead for life with a robber, saying, "I have a family, I have kids," but cancer is ruthless and blind. It doesn't care how bad your life already is, or what good you have done for the world.

It's hard to overstate the influence my dad had on my life. His mannerisms, morals, perspectives, how he battled his foes—they've been baked into my head since I was a kid. I walked into his arms when I took my first steps; he saw my first smile; he was there for my first words—that's the kind of love a parent has for their child, and speaking for myself, it's as surreal as it gets. The only thing more real is watching yourself fade to black.

When you have a connection like that with someone, you feel their pain as if it were your own. Dad's diagnosis was just as real as if I had gotten the diagnosis myself. My mind snapped, and one realization started plaguing my brain and hasn't left since: "I don't have much time."

That thought nags me every night as I drift off to sleep. It greets me every morning when I wake up.

Even since the motorcycle suicide bombing I could have prevented, my mind had begun to rewire itself to pay extreme attention to the little things, and to be aware that I never have enough time on this earth to do what I need to do.

I had seen the cost of little oversights, and now saw the cost of the "that can't happen to me" mentality. This sparked an obsession to challenge myself to accept nothing but excellence in the things I do. And I mean *everything* that I do.

Everything is broken in my eyes. The cracked paint on the walls or the drips where it bled onto the baseboards. The key tolerances on my keyboard. The way those sentences were structured to be broken up into two, rather than with a semicolon. Everything. Everything I do I see as broken first; the imperfections glare at me so hard that sometimes it blinds me to what's truly important.

Those crossed wires in my head have me doing basic tasks like I'm diffusing a bomb. I still shake from anxiety when engraving items on a laser, because the thought of failure and wasting my limited time is unbearable to fathom.

Recently a local police officer was killed in the line of duty, and his department asked my team to engrave his handcuffs to give to his kids. My team did a sample run on some scrap steel for my review. They expected me to go over it with a fine-tooth comb, poring over every line and letter to make sure it was up to snuff.

Here's what they didn't expect—although maybe they should have since they know me well. I took my phone out, opened the camera app, and zoomed in as close as I could on the engraving to see how good of a job they did.

"The text is shadowed here, here, and here," I said, pointing at the blown-up image on my phone.

"Oh man, I didn't see that!"

But I did. And it wasn't acceptable.

I kid you not, I took those cuffs and spent three hours getting them redesigned and engraved. I aimed for perfection, hoping to achieve greatness. Doing so probably pulled me away from some other critical task I was working on. But I couldn't bear the thought of knowing that an ignored discrepancy was visible, even if no one would ever see it except under a magnifying glass.

This is part of that Hero's legacy; I cannot turn a blind eye to it. That's like asking a fish to breathe out of water.

At first, I was upset with my team for presenting me with a problem that I felt they all should have applied enough attention to detail to solve on their own, instead of relying on what they knew was my own obsessive attention. But I love my staff, and I understand that we approach projects differently, because we all come with different life experiences and different lessons gained from them.

After completing the project, I looked at my vice president and he apologized, because he knew I wouldn't be able to let them proceed once I was involved.

"I should have known not to bring them to you," he said. "But I'm glad I did, because now they're perfect."

Ultimately, I knew I wasn't going to lose sleep over this project because I did that Hero justice in my mind.

I've come to realize that my obsessive striving toward perfection is ultimately a defense mechanism for taking control of my remaining time on earth. That, and I want to show that even a kid who was in special ed classes can exceed on the right task. If I can do it, so can you. I've simply decided that everything I do, I will do *right*, above the standards set by society.

If you say a three-inch tolerance is good, I want to give you sub-one inch.

If you say you can't find a discrepancy, I want to find one.

If you say you're a professional, I want to prove you wrong through my own knowledge of your profession.

You can imagine how exhausting this mentality is for not only myself but the people around me, because I pick everything apart and highlight every flaw.

As someone who has done home renovations on my investment properties, I have had to paint a few walls in my life. However, If I went and repainted a textured wall, how much time would I waste to avoid those pin-sized, unnoticeable dips?

If it was perfect, it would have no dips, drips, or pinholes, I would think to myself.

But then you figure out something annoying after looking at forums, desperate to find a solution: that's just how that type of paint is.

"But it's not right! Why are they even in business if they're not going to chase perfection?" I'd turn my head and say to Tiffany, who always reinforced my logic.

But the reality? No one cares. The paint would have 5000 five-star reviews, and to them it was good enough.

If I took apart this keyboard and made a comparison chart with another of comparable value to determine which had a better tolerance-to-response ratio, what on earth would I be doing other than avoiding writing?

I could say that stuff is "noise," but I'd still have to investigate further. Why is it so noisy to me in particular? Why do I keep seeing the cracks, smudges, and flaws? These small things, and they are small, make me so obsessive that I lose sleep. All I want to do is fix them.

When I looked at Dunston's plaque that morning after the drunken bender of making it, I didn't like what I saw. My mistakes glared at me, and it was all I could focus on. But when I gave that plaque away, none of those mistakes were ever brought up. It's possible they were noticed and Dunston's mom is just incredibly nice, but it might also be that I was looking for the problems. Sometimes, those problems are just noise. Other times, those problems are real opportunities for personal growth.

The question you must ask yourself when facing imperfection is: Am I feeling passion? Or is this just noise?

The answer for the officer's cuff and Dunston's plaque was easy: passion. This is what I'm here to do, and this is what I want to do, to the best of my abilities.

But what about noise?

A few moments ago, I talked about the pinholes in the paint on the wall. Well, the other day, I walked through one of my rental properties and told the contractors I had hired that I could see all the imperfections as if they were highlighted.

"What imperfections?" they asked.

Then I proceeded to point out all these alignment issues, gaps in the caulk, paint runs, etc. But they couldn't see what I was talking about. It was like we were looking at two different walls.

It drove me nuts because these guys weren't cheap, and it felt like I was only paying them for their brave attempt rather than the finished work of "professionals," as their title unfairly boasted to their customers.

I try to look at everything at a micro level, like a machinist who identifies the difference between a great job and an awful job at a scale of a thousandth of an inch, which is inconceivable to most. I don't know how to ignore problems and go to sleep at night. I have always thought that a problem implies the existence of a solution. When someone claims, "That's impossible," it signifies that an answer exists but isn't being sought. I can't stand knowing there's a solution that no one is pursuing.

But it was either right or wrong in my eyes. Black or white, ones or zeros.

An outlet cover that's slightly crooked may be functional, but it's still wrong, and if someone is going to call themselves a professional, then they should take pride and passion in the little things.

A passionate person who knows the difference between right and wrong will approve their work under a microscope and be their own worst critic. But if you judge your work by standing ten-feet back "because no one will notice," then you're not actually passionate about it.

I've legitimately felt that I'll leave a bad legacy if I don't pay attention to things on a micro level. But my "chase perfection," "never rest" mindset has sometimes been so overwhelming that it can take over my life. In fact, I've taught myself to work in my sleep, even engineering a desk that I sit at in my dreams. Upon waking after this deep planning, I write down the plans on paper, then try to go back to sleep.

I've come to realize, though, that it's not actually "perfection" I'm seeking; it's merely a desire to do the *right thing*. The search for perfection is ego-driven and, as Vince Lombardi has reminded us, an impossible task anyway. No, it's not perfection I'm really chasing—it's obeying a moral code, a code of right and wrong, a code about serving others—even if no one is watching and most people won't even notice those little flaws that you see. If you only serve others when it's convenient to you—if your work is only good enough so that *most* people won't notice its undeniable flaws—that's not a Legacy Mindset.

Perfection drives us back to ourselves and demands us to achieve the impossible. Right and wrong, though, propels us toward *other people*, and asks us to accept *only the very best we know we can do*. That's why, recently, I've had to adopt a 90% rule. The 90% rule is that, if a particular project is 90% to the standard you accept, leave it, or evaluate whether the impact of getting it to 100% is worth the time—because only one person can get it to your standards: you.

I know that not everyone is driven by an internal sense of right and wrong and are not able to see when others choose right, but there are cases in which it *is* recognized, and that is enough—one person seeing the passion with which you approach life.

But what about your work that's attention to detail no one will recognize but yourself? And is every flaw you see worth losing sleep over?

It's crucial to zoom out your focus and pick your battles with a Legacy Mindset, to take a moment to ponder whether 90% will suffice and if the extra hours (or days) it'll take you to chase down that last 10% are really worth the time, effort, and stress.

Recently, (yet again) I was overcome with fury about the quality of work that was being done by another contracting group at one my rental properties, from the caulking to the painting and more. Toward the end of the project, I was going around the house myself in pure ire, straightening screws on all the outlet covers behind the contractors' work and voicing my frustrations to Tiffany. I was not working on what I wanted to, Honoring Heroes with my team at Til Valhalla Project. I kept pacing through the house, making my disdain known . . .

And then I realized my wife was witnessing me having a meltdown, losing my mind over some screws.

"Why am I like this?" I asked out loud. "Why does no one care?"

I continued, "I just want to stop obsessing over small things and live a fulfilled life!"

Just before I thought I was going to break out in a scream while ripping an outlet off the wall, it hit me.

THIS IS NOT MY LEGACY! I thought to myself, managing internally to avert what was about to be a real crisis.

Jesus, that's it, I thought. *That's what I needed to hear.* "This is not my legacy."

I felt a monumental weight lift off me, like I had just found a new way through life.

Yes, I was still going to make my screws straight when I could, because that's who I am. *But*—I was now given permission to sleep in a flawed home, on a flawed street, in a flawed world, because I realized the more I managed to divert my focus from what was not truly important, the more my legacy was actually going to benefit others.

Obsession is a blessing and a curse, because if channeled uselessly, it will do nothing other than paralyze you, make you hate the way people are, and make you spend the time you *don't* have chasing unattainable perfection.

Out loud, I must tell myself, "Don't worry about the alignment of the screw. Worry about Honoring Heroes. Worry about *legacy*."

Then I end up tightening the screw anyways . . .

I ask you to seek the right path in everything you do, even if you think to yourself, just as I have at times: "*I* didn't pass society's standards, *I* never excelled in school, *I'm* the broken one!"

But it is *only* up to you to obey that moral code, because no one can do it for you, and many others simply will not for themselves.

So, challenge everything, but pick your battles on what you choose to fix.

There is not enough time to fix every flaw in a flawed world.

But then again, there is time to fix a few.

Summary:

- Weigh the value of time invested in seeking perfection against the actual gains. If something is 90% up to standard, evaluate if the effort needed for that extra 10% is worth the time or if it's better to move on.
- What might seem like a glaring mistake or imperfection to you might not be noticeable or significant to others. It's important to sometimes step back and see things from a different perspective.
- Seeing problems or imperfections doesn't always have to be negative. These can be opportunities to improve or create something beneficial.
- Obsession can be both a blessing and a curse. If channeled properly, it can lead to phenomenal work. However, if channeled incorrectly, it can be paralyzing and harmful.

Chapter 16 Exercise

Make a list of your daily tasks that fit into two categories: passion and noise. Then, take the tasks that are noise, and write down what you can do to remove them from your plate so you can focus more on passion. Make a goal to keep a small diary or note on your phone where you can quickly jot down tasks, issues, and other obligations that arise during the day. At the end of the day, spend a few minutes reviewing the list, categorizing each as passion or noise, and decide where your energy is best spent.

CHAPTER 17

TURNING POINTS

Life-changing opportunities often come cloaked in a blanket of misfortune. You need to be able to navigate and extrapolate the lessons within to move forward accordingly.

Not every story of change needs to be as dramatic as war or a cancer diagnosis. As a matter of fact, one of the biggest changes in my life came from a hotel room. One little fifty-dollar hotel room put me on a relentless path of success and personal growth that I will fight with every last fiber of my being to hold on to, because the alternative almost put me in the grave.

After Dunston's suicide, I started Til Valhalla Project. The goal remained the same: create plaques to Honor Heroes and preserve their legacy. Til Valhalla Project became a way to fund those plaques, allowing families of military, first-responders, and others to show support in ending the epidemic of veteran suicide. To fund those plaques, we sold impactful T-shirts, and as more people heard about the T-shirts and the project, we were able to make more plaques.

The two worked in tandem and the project, with its mission I believed in with all my heart, naturally transformed into a business. In early 2017, this new mission of delivering memorial plaques to the families of Fallen Heroes was starting to get off the ground, and people were slowly beginning to recognize my wife and me for the work we were doing free of charge.

Then my dad got his cancer diagnosis. And that's when a switch flipped.

It was time to leap and grow wings on the way down.

The mission was helping me fight the demons in my head, but I realized the business aspects of the project could help more than just me—it could help my wife and our relationship, it could help my father and his medical bills, and it could help countless more families and veteran supporters. So, I realized the opportunity I had inadvertently created:

This could be bigger than just a few plaques. We could reach more people and make a sizeable impact on this epidemic of veteran suicide. I needed to succeed not just for me, but for them.

The only question was how.

I wanted this mission to work; but for it to work, I had to devote my most valuable currency: time. That also meant funding was tight, as I had just quit my nine-dollars-an-hour associate position at AutoZone and dropped out of college. Til Valhalla Project became my focus, but I had no connections, no circle, and felt like a small fish in a big ocean of business that I didn't fully understand. Depression and drinking compounded those feelings, convincing me I had made a horrible mistake and clamoring for me to turn back. These feelings tainted everything we had done up to that point and everything we might do like a film negative—and I felt alone because of it.

But Tiffany helped me. She encouraged me by showing me all the families we had already helped together and let me know there were more out there.

"We can help them too."

And that created our strategy for business growth: reciprocity. With my equipment in my garage, it costs virtually nothing to make a gift for neighbors or go the extra mile to honor a particular Hero with my products. Even though I needed to sustain larger orders to pay the bills, I could not help the warm and fuzzy feeling I'd get when I discovered something a neighbor was passionate about, like a sports team. I'd hurry inside, rip the team logo off Google, then laser out something cool on glassware procured from the dollar store. I would do all this simply to knock on their door and hand it to them as a surprise. It was euphoric!

Sure, I didn't have much money to offer, but I offered all my time and passion. Because of that simple equation, the perceived value of my goods was worth more than the monetary investment. I could make the people around me happy by hand-engraving unique items out of my garage with my wife by my side, driving me to get even more materials.

Then something funny happened. The more we offered out of kindness, the more people asked for custom items, for which they happily paid full price. And what started as personalized items transformed into something more commercial that put income into the business, which then funded more giving, and so on—just like that first memorial plaque for Dunston.

From that point forward, I knew that giving was the only way to go, and if I couldn't give to others and have faith in the reciprocity model, then I didn't want to be in business. Or alive, honestly.

However, there was still a problem—my circle was limited. I had yet to learn how to utilize social media, market these items, reach out to support centers, and scale this business. I wanted this mission we believed in to help more people but didn't know how to reach them.

So I studied.

I read books, watched videos, and analyzed market trends until some iota of this digital world made sense to me. I researched profiles on social media of people with similar goals who were already successful at what they were doing. If I was a small fish in this big ocean, I wanted to grow—that made me hungry to consume as much as possible.

But there was a limit to how much I could do and understand myself.

And here's something that I came to understand about myself during this time: when I make my giant leaps, I do whatever it takes to grow wings on the way down—even if growing those wings is uncomfortable or embarrassing to some.

What I realized I needed was a mentor.

To find one, I emailed authors, DM'd celebrities, wrote letters to business owners, and in all my attempts, I never got anything back. Then one day in 2018, while researching marketing strategies on ClickFunnels's Facebook page, I saw a guy named Colin Wayne come across my feed. A veteran himself who seemed to have it all: the cars, the house, the attire, the looks. And I thought, "If I had even a fraction of the money this guy had, imagine the impact I could make and the plaques I could deliver." Sure, we all want nice things, and I'm not excluded from that, but I know that when I see a lavish life, opportunities for real impact come with it.

How the hell is he so successful? I wondered.

I clicked on Colin's profile and started to dig in. He looked about my age, his profile said he was in the Army, and he was clearly a fitness model. I know I say not to compare yourself to anyone else, but that's all I did at the time. Compared to Colin, I felt like scum on a boot heel. He had been critically injured in Afghanistan when an RPG hit his base and impacted just a few feet from where he was standing, sending shrapnel through his legs and abdomen. But it never slowed him down. He was the epitome of resilience in my eyes.

To go through all that and become that successful at twenty-eight years old—I was in awe. My injuries felt minimal compared to his, but I never saw him use them as an excuse, only motivation. So, from a distance, I had this immense respect for a man I had never spoken to.

But one thing was for sure: I wanted to.

I sent a friend request in the hopes he would approve.

And for days, weeks, months, he didn't. As I worked on Til Valhalla Project, I began following Colin's profile daily, watching the amazing things he did in his shop at Redline Steel—where he and his team manufactured customized wall art in the form of steel signs—to see how I could improve. One day I worked up enough courage to message him, but he already had a successful business; I had nothing to offer him. The message was left unread.

But again, I *needed* to grow those wings. *Find a breaching point*, I thought.

So, I used some tactics probably indicative of a crazy ex, adding all his top friends on Facebook and waiting for one of them to blindly accept my request—accuracy by shameless volume. Akbar Sheikh was the first who responded, and I started sharing my mission with him and asked if he could connect me to Colin. I put on a facade like I fit in with those guys, even though they were marketing giants compared to me.

But guess what? It worked!

Colin got back to me.

After honestly coming clean to Colin about what I did to get ahold of him, I expected him to turn me away and block me, but that couldn't have been further from the truth. Not only did he appreciate my drive, but he offered me the opportunity to come to his massive warehouse in Alabama so that he could mentor me for the day. I was completely stoked—but then he added: "I'll only charge you $5,000 for the day."

My heart sank. Five thousand dollars was damn near all I had in the bank. But I needed this. We needed this. My mission needed this. But it was a risk—a big one. If I failed after giving him that money, then I wouldn't be able to Honor any more Heroes and likely would have to focus on something else, something I was nowhere near as passionate about.

My mind started racing on what-ifs that quickly turned negative, even if they started off positively.

Five thousand dollars is not $100K, so that's good.

But $5,000 is all I have, so that's bad.

Til Valhalla Project LLC was established a year ago and has turned a profit. That's good.

But the profit is for the Heroes you're trying to help, Korey. It's not "yours."

I could help more people if this worked out!

But you could put your family in the red if you failed.

Mostly, I was just impressed that someone's time could be that valuable.

Fear set in, and I decided only a few things clearly: Five thousand dollars was a lot. Absolutely none of it would come from Til Valhalla Project. And, maybe Tiffany could decide . . .

Tiffany said she would back me either way, but it was my decision to make.

All right, back to me.

I messaged Colin back.

"I can't afford that, man. And what would I learn? Is there a guarantee?"

Today, I understand how silly these questions are if you genuinely want to connect with someone, but $5,000 is still $5,000. He didn't appreciate how I was wasting his time and redacted the offer almost immediately, which instantly gave me the fear of missing out. With everything to lose, I mustered up a response, before I could think of another opportunity to get cold feet.

I said yes and hit send before I could backtrack. Forced discipline and three-second rule, all wrapped up in one. I knew it was good for me, for everyone, but I was scared. So, I hit send before I could change my mind.

My body was visibly shaking.

I asked for an opportunity and got it, but it would cost me everything if I didn't take it seriously. Being broke demanded discipline from me, a back-against-the-wall situation, and I knew this risk was considerable. I just hoped it would pay off.

A few weeks later, my wife and I loaded our little Mazda and started the seven-hour drive to Alabama. All I thought about the entire ride was how big of a mistake this was. Ahead of the drive, Colin and I hadn't discussed the mentorship details and whether he would follow up after. In truth, we talked about damn near nothing except the $5,000 cost of entry.

I'm an idiot, I thought to myself. I was on the road with my wife with our last $5,000 in my pocket, trying to imagine how to transform this experience into something worth $5 million. We arrived late at night in Alabama, and the reality of my decision set in.

I was meeting Colin in the morning and we needed rest to make the best of it, but I had almost no money left. I kicked around the idea of us sleeping in the car, but my PTSD wouldn't allow it, and the thought of putting my wife through that was not okay. Being that exposed in a parking lot didn't sit well in my head.

We found a hotel that could fit my fifty-dollar budget (I still needed gas for the drive home). If you aren't aware, fifty dollars a night for a hotel, or motel as this was, is very likely not in a safe area. And, as we stared at our soon-to-be residence, I could tell Tiffany was uncomfortable.

The siding was cracked, the sign glitched neon light, and it looked like it was sporting rust from before my dad was born. Tiffany and I walked up to the front counter, exhausted from the nighttime drive and my nerves firing on all cylinders for seven hours. The lady that greeted us at the reception desk could probably write her own book on her experiences, which she carried in her eyes. A wife. A mother. A grandmother.

She smiled through her exhaustion, likely after a long shift, and took our payment.

I still think about how she carried herself and hope she's doing better.

But right after walking in and being greeted, we should have known this was a mistake. The inside, the desk, and the grime on the floor felt equal to the outside. I just wanted my wife to have a bed, and it was only for a short night, so I followed through, thinking the exterior and the check-in didn't necessarily mean the rooms weren't taken care of—it's still a motel and a business, after all. We got the key to our room and walked down the hall of peeling paint and torn-up carpets as the pervasive smell of mildew, or something worse, filled our noses.

Then we opened the door to our room.

I had slept in bad situations overseas but could not believe a place like this could stay in business! In plain sight, dead cockroaches were on the floor beside a huge stain of dried vomit. Dead bugs lined the walls with obvious dirt all over the place.

"What the f—k is this?" I said. "Is this even legal?"

My wife didn't say a word. We just walked into the potent smell of mildew and pure neglect. Side by side, we took it all in, amazed that a place like this existed in the modern age. But then that initial shock turned to panic because I started thinking, *I brought my wife here. How could I let this become a reality for us?*

These thoughts cascaded, and I was bombarded with feelings of being a lousy husband, chasing unrealistic dreams, and dragging my amazing wife into a place I wouldn't even have wanted to sleep in a war zone. If I didn't make this opportunity work, this could be our new reality. That's how broke we would be if this gamble didn't pay off. It took every iota of my being not to say "screw this" out loud, deposit the check back into my account, give up on the mission, and return to my old job, hoping for some semblance of stability.

"We're not staying here," I said, grabbing our stuff and heading back toward the front desk for a refund. My wife didn't stop me, but the lady told me I couldn't have a refund for whatever reason, and I almost broke down at the check-in counter.

I can't express to you how much I didn't want my wife sleeping like she was in a bombed-out house overseas, but I knew that I couldn't mentally handle sleeping in the car exposed. I felt stuck, and barely above a whisper, I asked Tiffany if she would be willing to sleep in that room. Without any hesitation, she just said, "Yes." And if that's not what it means to have someone by your side through thick and thin, I don't know what is.

But then it got worse.

We returned to the room and pulled back the blankets, revealing dried blood all over the sheets. I was beyond embarrassed at this point. I was embarrassed for my wife to be in this situation and to have a husband like me. If there was ever a time that I wanted her to move on because she deserved better than to follow me down this psychotic path, that was it. I wouldn't have blamed her in the slightest.

But she stayed with me. And she's still with me.

That night we slept on top of the covers, used each other as pillows, and felt disgusted, like bugs were crawling all over us. But I will tell you one thing: I woke with a f—ing *fire* in my heart that hasn't been quenched since that night. Even if I hadn't met Colin, I came face-to-face with my limits and knew exactly what I had to do to confront them.

I knew even if Colin didn't work out, I'd still find a way.

I knew if he didn't have the answers I needed, we'd discover them elsewhere, together.

But then, that morning, we did meet Colin. And, to be honest, there's not enough time to go into everything I learned from him in that one day, but I can tell you it was so much more than I expected. It was a gamble, a risk, but just from that first talk, I knew the knowledge I was absorbing was paying off. I sat near Colin in his office as he analyzed my business practices, numbers, overhead, and goals, and he showed us exactly how he used to be where we were and what he did to expand. It wasn't just about marketing, either—it was about reciprocity, being fruitful so others can benefit too, and he showed me how to make that a reality firsthand.

What I didn't expect, however, is how he empathized with me and my wife and our mission on the highest level. He was kind and generous, and from his demeanor and evident breadth of knowledge, I treated every word from him like it was sacred, writing it all down and making plans in my head on how to implement it. Then Colin surprised me again. He acknowledged the relentless determination and passion we both had for this mission and asked:

"Why don't you come back tomorrow, and we can keep going?"

As much as I wanted to, I told him I couldn't pay for another day.

He graciously offered us another day with him free of charge, as he said it wasn't often that he saw such purpose-driven people who took action as we did. And guess what? He even invited us to his beautiful mansion for dinner and put my wife and me up in a bada— hotel.

That night, we slept like royalty for the first time in our lives.

The culmination of those two nights felt surreal—like a dream.

And that was it. That horrible night followed by that wonderful day was my turning point—the moment everything changed. With his insights and the new fire under my butt, our mission had grown by over 300% every year since.

And all because one man gave me the chance to learn from him.

What he had gained, he gave back. He gave me an example not of business metrics and tactics but of what it means to build a legacy. It's what we offer of our passion that lives on in those lives we impact. "Korey, there is nothing to it but to do it," he would say. And something as simple as that is all you need. *You* are the only person who can make the future you want.

Because you're the only one who sees that future.

Do you need help on the journey? Absolutely.

But your passion for taking that journey is going to inspire others. It's going to show them that they can do this too. They can overcome adversity. They can find ways to push back the demons and make the time they spend meaningful.

In twenty-four hours, I risked everything for a moment with someone I didn't know, saw my wife endure something I would cry at the thought of exposing her to again, and witnessed what impact you can have on others when you are in a better place and have a good heart to accompany it. That was a unique power to harness, positively changing lives. Colin was a young millionaire that owed me nothing, but being financially stable allowed him to put me in the best hotel and spend time with me without batting an eye.

Today, my wife and I only stay in the best hotel rooms. No, it's not because we're too good for an average hotel, but because it's important for us to celebrate that life-changing day years ago. And when people come to visit, or I invite families of Fallen Heroes, I do the same for them. If you don't know us personally, know we live pretty humbly in all aspects of life, enjoying only specific luxuries that we can share with others. But now, when I get to a five-star hotel while traveling for impact, I ask, "What's your best room?" regardless of price.

That's our one nonnegotiable.

When you have your turning point, or if you have had it already, celebrate your wins and set ongoing rewards to remind yourself of where you came from. I refuse to regard myself as someone special, because then I would no longer be a student. By always looking for lessons, you remain a perpetual student and recognize the people and the world around you as your teachers. When the world is your teacher, you are never above those around you—they are integral to your learning journey. That night and that turning point showed me I was capable, showed me fear slows us all down, and showed me that financial success, when appropriately utilized, can amplify your true intentions.

Without days like that, turning points to reignite our focus, Til Valhalla Project would never have been able to donate millions of dollars or donate clothing to people experiencing homelessness; give money toward therapy, housing, and furniture for veterans; and cover the costs of funerals and plaques for families of Fallen Heroes. Recently, my wife and I also invested in a mental-health retreat on the water to invite struggling veterans and first responders out to unwind, relax, and gather themselves again. It's a property most of the people we speak to would never have an opportunity to set foot in, some of them only being able to afford a fifty dollars per night motel or sleeping on the streets—but we wanted to give them the same feeling Colin gave us after that one dreadful night: hope.

So, whenever you find yourself struggling with adversity, remember that each challenge you face adds depth to your journey. Embrace these moments, for each moment of adversity makes your underdog story that much sweeter.

Summary:

- Sometimes in life, taking a calculated risk can lead to incredible opportunities. Weigh the risks and rewards and be willing to step out of your comfort zone when it counts.
- Recognize when you are at a turning point in your life. These moments can significantly change the course of your life, and acknowledging them can help you understand what their impact could be.
- Turning points can serve as markers in your journey. Set new goals based on where you are after a turning point, and let them guide you toward your next steps.
- While celebrating turning points and wins, remember to keep a balanced perspective. Celebrate, but also prepare for future challenges. The journey continues, and being adaptable and ready for what's next is crucial.

Chapter 17 Exercise

Write down a major turning point in your life. Then add a sentence or two about how that turning point impacted your journey.

_____

_____

_____

_____

_____

_____

_____

_____

_____

_____

_____

_____

CHAPTER 18

HARNESSING MOMENTUM

> Legacy is a shared perspective. It's building others up and encouraging them to build others up. You build that foundation of people lifting people, and you create a community.

A few months after meeting with Colin, I was on a business high. Sales were coming in, and our mission was exploding from all the "Do Good, Be Good" knowledge I had obtained from Colin, which had latched its way onto every new decision we made. My wife and I would wake up every morning to hundreds of orders in Shopify and Etsy, to the point that we would have to mute our notifications from the constant dinging.

My dad's garage was absolutely filled with little yellow bubble envelopes of laser-engraved items sent out to people all over the US. We bought an even bigger laser to take on bigger jobs and build multiple plaques at once. And I couldn't quite get over this amazing feeling of shifting from feeling hopeless to valuable in such a short time.

All it took was reaching out.

I went from one plaque a month to one a week, to sixteen a month, and so on. Each memorial was surprise-delivered to the families of Fallen Heroes based on applications we received from the general public. But in my heart, I knew that laser-etched goods were of limited use; we were lucky that our products were in high demand, but we still didn't have anything that made us stand out besides some Facebook ads

I set up that were doing very well. That's not business stability. I'd call it beginner's luck—and luck can happen to anyone.

The question is: How do you utilize that initial boost? How do you be the person that hits the lottery and actually grows their winnings, rather than depletes them? Or in my case, how do I take this lucky scenario of sales and use it as my start-up funds toward a bigger vision?

As we were riding this high, I set my eyes on new ways to keep it going once the products started to saturate the market, attempting to stay a few steps ahead and maintain the "It won't last forever" mindset. And that's when I sat down and thought of something everyone needed that had a low barrier to entry: apparel. What I liked about clothing was that it could communicate some powerful and positive messages to people who needed it (including myself). We all wear clothes, and if I could make mine different and impactful enough, we could scale that side and change lives in more ways than one.

So, the mission got its new label: clothing brand.

The only problem was that I knew jack s—t about making T-shirts.

What we did know, however, and could never forget, is that over 60% of the memorials we were making were for Heroes dying by suicide. Because of that, I wanted to put out strong, impactful, tasteful designs that would also be proactive in encouraging veterans—and anyone else—to reach out. I defined three pillars for my brand: awareness, motivation, and tribute. With those pillars in mind, we designed shirts with messages like:

Do not give in to the war within

Honor their sacrifice

Don't let the hard days win

You have value

We Live Among Giants

Be kind, you never know what someone is going through

These were all designs made from the heart as outward-facing messages to my brothers and sisters battling, and an opportunity for those already supporting them day in and day out to show that support. And beyond that, they were also messages I needed to hear personally—I was my own demographic. I constantly govern my designs by doing what I believe would make my Fallen brothers proud. This approach makes most design decisions easy and keeps my moral compass aligned, even when it's difficult. Call me insane, but I have a mental roundtable with each person I lost to ensure they would be proud of whatever work I am putting out. If they disagree, then it doesn't launch.

So that became what set Til Valhalla Project products apart; well that and surprise-delivering thousands of memorials, of course. Unlike others, I didn't want to put out cringy T-shirts that we're more destructive to people's mentality than constructive just to make a quick buck. I could never live with myself knowing that, if I put a bad message out there and a person took their life wearing that tee, I would have to make a plaque knowing I participated in some cringey dark humor BS that only hindered their growth vs helping them grow.

The thought of that possibility destroyed me emotionally.

To battle that fear, my pillars containing messages of motivation, tribute, and awareness added positivity to a historically embattled group of people. It wasn't about the money; it was about serving people and pursuing personal growth for as long as I can. The idea of wasting my life for personal gain was unbearable. While the numbers in the bank are important to track and grow, the true reward lies in the widespread success of an idea or invention. But, as you might imagine, that message wasn't received very well by everyone initially.

The clothing portion of our mission started slow. I had to sell seventy-five T-shirts monthly to fulfill my contract with the company that made them for us. Seventy-five . . . that was a lot. For several months, I would put in my own orders or plead forgiveness to not get booted from their service for not meeting their quota. I just wanted them to believe I could do it and that the message would eventually resonate with the people out there. Thankfully they never shut us down, and after about five months of barely making it, I discovered the art of digital marketing and hired a personal mentor (Colin). Finally, the clothing brand saw a change.

We all did.

Furthermore, I started to feel valuable for the first time beyond the battlefield. With people now starting to rave over my designs and commend me on the noble mission, I began to think to myself, *Maybe my perspectives are valuable to people. Maybe I can serve at a higher capacity than the Marine Corps. Maybe, just maybe I could impact millions of people in a positive way. Maybe I could even save lives.*

When those thoughts came flooding in like a broken dam, it was almost as if my trauma got pushed to the back of my mind. Instead of my first thoughts upon waking up being *My body hurts. Last night's nightmare sucked. I miss my friends. I wonder what I'll drink tonight?* they slowly transitioned into *I wonder how many orders came in? What's my next impactful shirt going to be? I wonder if that family received their memorial? I bet my Fallen brothers are proud.*

The less idle time my mind had, the fewer demons crept up on me. Weird.

These new thoughts and feelings helped me begin to realize that I am capable of something bigger than what I had already done with my life. All I needed to do was channel that pain.

But why me? I'm a nobody, I would think. I often still do.

I grew up poor, failed in school, was deemed in need of special education, joined the Marines only to do half of what I expected and get injured in the process. Plus, I annoyed most people with my obsession over seemingly unimportant objectives, so I could count my friends on one hand.

The thoughts of obtaining this newfound value and imposter syndrome played tug-of-war in my brain. Like my mind would not permit me to feel loved and needed for any respectable length of time. But I kept going and continued making products that made me feel good, in turn making others feel good.

When I started getting messages from friends and family across the nation sending me pictures of a spotted TVP T-shirt in their local gym, grocery store, or airport, followed by pure excitement and stories of "I know that guy who made that T-shirt!" I began to think to myself, *Korey, you may not be worthy of this mission, but you need to take it as far as you can until someone else comes along and does it better.*

That mindset gave me permission to put *everything* I had into my company, because no one had done it yet, and that was one thing I could not deny made me and my situation special. I had invented a concept that was helping people, even if I felt odd being the one creating the path.

That's the thing about establishing value; I knew that if I stopped, then memorials would stop being delivered, and people would stop receiving their tees that helped them get through the day—and to me, that was not an option.

My confidence grew with the sales, and my sense of worthiness, which came with bringing Honor to the brothers I had lost, was improving. Mentally, I was having more up days than down days, but still I would find myself thinking, *I'm not supposed to be okay. I have depression and PTSD attached to my name. What's going on?* Even as my morale was improving, I started to feel guilty knowing that most people would likely never experience an opportunity like I had. So, every chance I got, I tried balancing the scales by sharing any knowledge I had with anyone who would listen. I was becoming a motivator and an advocate without even knowing it at the time.

Meanwhile, my dad's cancer was getting progressively worse. He started to lose a lot of body mass—and he didn't have much to begin with because of all the running. His loss of mass was coming from chemo, and things started to get worse by the day. This was now the second year of his diagnosis, and the effects from chemo seemed worse than the cancer itself.

Chemo messed with his senses, and he was so cold most days that even prolonged contact with boiling water wasn't giving him a sense of warmth; he would shiver all night. And due to the circumstances of his colon repair, he'd constantly need to rush to the bathroom, destroying his ability to go anywhere for fun or visit the people he cared about.

But he still insisted on his work as a mechanic, which was nonnegotiable.

He had a weekly to-do list, and I would find nonchalant ways to keep his finances straight, like figuring out his groceries and buying them with mine or replacing some appliance on the preface that I broke it. I did everything I could to help my dad preserve his dignity, even if it made me look dumb, like I was going around his house breaking things by accident all the time. His dignity meant everything to him—and so it did to me.

If Dad couldn't work, he had no value. That's how he saw things, and if he didn't have value, he didn't want to be here. I could relate, so

I tried to alleviate his financial stress, but I knew the more I helped, the worse it made him feel, unless my gestures were nonchalant or secretive. But I knew it helped him, and he appreciated it, even if it was unspoken. Once again, my dad was a man of strict principles, so if he could justify it, it was okay. I was always finding ways to justify my help to him.

But there were a few things my dad would do, like mowing the lawn, that I saw were very taxing on him. He was getting lethargic, and he would start sleeping for entire days at a time because he needed a whole weekend of sleep to wake up to that 5:30 a.m. alarm and get ready to put cars together in the blistering heat or freezing cold—even though he couldn't regulate his temperature because of the chemo. It would drive him to the point of tears.

He didn't understand how much he was exhausting himself, but I knew, and so did the people around him. But he had his dignity and a sense of self-accomplishment to uphold, so we didn't dare ask him to take it easier on himself.

I would watch him stumbling to mow the lawn, using as much of what was left of his body weight to keep the mower going. A man that was 205 pounds for almost as long as I'd known him was now 135 pounds and losing weight fast. He would go in the house, lock himself in the room, only to come out three days later looking skinnier and more tired—revealing more and more of his skeleton each time. I feared every time he went in there, because I knew I would have to pull him out one day unless a miracle happened.

But he was persistent and needed independence—that's how he valued himself. So, when he would get up and do things like mowing the lawn, I would continue working at my desk with the blinds open to watch and help if he needed it.

One day, he looked extremely rough and struggled a lot to keep up with the mower. I went outside and waited for him to notice me as he made his second pass in the front yard, and waved at him to cut off the mower.

"Hey, Dad, let me take care of that for you," I said, following with, "It's hot as hell out here, and my fat a— needs the exercise and sun."

He knew what I was doing, but prefacing a benefit to me meant he couldn't decline, or it would go against his fatherly instinct to help his son. Instead of arguing with me, he looked down at the mower briefly, almost as if to convey the thought, *Wow, I can't believe I can't even mow the lawn. This is it. This is really happening,* but instead just said in utter defeat, "Thanks, son, that sounds like a plan," stepping away to let me have the mower with no fuss. It's tough to even describe what it felt like. I was happy he actually let me do the job for him but felt like I was pulling one of his last bits of independence and purpose right out of his hands. It tore me up inside. I knew the cancer was winning this battle and that the signs of pullback, or the acknowledgment of his body's limitations, would get more frequent. To me, mowing the lawn was *noise*, especially for someone like him with little time and little finances left because of this damn sickness, but he was still using his time to make the front yard look good because that's what his ethics—and the homeowners association—required of him.

As I grabbed the grips of the mower, worn from years of use, I said, "Go relax so you can focus on fighting this battle. I'll take care of this, and you can take it back from me when you get better." Which sounded like a positive goal for both of us. He could focus on his health, and I could focus on optimizing the environment around us to build more memories and create more streamlined processes.

Let's talk about opportunity cost for a moment, both financial and time-based. Because, even when you are doing favors or simply the right thing to help someone in need, you still need to be aware of the costs.

As Til Valhalla Project grew in an increasingly digital marketplace, every time I opened my computer, I found myself able to help people, and that sense of responsibility to do so just kept growing. So I would (and still do to this day) keep my computer open and hustle, all in the hopes that someone benefited from it. But I needed to *keep* all the time I could and reduce the noise of the universe outside my life to focus on funding the extra medical finances for my dad, our lives, and our mission. I was committed eighteen hours a day, seven days a week. (Disclaimer: As of writing this it has been several years, and Tiffany and I have not taken a single day off—through everything, whether sickness or deaths. I've been so lucky to have a life partner who's been willing to walk through hell with me.) But that's what my mind needed to stay alive.

I had agreed to take over the lawn for my dad, but I also knew the lawn and appeasing the HOA was not my legacy in any way—so I ultimately decided to call a company to cut it every week. Though I may have financial freedom today, I remember what it was like to struggle financially. By no means am I saying you should "buy" yourself out of all situations, but I am saying this: My opportunity cost at that point had a real impact on people, and I only had limited time left with my dad. Fewer Heroes would be Honored, fewer memories with my father would be created, fewer veterans would have their therapy covered, and the mission/company would grow at a slower pace if I undertook these tasks myself. I would have paid even more to eliminate that noise from my life and his and continue helping people while building memories with my dad.

However, as you might expect, my dad had some conflict with this.

He knew I had found a new calling and was glad I had established a new way to quantify my value. For years since returning home he had watched me struggle daily in life, with my injuries and PTSD from overseas. And in those few months, he probably felt a dissonance between what he expected from me and what I actually did—as if, as a veteran, I was supposed to feel hatred and anger about the world. My dad was proud but couldn't shake the mentality of someone else doing the work I could do—for something like $140 a month.

A proud moment for me was responding, "I have enough value to people in my life to say that it's better for me to sit here hustling than it is for me to be outside mowing the lawn."

In those days, I felt like I was moving closer to reestablishing my value, something I had lost when I left the service. At the same time, I absolutely understood where my dad was coming from: "That just isn't the life we live." And historically, it wasn't. We never had the option before of hiring out such work. Growing up in a community where a neighbor fixed your car or you didn't go to work, it was either figure it out or deal with the consequences.

My dad was the neighbor who fixed cars. He was the one offering help. He wasn't receiving it.

But I had become obsessed with my mission, my legacy, being financially free to serve others, addressing my mental health, and how I used my time be a benefit to the world. I wanted to free up even more time to spend with my dad and wife, and to improve people's lives. That wasn't necessarily unlike my father's goals, either. The difference was that I had gained these values from a computer instead of twisting wrenches.

But that realization was hard for both of us. At the same time my dad's life was crumbling to pieces, I had just discovered a level of value and self-pride that he had been striving for all along. It felt like a slap in the face, but he never stopped talking about how proud he was of me. He kept me inspired and reminded me that success is my responsibility, and that he never wanted me to become a "grease monkey" like him, despite me constantly saying I would follow in his footsteps. No real conversation was needed to tell me that my dad hated being a mechanic. Any time I would mention becoming a mechanic, he would go on to tell me horror stories.

"Son, you want nothing to do with this industry and can apply yourself to be more than a grease monkey. Do you want to spend the rest of your life in people's roach-infested cars, fixing their gross negligence, only for them to not want to pay you?"

"I like fixing things others can't," I replied. "I think that's what I want to do."

Then he would shake his head in disappointment.

I used to think it was because he disliked serving people, but now I realize he was afraid I wouldn't serve enough. He wasn't against impact; he feared that I would not achieve the level of impact I was aiming for, and finding that out the hard way would be a long road.

To my dad, a good, steady paycheck equaled freedom. If you had the money, you had the means. The challenge for my father was sacrificing what he wanted to do, what he dreamed of doing, in service of that steady paycheck. I'm not knocking him for this decision. So many parents across the world and across time have done this to offer their children the opportunities they never had. What they don't expect, however, is for their children to idolize them for what they do and all they are already.

I wanted to be a mechanic like my father. That was my dream for a long time, because it seemed like he had everything figured out. Only he didn't want to be a mechanic. He wanted to go to school and study to be an engineer. He was passionate about fixing things but wanted to make a more significant impact. Fix more. Help more. Be more.

Until that day, I never realized it. And at the end of that day, I realized his passion became a daily slog because it didn't quite live up to his goals, and being "just a mechanic" in the face of the future he once saw for himself made work feel like just more *noise*. Maybe that's why, even then, he constantly pushed me to build a life I could be happy with.

As the months went on, I now had my dad's busywork outsourced, and he slowly came around to the idea. He rested more and began having some positive days, since he wasn't depleted physically and emotionally from mundane tasks. This led to us spending more time together after my long workdays, and I felt like I was making a difference. To top it all off, remember how I needed seventy-five tees to keep my contract? Well, after freeing up that time to double down and obsess over becoming extremely proficient in digital advertising all over the US, we went from seventy-five to several thousand tees sold each month! Eventually, the T-shirt company actually *lost* our contract because we *outgrew* their shop.

It was a new high for all of us, and the growth meant we would need to establish our first shop and finally get out of my dad's garage. But a bitter reality appeared, like a cruel joke, when just as my business started to expand, so did my father's cancer.

We went in for a routine appointment and expected good news from my dad's recent burst of energy: "Everything is great, and his cancer has completely disappeared!" And somehow it made sense to hope that good news would keep compounding, like the climax of a movie. But life isn't like a movie. Things aren't tied with a bow and resolved, and we must deal with whatever is thrown our way.

The cancer had now spread to his lungs, and the once microscopic spot on his liver had taken over 40 percent of the organ. The doctors recommended he go into immediate surgery to cut out at least half of his liver and stop the spread—followed by more chemo afterward to hopefully clear up the dots in the lung. They made it sound like this was our best chance for a normal life and gave us another glimmer of hope. So, with this news, our minds dwelled on daydreams that he would one day become a grandparent and we could reflect on these hard times of resilience and challenge. We opted for the surgery and were briefed that an operation of this magnitude was no joke—if not done perfectly, it was possible that he could die on the table.

Without hesitation, my dad said, "Let's do this."

He signed the paperwork, and they rolled him to surgery.

I stayed with him all the way to the back. We knew the risk and knew it was our best shot, but even then, neither of us said, "I love you." I remember wanting to turn around before I walked out to let him know that I did, but they were already getting him prepped. We were always weird like that—the uncomfortable old-school masculinity not letting us express our love for each other with such explicit words, always coming out in some tough-guy, "Luv ya" sort of way.

I will tell you right now that I don't have that problem anymore.

Dad was in surgery for what felt like an eternity. We were given a rough timeline of when he would be out of the operating room if all went well. When that time passed by several hours, my family became distraught. I still had the perspective of "It's my dad. He's not going anywhere," which kept me blissfully ignorant of the negative possibilities. It's strange; for so much of my life I focused and dwelled on the negative, but when it came to my dad, the negative rarely came to mind. *He always pulls through.*

And he did. He pulled through the surgery like I knew he would, but the doctors said it was close. Someone had slipped up and nicked an artery, and he almost bled out then and there on the table, but they sprang into action to bring him back to stable. Hearing that helped me realize this mindset I've always had about my dad, and it made me regret not being able to tell him how I felt as plainly and clearly as, "I love you, Dad."

Whenever you can, never miss an opportunity to let someone know how they changed your life. Because the feeling of thoughts gone unsaid after losing someone you care about is one of the worst feelings.

But my dad's surgery was a success. They removed the cancer from his liver. It was huge news and my entire family was riding high, because maybe everything else would fade away with chemo. Then we went in to see him. His eyes were sunken in, his skin was damn near blue, and he was stapled all the way up his chest because, when the accident happened in surgery, they had to open him all the way up to fix their mistake. He was a mess—and he looked it.

I went around to grab his hand, but it was so cold it didn't even feel like he was alive. He was stiff, and his fingers were hard. It didn't even feel like a hand. Between the working man's hands and the cold, it felt like frozen leather. And for the first time since my dad's illness, I felt like crying for him. I felt so bad that this was happening to him, and seeing him unconscious and torn apart like Frankenstein's monster hurt me in ways I couldn't express. The only thing that convinced me he wasn't dead was the rise and fall of his chest as he struggled to breathe.

After a while, he started to wake up and asked quietly: "Did they get it all?"

"Yes!" we told him. "They said they felt really strongly that they got it all."

He didn't open his eyes. "Good," he said.

"We almost lost you, Dad," I said. "But you're here now. You made it."

He didn't say anything back, but just seemed to be taking in the shock of being almost cancer-free after such a close call. But it felt like the battle was over, and we could start talking about a normal life again.

Then, as my dad started to come to, he started getting visibly angry. I couldn't figure out what he was so upset about, but he kept asking for the date and saying he needed his laptop from his bag.

Eventually he mumbled something about a late payment, and that he needed to log in or they would charge him even more. We were all dumbfounded.

A late payment?

He had just been given what seemed like a clean bill of health and survived a gut-wrenching surgery, and he was mad about some bill? Now wasn't the time to challenge his thinking, though, so in the hopes of getting him back into good spirits to appreciate the news with us, I got him his laptop so he could handle whatever it was and we could get back to celebrating. But he was on some heavy pain meds. His vision was foggy, and I could see him rapidly blinking to try to get his eyes to focus while shaking his head.

With the laptop on his chest, he used his cold, stiff, drugged-up fingers to try and type in his password, but it wasn't working—so now he was getting even more upset. I offered to type his password in and he told me what it was, but it didn't work—and then he was freaking out suddenly and shifting his body, tapping his head with his hands to eke out some memory through the fog. And I thought: *What the heck is so important right now? You're alive, the people around you care, and you just got a clean bill of health. What bill is so important?*

"Dad," I said. "You don't have any bills that I can't afford. Don't worry about it right now. We'll get it sorted soon."

He still wasn't having it. His visible anger with the whole family standing around him became uncomfortable, but we were also used to his demeanor when he got locked in on something. After twenty minutes we surrendered to his ire and just let him "blow a gasket," as my dad would usually say—yet another reference to how our lives are like the engine of a car.

He finally found the correct password and paid the bill.

How much was the bill?

The house's termite bond was $170.22, to which another fifty dollars would be added if he was late.

I couldn't believe it. The idea of a late payment was enough to overshadow the gift of life and a future with his family. He was so strapped for cash, so afraid of debt, that he disregarded all of the good news he had just been given to avoid a fifty-dollar fine. And that was his whole life, I realized, counting every penny, hand-to-mouth, providing. Money wasn't just making a living; it was life. Wasted money was wasted life. With the new bills, his sickness, and us living under his roof, he counted every cent. That was the noise he couldn't let go of.

And it's the noise, when we're broke, that most of us can't let go of.

Dad had just been given a gift and wanted to return to work, not to life.

When the doctors finally came in, he was relieved because of finally having paid that stupid bill. They told us that they worked on him as if he were their own family, which was one of the most beautiful things anyone has ever said to me. Then they ran some breathing tests and said he would have to stay there for a few more days.

I told him I would get some rest and then do all my work by his bedside the next day since my workload was mobile. But, as I headed downstairs, I couldn't shake what had just happened.

That moment in that hospital room was traumatic if I'm being honest. I watched the strongest man I know push everything away for fifty dollars. There's a part of me that knows he was drugged up, but there's also a part of me that knows if he were financially free, he would have been able to appreciate the time he had left. Ninety-nine percent of my dad's struggles through life had been about money. He knew the reality of working your entire life only to see all of your finances crumble around you.

This is the part that comes full circle for me. Outside, as I was holding back tears, angry at my dad's anger, I turned toward the hospital and said to my wife:

"I'm going to make sure that no one goes through that. I'm going to help people get free of that mentality. No one should live in fear like that."

Then, I turned back and started walking toward the car.

I honestly meant it. I didn't know how to do it, but if people wanted to change, I wanted to find a way to inspire that change. If they wanted financial freedom, I wanted to give them the tools I used to feel financially free. If they wanted better mental health, I wanted to show them how I went from crippling PTSD, suicidal thoughts, depression, and lack of self-value to helping others establish a new mindset that keeps them moving forward. But most importantly, I wanted to help them see that legacy extends beyond the monetary. It extends beyond financial success.

Our legacy lives on in the lives we inspire.

We can start doing that right now. We can make an impact today.

The key to leaving the legacy we want is being able to analyze the opportunity cost of any decision we make. My dad made the decision to choose family and the security of stable work. With that choice, he was able to keep a home for his family and serve others as a mechanic. But in doing so, he felt like he missed out on the "next best" life of being a financially successful engineer. What I don't think he could see is how his choices provided *me* with that kind of opportunity.

Dad was still stuck in that famous "two roads diverging" feeling, like he made a mistake choosing left instead of right and didn't want to continue on the burdensome path he chose. I wish he could have known that when that road diverged in his yellow wood and he walked left, deciding to protect and love his family, it meant that others, like myself, would later have the opportunity and the inspiration to walk right and leave the legacy we wanted to leave. This is something I should have made sure he understood.

Don't make the same mistake I did and wait to let people know how they've changed your life, because they might be going through their own life feeling like a burden, like a failure, like a person who missed their shot. Legacy is a shared experience. It's building others up and encouraging them to build others up, empowering them to leave their own desired legacy. Legacy doesn't mean making a global or a spectacular mark—perhaps the kind of mark my dad envisioned for himself. It just has to make a mark.

Because then you won't have to worry about opportunity cost. Your road may have diverged in a yellow wood, and you may have walked left, but the others you inspired, cared for, protected, and loved—well, maybe they had the opportunity to walk right.

And they have you to thank for it.

So, if I haven't said it enough, let me write it here.

Thank you, Mom. Thank you, Dad.

For everything.

Summary:

- Understand the importance of your time and what you choose to focus on. If you have the means, don't be afraid to delegate or outsource less important tasks that can free up your time.
- Time and resources are limited. Weigh the trade-offs and understand what you might be giving up when you spend your time or money in a certain way.
- Never miss an opportunity to express your love and gratitude to those who matter in your life.

Chapter 18 Exercise

Take a moment to call or text a friend or loved one and remind them what they mean to you. Consider how they've helped you on your path of personal growth, and tell them how.

_____

_____

_____

_____

_____

_____

_____

_____

_____

_____

_____

_____

_____

CHAPTER 19

UNTESTED VALOR

There's more than one way to test your valor—

the key is discovering how you will do it.

A few years ago, I was scrolling on Facebook when a short clip from the Iraq War came across my feed: an in-combat interview of a battered Marine named William Wold. The video was short, but you could tell they were in the heat of war by the sounds of explosions and gunfire in the background. There are other videos of Wold and his unit in Iraq on YouTube, showing him room-clearing during the peak of violence in 2004. One such video features the Marines scooping pieces of Iraqi fighters into bags, followed by an interview in which Wold tells the embedded reporter filming him that he killed twelve insurgents in just a few short months. Wold explains that he is leaving operations soon, and the reporter asks him, "Why are you getting out?"

Wold tells the reporter, "I just wanna be normal. I wanna live a normal life."*

What they don't tell you is that William Wold did not come back "normal" as he had hoped. He struggled with anger and PTSD. He found himself wanting to return to the war, where he'd felt valuable, as the other "world" of civilian life wasn't meant for him anymore.

---

* William Wold, "William Wold Interview," interview by embedded reporter, posted July 6, 2019, video, 3:00, *YouTube*, https://www.youtube.com/watch?v=x24cLbwPWqc.

He was too conditioned to violence and tainted by the horrors he saw. And when I heard that, I knew exactly what he was talking about.

I related to this feeling and even revered Wold for saying it.

But when Wold rejoined the Marine Corps brotherhood, he was physically beaten by some other Marines who were upset about his continual night terrors keeping them up at night, to the point that he developed a stutter. Wold was betrayed by his kind because of the battles he had seen and was incapable of leaving behind.

He would go on to need medication to keep him level enough to operate outside of a war zone. He was sedated to survive "normal" life again—that is until one night when he was so high on drugs that he forgot he took his dose and ended up double-dosing.

William Wold died in his barracks that night. A Hero whose actions and experiences dwarfed many others, he died because of the response he received from what should've been his brotherhood, from a system that failed him. A Hero, who wasn't given the Honor so many others received, and which he deserved as well.

That story killed me. Not just because it was sad but because it was something you had to dig in a reporter's archives to find. Imagine serving your nation in a capacity that almost kills you only to be betrayed and failed by the very system you fought to protect. After reading that story, I couldn't eat. I didn't want to hang out with my wife. I just wanted to be left alone. I wanted to feel a connection to Wold and give him the consideration he deserved, consideration that not many others outside his family likely had the experience or empathy to provide. It felt like I owed it to him to feel his sadness, to imagine what it was like to be in his shoes, betrayed by our brotherhood. And I did. I felt it deep.

Whatever connection I had through the fabric of space, I felt I needed the connection to happen and continue, no matter what anyone believed in. So, when I said before that empathy is a tool, I meant it. A connection can be made to others, even those we've never met, by sharing their pain and trying to help them if we can.

After all, what is the point of life if it's not to make it better for each other?

Valor is not just a concept a service member strives to live up to. It is a concept that applies to *everyone* who is tasked with facing *any* challenge in their lives with courage and determination. Many of us like to believe valor is within us, but only some of us will truly get to prove it. Just think about it, every time someone's misfortune is captured on camera and presented for the world to see on social media, there are always people raving about, "If I were in the same situation, I would do X, Y, or Z." The difference is that when you are watching a high-stress situation from the outside, you can see the whole picture and make decisions off your cold observations, but when you're in the stressful situation yourself, you have tunnel vision, feel the actual risk—and all of that factors into your decisions. But valor is something many of us want to be able to say that we have.

Courage, fortitude, the willingness to charge headstrong into the unknown.

As I was sitting in my dad's garage building the memorial plaques for families of Fallen Heroes, I grew more and more intrigued by their stories.

"Why are they not here right now?"

I knew that behind every grieving family was a story that ended with their Hero no longer with us. With more memorial requests coming in, I started asking for stories about the Heroes so that I could bond with them while building the plaque. After a few dozen plaque requests, I discovered something that hit me as hard as the documentary on William Wold.

Where are the KIAs?

Where are the Fallen Heroes who died overseas?

Over 60 percent of my memorials were from Heroes who committed suicide. Suicides from across all branches—some who had deployed to combat and some who had never set foot in a combat zone. I thought what my unit was going through with suicide was unique—like we were just a broken unit. But the more memorial plaques I built, the more I realized something was wrong. We couldn't just write each of these Heroes off as a suicide due to combat-related PTSD; many had never left the States.

What the hell is going on? I asked myself.

I sat at my woodworking bench, reading a Fallen Hero's story, covered in wood stain and surrounded by plaque supplies. This Hero had never left the States, never been deployed, and only recently graduated from basic. I got up, knocked the sawdust off my shirt, walked to my beat-up work computer, and typed, "How many veterans take their lives?"

According to the Veterans Administration, eighteen to twenty-five per day. On average, twenty-two. While this number has faced a ton of controversy for being reported as either too high or too low, one thing is for sure, we are looking at thousands—and just one was too many.

This number awoke a slight panic in my chest—because my goal was to Honor all Heroes.

Thousands of veterans per year are taking their lives.

To put that in perspective, we almost lose more veterans to suicide in one year than we did fighting insurgents during the *entire* global war on terror.

Are you kidding me? Which f——ing war are we fighting? The one over there or the one at home?

The more I looked at the numbers, I realized my friends, my brothers, and all these Heroes waiting to be Honored in my small workshop are part of that number—that statistic. There is almost no way to describe how I felt at that moment other than sad and defeated. I had no idea that the number of suicides outweighed those who even died to combat—I felt like my mission was over before it started. How the heck can I Honor all those warriors? And even more so, why are they taking their lives even when they are not going to combat zones?

Then it hit me—untested valor.

I thought back to how I felt before ever doing any combat operations. All I wanted was to prove that I was capable of great things and Heroic actions. I wanted it to be known that if a brother was under fire, I would go through brazing fire myself to get there and support him. I didn't just want to "serve," I wanted *to prove my worth* through actions, or die trying. In the back of my mind I also knew that if I didn't get to prove it in the military, then odds were I would go the rest of my life not knowing what kind of man I was, and the thought of that was unbearable. *Who are you? Who are you really?*

These are questions that you think you know the answer to—but until they are proven, you never truly know. You may say you're a fighter, then turn the other cheek. You may say you're courageous, but find yourself watching someone slowly die just outside of cover as you hide behind yours. You just don't know until you know for sure.

We joined the military so that we could find out who we really were, but some of us did not get that chance to test our fortitude. And when an awareness of untested valor begins to eat away at your mind, you might find yourself seeking other ways to test yourself—and most of those ways are not healthy.

I stared at the half-empty bottle of Jack Daniels beside my workstation. I wasn't working on a plaque anymore. I wasn't looking up more debilitating facts on my computer. In a trance, I was staring at the other side of the garage, replaying what I imagined were those Heroes' final moments and what they were thinking.

I have no value.
I'll never get to prove myself.
If this didn't work, then nothing will.
The best part of my life is behind me.
I miss having a place to belong.

And as every one of those thoughts crossed my mind, imagining the Heroes and the faces on the many plaques I had made, I realized they were my thoughts too.

Was my valor tested? Am I the person I thought I was? Am I a fraud?

The struggle of a veteran is complicated. You experience so much trauma that you must constantly fight to keep those haunting memories out of your mind, and this sometimes results in thoughts of suicide and the need to self-medicate. Meanwhile, on the other side of your mind you're missing a place where you feel you truly belong, where you feel alive—a place to test your worth to the world.

Getting out of the military is like getting the largest demotion of your life.

Imagine life for veterans post-deployment. A few months ago, you had thousands of brothers you could lean on, you were trusted to serve your nation overseas, you had millions of dollars' worth of gear, you had other people's lives in your hands, and at some wildly young age, you were shown what the peak of your value looks like on a global scale.

And then you leave. You go home. You get out.

Suddenly you're stripped of all of it, and are no more qualified for the workforce at home than an eighteen-year-old flipping patties at Burger King. How are these Heroes supposed to move forward in life, thinking the best days of their lives are already behind them?

The good times and the bad. The adrenaline and the shared pain of loss.

It starts to make sense, doesn't it? *Life is over.*

In an interview I held with former NFL athlete Anthony Trucks, I asked him, "What if you always dreamed and fantasized about getting a game-winning touchdown? And you trained day in and day out, conditioning yourself to be ready for greatness? Then, over the years, they never play you, and now you're too old to play the game?"

There's the feeling again of missing the boat. *Life is over.*

My wife opened the garage door and I snapped back into reality, acting like I was doing something productive—picking up a nearby plaque and peering at it as if inspecting it for imperfections. Normally if I was interrupted during a flashback, I reacted horribly to whoever had interrupted me—especially when someone looked at me like I was a monster when I told them to leave me alone. Something about being pulled out of a place you want to be in your mind brings out the worst; and then when they look at you like you're a monster, you want to unshackle your demons right then and there and show them what a monster really looks like, show them a glimpse of the demons you brought home, so they really understand.

But with Tiffany, it was different. And this time—it *was* different.

I almost felt embarrassed that I hadn't built my first plaque of the night yet, almost like my boss walked in on me texting or something.

"How's it going in here?" she asked.

"Great!"

"Need anything?"

"Nope, I'm all set. Thanks!"

She closed the door, and I realized I let this new information about veteran suicide consume almost all my time. Hours had passed. I started building again, because I knew I had to work in the morning. But something felt off as I began to assemble the plaque—I knew I was helping to carry on the legacy of these Fallen Heroes, but for a moment, it almost felt pointless, because they would never stop arriving.

Sure, I was telling grieving families that I would Honor their Fallen son or daughter, but what was I doing to help their names from ending up on my plaques in the first place? More warriors like Dunston. More friends, brothers, sisters, fathers, mothers—and at the end, families. It didn't feel good knowing that I could help more of these Heroes stay alive by helping them find value. If I didn't take real action, I was basically saying, "I know these veterans are struggling and many will likely take their lives, but I have a really nice plaque for their family when they do."

I made a commitment that night without knowing how I would pull it off. I planned to share a percentage of my mission's proceeds toward providing therapy for struggling veterans. I could try to save as many veterans as possible, and I would carry their legacy when I failed. That was my purpose. I made plaques to Honor these Fallen Heroes, but I wanted to be able to make fewer of them.

I know everything I've said so far relates to the challenges of veterans and the endemic of suicide we've faced in recent years, but these words apply to everyone. Just like the example of a football player, untested valor can affect any of us. We all want to feel valuable, and we all want to know that we are capable of what we think we are.

Veterans, in particular, just have a smaller window of time to prove their valor, and combat is often seen as the only opportunity to do so. At least, that's what training imprints on them and society echoes. There is an extreme sense of unity in the military, where we look at each other as one and the same. Of course, there are cultural, ethnic, religious, and age differences—but the uniform unites us in our desire to show our worth. We all have a similar expectation of what we are there to do. If you are in the infantry and have never thought of getting pinned down, jumping on a grenade, clearing a room of enemies, or saving the life of a brother, then what the hell were you doing there? All troops share a similar understanding of what we call valor, what it looks and might feel like. There are medals for valor and endless presentations on the acts of valor of Heroes who came before us.

Boy, I hope that's me one day.

Then you realize your service will not be anything like theirs. That's what happens when you hand-pick a few extraordinary people or instances to represent valorous service: we walk away from our own service with our heads hung low, going home to a family that treats us like the Heroes we don't believe ourselves to be. For some, it feels like stolen valor. It makes us feel dishonest, and we sense an uncomfortable dissonance within. When building memorial plaques, I couldn't escape this feeling of guilt and unworthiness.

We set an unrealistic standard, and when we return home any chance to reach it is left in the past.

But the brotherhood, at least, was real no matter what.

We are connected by the uniform and what it means to wear it. The hardest part about seeing your friends or other service members commit suicide is empathizing with why they did it, understanding them and feeling it so close that you know it could just as easily have been you.

If they died overseas after I left, then I'd say, "I should have stayed and fought more."

If it was a suicide before I founded my company, then I'd say, "I should have started sooner." And if it was after, then: "My message isn't strong enough."

It's easy to obsess over what you could or should have done differently, to criticize yourself for the valor you feel you have not been able to show—but in doing so, you might neglect the impact you've made and are still making in the lives of those around you. We are often simply unable to see the impact we are making on the world, especially if we feel we must compare ourselves to the service done by others. One person's "service," one person's "valor" may look different than another's, but all of us are able to leave our legacies in different ways.

As my mission and company grew, I received thousands of letters from veterans, first responders, and civilians alike, thanking us for helping them feel that they still had value and that their best life was still ahead of them.

The more I grew my company the less I told people that I was a veteran, because it didn't matter to me anymore. The service I was providing for others was born out of my service in the Marines, but it was a *new* calling as I went forward in my life.

Go out there and find your own calling, a way to serve others. Put one foot in front of the other and start failing forward, until you build something that makes you see and feel your direct impact on people. That's when you'll feel the curse of untested valor begin to lift.

Military or civilian, your valor isn't defined by your past; it's defined by your choices. We face tests of valor everyday—you just have to see them and accept their challenges.

Just remember: your untested valor is not a deficit, but an opportunity.

Summary:

- Whether you're a veteran or a civilian, the need to feel valuable is universal. Valor that never gets put to the test can lead to feelings of worthlessness and despair.
- Courage is as much about the internal battles we face as it is about the external ones. It's not just about heroic actions in moments of danger, but about having the strength to confront the issues we struggle with personally.
- It's easy to be critical of ourselves and focus on what we should have done differently. Instead, acknowledge your positive contributions and understand that *not* finding yourself in critical situations is a sign that you're doing well.
- Be aware of what's in your power to change and what's not, and don't beat yourself up over things beyond your control. The aim is to keep moving forward, not to be paralyzed by guilt or regret.

Chapter 19 Exercise

Circle or highlight the following mantra:

True valor, for everyone, lies not in the battles we face, but in our willingness to face them.

Then, find the pride in yourself to consider one example of how you've shown valor in your own life and write about it. There is no example too small.

_____

_____

_____

_____

_____

_____

_____

_____

_____

_____

LEGACY MINDSET

CHAPTER 20

WHAT LIVES ON

Wealth is what will be left behind in the form of assets. Legacy is what lives on in the hearts and minds of those impacted by your existence.

We all have our own vision of success, and in this vision we imagine a future that embodies that success.

Where do you see yourself? Are you on a yacht popping champagne? Are you living in a penthouse in New York? Do you have a big plot of land in the country where you tend to animals and a small farm, even though you don't have to because it's not your sole source of income? Do you have a spouse in a comfortable home with a white picket fence and 2.5 kids?

It's hard to pinpoint exactly how we all cultivate our visions of success, but we all sort of "know it when we see it." The trouble is, in a world of social media, with its constant inundation of other people's lives, our visions of success might come barreling at our heads and change every day, with subliminal messages of *This is what you really want. This is what you really need.*

Truthfully, my own image of success wasn't hard to build. My dad was a mechanic. He loved vehicles, so I loved vehicles, and when I was a kid, I wanted a dirt bike. You already know that story, but nothing about that "image" of success changed when I grew up. I still wanted a vehicle—only it was a dream car this time. A Nissan GTR, as seen *on every young man's wall,* and driven by yours truly in the game *Need for Speed.*

That was my dream car. It was always my dream car.

The trouble is, as I grew up, went overseas, came back and got married, started a company, and then dealt with my dad getting sick, I always found reasons not to get it. By the time I was twenty-eight years old and my company was doing well, I could afford the car, but I still didn't feel like I'd earned it. I always struggled desperately with my sense of value, never feeling like I had done enough to justify treating myself or my family to any of the success we had. There was this expectation ingrained in me that only once I had Honored every Fallen Hero and saved every veteran from suicide would I have earned this car. Only then would I be valuable.

So, I set an impossible goal and said, "If I don't do this, I don't deserve happiness." It was an all-or-nothing mindset—and not a healthy one at that. I will say, however, that we had had done an outstanding job on our mission by this point in my life. We were close to $400,000 donated and over 600 memorial plaques delivered, which was another $350,000 contributed. I now received countless letters from struggling veterans, talking about how I or the mission inspired them or saved their lives—to the point where the letters were pinned up to line the walls of our production facility.

But how did I feel about this success? *Meh.*

Heroes were still dying. Veterans were still taking their lives.

And you know that clean bill of health my dad received after surgery? It was a false alarm. The follow-up visit showed dime-sized masses on his liver and lungs.

What was there to celebrate?

At twenty-eight years old, I had big dreams and visions on my vision board, like houses for veteran retreats, a big plot of land for my family and me, my dream car, standing on stage speaking to struggling veterans, and writing a book. But a vision is only a dream until you quantify it into actionable steps. Then it becomes a *goal.*

A big home or plot of land far away was out of the question, because I needed to be there for my dad to help him fight his ever-present battle. And the rest were just big moves for the more established people who provided *real* value to the world and solved problems at a high level, which I did not feel I did. So, the easiest thing to cross off the vision board was the dream car: a brand-new Nissan GTR. From the first time I saw Paul Walker drive it on VHS, I had obsessed over this car. Of course, it was the older version that sparked the initial vision, but the spirit of the car was what I fell in love with.

And that spirit didn't dim with age. That car was on my phone and computer background, my mouse pad, and was always the first one I picked in any video game. Using manifestation and the law of attraction, I ensured it was never out of sight. Even so, the timing never seemed appropriate, as most goals never do. Those of us who set a lot of goals tend to just keep moving the bar, because it's never quite high enough.

I also felt immense guilt, as the thought of buying a six-figure car made possible only through an integrity-based mission did not make sense to me. The dissonance paralyzed me for a long time, because I was always scared that I would be seen as vain or doing things for the wrong reasons. *Not yet, not until I Honor more Heroes and save more lives,* I would tell myself, knowing that I would always move the bar higher every time I got close. Despite my hesitancy, my team and family members encouraged me to buy it, telling me that I *had* provided value and that I deserved to be happy.

It didn't change my mind. I didn't believe them, and most days I still don't. Their image wasn't mine. But when my dad got sick again, it was clear that time was limited. This led to a sort of "f—k it" moment, and I resolved that I wanted him to see me put my mind toward a big dream and check it off my list—the same thing he always wanted to do.

So, I approached my wife and said, "I'm going to get a GTR before my dad passes."

"I think that's a good idea. He'll like that."

Then in a few minutes, she found two GTRs at two different dealerships that seemed like the best bang for our buck. With that, we headed to the first dealership.

Just to give you an idea, I've dressed the same way since high school. That means basketball shorts (usually with paint splatters from DIY endeavors); a T-shirt (nowadays usually from my company); a crusty old hat with a Velcro American flag patch; beat-up Walmart shoes that should have been tossed out years ago; a memorial bracelet for the guys I lost and continue to lose; a scraggly beard that just never entirely filled in; and hair that's about three months late for a cut, as per usual.

And it was in this state that that I headed into that dealership. I tell you this because how I dressed did *not* fit the image of success reflected in that first dealership. And truth be told, at twenty-eight, and maybe even now, I wasn't going to get a haircut, buy a suit and tie, or play Beethoven to feel worthy of buying a car. I had a goal and was not interested in fitting a narrative of success to buy it.

The first associate saw us pull up and met us at the door.

"Hello! What are you looking for today?"

"The silver GTR, please. My wife found it online."

He nodded and headed over to the manager for the keys.

The manager peered over the desk divider at me and my wife.

"They can't drive it," he said to his associate while handing over the keys.

I waved it off, and the associate guided us to the car. I started it up, sitting inside to feel all the beautiful craftsmanship and listen to the sound of the engine.

"Give it a rev," the associate said.

I tapped the throttle lightly, knowing the car wasn't warmed up yet, as I didn't want to damage the engine of my potentially new car.

The manager ran out to us.

"What are you doing? Don't rev it!"

I understood they must have had many window-shoppers who kicked tires—but all the guy had to do was give me the time of day and see that I was a serious buyer just trying to make my dad proud. But I was over it, and even my wife felt uncomfortable.

"That dude's a jerk," I said to the associate. "I'm going to look at another dealer."

He agreed and apologized.

I felt terrible that my wife even had to witness that type of disrespect, just because we didn't "look the part." It served as a reminder: Don't judge a book by its cover, because you have no idea what's within its pages. I wasn't going to put on a dog and pony show or flash signs of success to plead with this guy to buy a car. We were people too, whether we had money or not. So, I changed my game plan for the next dealer. I walked in and saw the GTR indoors, and when the guy asked what we were looking for, I just walked over to the car and said, "I'll take this one." Everything got quiet, and the three guys at the desks turned around to see who was buying this car.

"Really?"

"Yes, sir."

"Want to test drive it?"

"No, sir."

"Do you need financing?"

"No, sir."

I bought it on the spot. But I was shaking as I signed, burdened with self-doubt: *People will think I'm a bad person. People will hate me. People will say I don't deserve it. My employees will lose respect for me.*

But all those feelings were overridden by, *Your dad needs to see this. He's getting worse.* Then a peace washed over me as I finished signing the paperwork, got in my new car, and drove home.

I didn't drive too crazy in my GTR (I had learned my lesson from the dirt bike). I just took the time to appreciate it and reflect on the choices that got me here. I wanted to go straight to my dad like a kid with a new toy—one I wouldn't take apart this time.

I arrived at my grandmother's house, where my dad was staying since the cancer had spread all over, spending his days waiting out the clock. He was so frail from losing mass that he couldn't walk much anymore. When I arrived, I made sure to park right in front of the door so he could see it.

My dad was on the couch watching Netflix, hooked up to oxygen, and could barely breathe. The last time I had seen him was a week before, and even then, the oxygen was on an as-needed basis. Now he needed it all the time. My dad was forty-nine years old, but once could have passed for mid-thirties with his health and running routine. Seeing him then, with his body shutting down to the point of oxygen dependence, hurt me. What hurt me worse was feeling that, for the first time, he didn't only look his age but older.

I didn't want him to see that pain, so I put on my typical facade.

"Hey, Dad! I got something!"

"Oh, yeah?" He took a breath through the machine. "What's that?"

I scooted up next to him like a little kid and pulled out my phone to show him the picture of the car I snapped just before I walked in the door.

"Hell yeeeeah!" he said, defying his oxygen to give me that notorious high-pitched "I'm celebrating with you" sort of tone. Admiring the picture of the GTR looking glorious on the front lawn, he realized—

"Wait, it's out front?"

"Hell yeah," I said. "You didn't hear it?"

"I didn't know it was yours!"

At that moment, I knew why I wanted the car—for that moment, right there.

I just wanted to make my dad proud, and he knew it too—call it a dad's intuition. So, when he asked to see more pictures of it versus going outside to see it for himself, he probably saw the light leave my eyes and my body physically slump. *I was too late.*

I scrolled through pictures of Tiffany and me at the dealership, and he saw the cracks in my facade as I felt them. He took a deep breath through the machine and said:

"Actually, can you push me out there to see it?"

I lit back up like a Christmas tree.

I grabbed a rolling office chair and his big oxygen tank, then lifted my dad for the first time in my life and set him in the chair. He felt light in my arms. Too light. It was heartbreaking. I rolled him through the living room, out the door, and he covered his eyes from the midday sun.

I got him as close to the car as possible, hoping he'd see the beauty of it.

I started rambling all technical about it, which was a language we spoke to each other often: "It's got a torque vectoring all-wheel drive system with 565 brake horsepower and a dual-clutch, six-speed transmission . . ." *Blah blah blah.* He just listened and smiled, indulging in my excitement. Finally, I ran out of facts and knew he'd catch me if I made anything up.

I turned to him and asked: "Want to drive it?"

Neither of us had ever owned a car like this in our lives. I owned a lot of clunkers, as I was constantly cycling through and flipping them, but my dad was always the first to give the "Dad Seal of Approval" to validate whether I did a good job on the acquisition. Most of the time he hated what I drove because, as a mechanic, he had that underlying knowledge and eye for perfection that outlined everything wrong with those clunkers in detail. Much like myself, he couldn't appreciate most things for what they were if he knew they were broken.

He knew they could be improved.

But this time was different.

I expected him to say no. I knew he was feeling too frail and weak for this, and I braced myself for the hit. *I bought the car too late, and he'll never get to drive it.* Then he looked down at his big green oxygen tank and said: "Sure, just hold my oxygen."

I cannot express the joy that overcame me as I smiled ear to ear.

Just as I'm doing right now, reflecting on this memory.

I loaded him into the driver's seat. He was breathing heavily with any added movement of his own, so I gave him a second to calm down and catch what little breath he could. I then ran to the passenger seat, trying to hurry in case he changed his mind. I plopped in, shut the door, and there I was, straddling a massive oxygen tank in the passenger seat, trying to walk my dad through the performance user interface on my new dream car and guiding him on how to get the most fun out of it.

He didn't need convincing.

He pushed the red start button like getting ready to launch a rocket, put it in drive, and softly pushed the throttle to feel out the catch points. The dirt kicked up behind us.

And we were off.

My dad and I both appreciated the performance, commenting on our speed as he started driving just a little crazier on the back roads, testing the limits of this new beast. As he started getting more comfortable with the throttle, winding us through the gears using paddle shifters, I became visibly more excited—hanging onto the "oh, s—t" handle for dear life.

1st . . .

2nd . . .

3rd . . .

As the engine screamed to 7,000 RPMs, he banged through the gears, both of us hooting at the raw power and freedom of that hand-built twin-turbo V-6. The speed climbed in tens of mph, not single digits. The road opened, free and clear.

60, 80, 100, 120, 140 . . .

He was getting it!

We laughed and smiled the whole time as he jacked up on the brake around the corners, like we were on a racetrack. Then I asked:

"Want to try launch control? It's the best part."

The car had a 0–60 time of 2.9 seconds, which most people won't experience in their life, so I wanted him to see what this beast could do.

"Hell yeah, how do I do it?"

Once again I lit up, knowing he wasn't holding back. We stopped in the middle of a long back road with no one around, and I pressed a few buttons to get the launch control set.

"Okay, now press the brake, smash the throttle, and when you're ready to go, release the brake!"

He followed the instructions perfectly as the car revved steadily to 3,000 RPM, then he let go of the brake, and we took off like a literal rocket!

We both sunk back into our seats from the force as all four wheels fought with the pavement to catch traction, and we were gone. Again, 60, 80, 100, 110—he was flying!

I know it was dangerous, but honestly, this was it—the moment I envisioned. It felt like there was nothing else in the world except me, my dad, that beautiful car, and an open road.

One hundred percent worth it.

He jacked up on the brakes as we came to the end of the road, and were both laughing and giggling like schoolgirls. Then he said something that will stick with me forever.

"Man, I'm breathing better already!"

There it was, all the value I ever needed. At that time it wasn't about me, but giving my dad a reason to really smile again, without a facade. A genuine smile I hadn't seen since he got the terminal news—it was worth more than anything I could imagine. It's the little things. I know he did a lot of that for me, but to see him genuinely enjoy something for the first time in years was healing for both of us—in more ways than one.

We pulled back up to my grandmother's house and were greeted by my wife and the rest of my family outside on the front lawn, smiling, both knowing (and hearing) the fun we had. Our faces were painted with big grins from the tomfoolery that had just ensued. We spent the rest of the night talking about it, then my wife and I had to get home and get to work.

The second I pulled the car into the driveway of my dad's home (where we still lived), I stepped out and looked at the GTR for the first time by myself, glistening in the light of "home." I got my phone out to get it prepped for the overwhelming sense of accomplishment and excitement I kept looking forward to. I snapped a picture.

And do you know what I felt?

Nothing.

There was no smile. No celebration. It just looked like a frame with paint, nuts, and bolts. I couldn't see its soul anymore; I couldn't anthropomorphize it anymore. It looked like an insane insurance payment; a sight for kids to gaze at. But with or without that car in the driveway, I still had to go in and bust my butt to make sure my mission stayed afloat. We went straight back into the eighteen-hour days the next morning. My nightmares still ran rampant in my mind, and I was still scared of sounds that weren't there. I still felt undeserving.

Don't get me wrong, I loved that time with my dad, and I would buy that car ten times over for that same experience. But I knew my dad wouldn't be around much longer and that this was realistically the last joyride he would ever have—once that realization set in, it became just a car. An expensive piece of metal that didn't improve my mental health—and, over time, even degraded it. Don't scratch the paint. Park it far away from other cars. Keep it detailed so it "looks the part." Watch the other people with the same car or a similar one put others down for not owning one, thinking they have life all figured out.

I realized in that moment of standing in the driveway, camera in hand, that it was possible to overcome adversity in many ways, but if you are a depressed person who doesn't really consider the core reason for your desires, then, like myself, you are just going to be a depressed person with a GTR in the driveway.

Nothing changes if you don't change.

We can never truly know the long-term effects of seeking and obtaining the things we value at any given time. However, we can always ensure that we are obtaining those things for the right reasons and minimizing the amount of "Oh s—t" realizations that could come with an achieved goal or small victory. I thought to myself, "Holy crap, what if I had waited until I was fifty years old to get that car and learn that lesson?" I realized that so much of my life had been tethered to the idea of possessing that GTR, and the rudest awaking possible was discovering it changed nothing about my life.

So many people think, "I'll be happy when I get . . . ," but it's often a joke because they're not identifying moments to be grateful for already each day. I'm not telling you not to strive for possessions you desire. Make your goals nonnegotiable, but reorganize your priorities according to value, always leading with legacy, family, and mental health. Then let your mind guide you to what you need for fulfillment, treating possessions as the tools for spending more time with the people in your vision of the future you're working toward.

And live for the moment, not the "when."

Summary:

- A vision is only a dream until you quantify it into actionable steps. Then it becomes a goal.
- Cherish special moments with loved ones and make time to create memories that will last a lifetime. Surround yourself with people who understand and support your dreams.
- Seize the moment (especially when time is limited) to experience joy and fulfillment.
- It's okay to have goals like achieving wealth and buying material possessions, but you should understand why you desire those things. True fulfillment comes from the emotional connections and shared experiences material possessions allow us to have, not from the objects themselves.

Chapter 20 Exercise

Take a minute to write down three things you're grateful for that aren't material possessions. These can be experiences, people in your life, personal achievements, or moments of peace and happiness.

_____

_____

_____

_____

_____

_____

_____

_____

_____

_____

_____

_____

CHAPTER 21

THE BREAKING POINT

Living for others saves our lives. Looking at others and asking, "How can I make their lives better?" will set your path for leaving a legacy you're proud of.

As I think back and reflect on who I was as a kid growing into an adult, there are countless moments when I felt that this world was not the place for me. Just like the cancer that was taking my dad, at one point I could've looked at you with tears in my eyes and told you that I was a cancer to the world. Even now, writing those words, I feel tears welling in my eyes.

But that's what reality was—my reality.

Looking at my childhood, I always felt that I was the cause of my parents' separation. If I had kept my mouth shut during that argument, they might have had more time to figure out their love for one another. Maybe my brother and sister would have had a closer relationship with their father. Even if all I wanted to do was connect with them, my presence felt destructive. I didn't mention this initially, but sometimes my mom would have to come get me because I was cutting myself in school. For as long as I can remember, my feelings drove me down a path of self-harm with only one visible outcome: suicide.

I look back on those days and want to say: "What the hell were you thinking, Korey?"

But the reality is, I was broken.

There was no value that I could put on myself.

There was no outlet that I could talk through.

I had no real friends to care about my well-being, and everyone in my family seemed to be constantly battling some external drama that made it seem like reaching out would be a burden on them. So, I did damage to myself, mentally and physically, to see if I could create some connection.

I have a hard time imagining other kids, or even adults, feeling the same way. That's what hurts me most—knowing someone out there thinks the world wouldn't miss them or that they have no value. It genuinely brings tears to my eyes. But that's the way it goes, right?

People who are empaths divert our pain to help others with their own.

One of the most common traits of empathetic people is wanting to steal pain from others at the cost of their own mind and body. Like we are a vessel that can absorb negativity from others. This is not something we do consciously. Whether your empathy developed from your own life experiences or you were simply born that way, once discovered, it makes us feel like we have value.

When does it stop? When have we taken on too much? What's our breaking point?

Throughout high school, thoughts of suicide always crept in any time my body went idle. If I had time to think, my mind would gravitate toward the negative and do its best to keep me there. That's why, to this day, I am always moving and doing something different—an idle mind is where the demons creep. In that way, the Marine Corps became my outlet. My alternative. If I was going to risk dying, I didn't want it to be by my own hand but for a purpose that would be remembered—for a legacy I wasn't even sure I wanted or deserved yet. And though the catalyst may differ between people, I don't think my mindset was so different from other eager young warriors who signed on the dotted line of the USMC contract. All driven by a subconscious, desperate desire to have purpose, willing to die rather than live a life of no significance.

I will tell you right now that my act of service began selfishly.

So many people have told me in different ways, "Oh, that's so great that you're willing to serve and fight for our freedom."

I just smiled and nodded. *No,* I thought, *I'm fighting to see if I belong in this world or die trying. Preserving freedom is just a bonus.*

Though it's not often said, my discussions later on in life with other veterans made me realize I wasn't alone. We felt desperate for purpose; and the military offered it, deployment provided it, and medals presented it—but what about when our time is up? What about when the "best days" are behind us? What is left but those same negative thoughts we never resolved? If our days of providing value have passed, what's left? We were ready to lay our lives on the line but walked away, having never had to. We were willing, sure, but is that enough? What does it mean that suicide and self-destruction among veterans is an epidemic? Why all of this untested valor?

How do we find new value?

How do we move on?

You might be battling these demons of self-value yourself, whether you've served or not, and could be battling them right now. I can tell you that the deepest, darkest time in my life was at the height of my alcohol addiction. But I can also tell you the day that addiction stopped. What I hate to admit, however, is that I only beat the addiction after almost everything I've told you I've encountered.

It was after my childhood, after my training, after my deployment, after my marriage, after Dunston, after founding Til Valhalla Project, after my father's diagnosis, after the business contributed millions to our mission, and after that beautiful day driving the GTR with my father. I tell you all this because I want to impress upon you the true and genuine dangers of addiction and alcohol abuse.

When the demons creep in, addiction provides the darkness for them to thrive.

On March 23rd, 2020, my life changed forever.

Like a snapshot of the day, I can tell you exactly what it looked like, as if a drone were flying through my home. I sat on the couch with a drink, cleaning one of the pistols I had just shot at the range. Koda is at my feet, and Tiffany, also on the couch, is helping me unpack the range gear. In the kitchen there are Crown Royal and Jack Daniels bottles on the counter—these were always full because they were the replacements for the bottles I drank the night before. In the fridge are several bottles of Coke Zero, the mixer I used for my liquor, and a large case of Bud Light "just in case" I needed something to hold me over until the next day's liquor run. Outside the garage are three large blue recycling containers, each one overflowing with bottles that smelled like a frat house, creating an ooze of smells from all the mixed drinks and beer baking in the heat.

My dad's old room down the hall is empty, except for an old 32-inch TV and his bed of fifteen years with a crucifix mounted to the wall above. His sheets look pressed because he has lived with my grandmother ever since his decline in health. Past that, the office in which I started building my company has a large safe full of guns, and there was always one I was working on across the table. Koda's bed isn't in there, though; it's now in our bedroom, because he has a tumor the size of a softball that is killing him quickly at only seven years old. Lastly, there are my memorial bracelets for the guys I lost sitting on my nightstand, reminding me daily that they were gone and I couldn't get them back.

That day my mind was idle, cleaning guns being second nature to me from the military, and it all hit me like a freight train as I locked eyes on my pistol, reflecting on the day before. I had been drinking in my office alone, and everyone else was distracted. I decided that day was the day I would test fate and see if it still wanted me here, if there was any difference I could make at all, or if I was disposable to the universe. I wasn't ready to go, but I needed to know if fate was ready for it. For some reason, I hoped that if I drank enough, one day, I would have the guts to do it straight out and rid these thoughts of pain, trauma, and worthlessness from my mind.

Almost as if I could kill my mind but keep my soul and body intact.

Really messed up thinking. Alcohol does that.

I unlocked my safe, loaded a single hollow-point round into my nickel-plated snub nose .357 Magnum, and spun the cylinder before closing it. I slowly put it to my head and took the slack out of the trigger. I needed to feel what the millions of people before me felt in their last moments. Drunk, with a loaded gun against their heads, noose around their necks, or pills in their hands. And I let my adrenaline build, seeing if I could get the fortitude to pull it, taking so much slack out of the trigger to the point where, if the blood in my finger pulsed the wrong way, the hammer would fall and seal my fate, whatever it was.

Here for a purpose or not?

Am I here to build a legacy and help people, or am I a nobody?

I thought of Dunston. I thought of the brothers I lost. I thought of my dad's inevitable passing. I thought of Koda's inevitable passing. I thought of the suicide bomber. I thought of the people I watched die. I thought of the people I hurt. I thought of my parents' separation. I thought of the lives I could never help. I thought of the countless torn-apart families that requested plaques for their sons and daughters lost to suicide or overseas. I thought of the guys who were doing the same thing in that exact moment.

Tears began to swell because I knew I wasn't right in the head, and the demons were winning. But I needed to see where I was and if my will to survive was stronger than my will to perish.

The last time I checked my will to live, right after I got out of the Marines, I put the gun in my mouth and almost threw up because of the taste of carbon and oil. With the fatigue in my finger, I knew that I needed to put the gun down and check my fate before it was sealed for good. What would have happened if I had pulled the trigger?

Nothing.

The round was at the bottom of the cylinder. My breathing shuttered as I exhaled.

I pointed it back at myself, still loaded, and pulled the trigger.

Click.

I began to cry softly so no one could hear. I was embarrassed that I was so broken. I was someone's son, husband, brother, and nephew, and to know that I would have selfishly taken my life right before all the pain that was about to hit my family in the upcoming weeks is just unbearable to think about, even today.

My dad would die two weeks after that day. Imagine how his heart would have broken, knowing his son killed himself, one less person to carry on his legacy while his vision faded to black. Even the idea of it makes me tear up; and the fact that it could have been a reality infuriates me. I could never do that to him, so why did I try to? He had been through so much already. And imagine my wife having to put our dog down alone, just a mere three months after my dad or even me. Koda would have wondered where I went as his sickness took over. I couldn't do that to her or him. To any of them. Imagine my staff of fifty plus people at the time, building memorials for Fallen Heroes and making shirts that change the world. They would have to shut the mission down, all due to another veteran who committed suicide. Funds would deplete immediately after my death, and there would be families who would never get their memorials, their closure. I couldn't do that to them.

"I'm here for a reason," I said aloud. "People need me even when it doesn't feel like it."

Then, after all that, I'm sitting on the couch cleaning the gun, a drink still in hand the very next day. I looked at that gun, and you could hear me whisper: "My decisions have an impact. I need to live for them, not for me."

On that day, March 23, 2020, I told myself: "Nope, I'm done with alcohol."

I bet myself that my dad would rather have a positive note to leave on versus a broken heart. I didn't pick the bottle up in hopes that I could tell him I hadn't drunk in several weeks before he passed, which is something he had not seen since I moved in with him.

And now you might be thinking: "It's not that easy to stop an addiction." And you're right; it's not. It took me gambling with my life, playing Russian roulette alone in my office adorned by plaques of Fallen Heroes, and doing some of the deepest soul searching—the kind that makes it hurt to breathe—to have enough fuel to overpower my desire to pick up another bottle. I rewired my brain on the spot in the face of all those possible realities: my dad's broken heart, Tiffany going through life alone, Koda fading out without me, and my team getting the news that they lost their founder and their jobs. It hit me like a f——ing ton of bricks, and the wires snapped and realigned.

I put my gun down for a second, looked over at my amazing wife, and said:

"I'm done drinking. Tonight is the last night. There's too much coming down the pipeline." Then I grabbed my phone and looked for any tools that could help me keep this commitment. I found a "Sober" app that tells you the day you quit, the money you saved, the units not drunk, and some motivation with sobriety coins. This gave me something to compete against: me versus it—or me versus me. The number going up daily meant I was winning the battle; and as one day turned to one week, one week turned to one month, and one month turned to one year, I felt like I had more people in my corner. It wasn't me versus it, or even me versus me. It was everyone I loved, every last part of the legacy I work every day to create, standing against this horrible amalgamation of pain I had fought all my life.

I won't say the battle is easy, and some days are harder than others, but as of today, I am three years sober and writing my first book. It floors me how things can change when you rewire your brain to think about the legacy you leave behind and truly appreciate your impact on others.

It was no longer debatable whether I was important to people—it was black and white, like the words on this page. And now that I had that information, I was able to make more progress in three years than I could with my old mindset in three lifetimes.

If you ask me, I did die that day. The version of me that could not perceive my own value and saw suicide as the most viable option. That Korey is gone but not forgotten. I realized something that I'm hesitant to put in writing because it can be misconstrued, but it went something like this: "It's okay to kill the old you, but not to kill yourself."

What I mean by that is that if you're at the point like I was, why not drop everything and try a new life versus dying with the hand you were dealt? It's the same thing as when people think once they're gone, "I'll come back in another life when the world needs me." Well, you can do that right now. You can change your life starting this instant. You can lift your head from this page with the mind of a completely different person, if your will to change for the better is strong enough.

Living for others is what saved my life. Looking at others and saying: "How can I make your life better?" at a large scale is the legacy

I want to create. I will invent life-changing devices and software. I will get on stage and inspire people. I will have coaching groups that help others find their value. I will create companies that never existed to help people in different ways—just like I did with Til Valhalla Project. My goal is to make an impact on people's lives, then move on to the next. Rinse and repeat until I die.

I will leave a legacy in the words on these pages and through the hearts of others.

Impact; that's my purpose, my legacy.

I was "cursed" with an over-analytical mind and dark thoughts that refuse to let me be idle. That's always going to be the case; whether I like it or not, I have empathy. And whether it's my own traumas or those of others, I have learned to accept them—despite how difficult this may be to endure. But I can tell you I no longer feel the need to test my fortitude. I have too much work to do for others in this lifetime to consider putting myself through all of that again. It's the same with drinking. Urges are there, and I always say, "I don't know that I'm sober for good, but until I get control of my mind and willpower, I will stay this way." And with humility, I can say that I'm not ready to open that box again, or possibly ever. Leaving the door cracked is a dangerous option. The odds are that if you have identified an addictive personality, the door, once shut, should be boarded up, nailed shut, and poured over with concrete.

Every choice I make today is based on the Legacy Mindset:

What demons do I have to overcome to build a legacy that leaves a positive impression behind?

So, lift your head from this page, and reflect on what that question means to you. If you find your mind flooded with negative thoughts about yourself, I'll say plainly that they're wrong, they're just wrong. You have value, just like I do.

But *you* need to see it for *yourself* by *living for others*.

Keep moving forward until you get there—because you will get there.

Summary:

- Be aware of the destructive power of addiction. If you find yourself dependent on a substance or habit, seek help to overcome it.
- Your life has intrinsic value. In times of despair, think about the potential for you to change and the positive impact you can make in the world.
- Be open to the idea of transforming yourself. You have the resilience and power to change the course of your life. Engage in self-reflection, set goals, and take steps toward becoming a better version of yourself.
- Don't be afraid to lean on tools (apps, books, support groups, etc.) in your personal development journey.
- It *is* possible to leave behind old habits and patterns of thinking. Think of this as a rebirth into a more positive and fulfilled life.
- If you find yourself struggling with thoughts of suicide, substance abuse, or mental health, seek help from the Suicide & Crisis Lifeline by dialing 9-8-8 or the Substance Abuse & Mental Health Services National Hotline by dialing 1-800-662-4357.

Chapter 21 Exercise

Prompt 1: Spend a few minutes writing in your journal about a moment in your life when you felt you had no value or purpose. Reflect on how you overcame that moment or how you're currently working to overcome it. Focus on identifying the small steps you took or can take to change your perspective.

_____

_____

_____

_____

_____

_____

_____

_____

_____

_____

_____

_____

_____

_____

_____

_____

_____

_____

_____

_____

_____

_____

Prompt 2: Ask yourself: What can I do today to live for others? Make a list of at least three things.

_____

_____

_____

_____

CHAPTER 22

KEEP MOVING FORWARD

Aim to have tough memories rather than no memories at all, because within the depth of those challenging experiences lie invaluable lessons, resilience, and profound growth.

I kept that low moment in my life quiet. I waited until I had something positive to share. Two weeks later, I felt like I did, so I picked up my phone. It was Wednesday, April 8, 2020.

I told my dad that I was sober as he sat in the hospital awaiting his fate.

I hope that I never find myself in a situation where people try to guess how much time I have left based on my body's physical degradation, because that's exactly what I did every time I saw my dad those last few weeks. I would see him after a day or so and try to figure out how much time I had left with him. This was mostly up to us, as no doctor gave us a timeline.

In three painful years, it went from "You'll be fine. We might see you back in ten years . . ." to "Let's fix this small issue and get you back on your feet . . ."

. . . to "Sorry, there's nothing more we can do."

In that way, our guesses were more of a defense mechanism, a sort of wishful thinking to help us decide how much time we should spend with him. I guessed that we probably had another year with him. But my dad had a contagious sense of faith when he spoke, saying things like "when I get older" or "maybe next year," when you knew damn well that unless the doctors came up with some miracle, it was nothing more than wishful thinking. I've never been one for wishful thinking, and it hurt me a lot to see him in such denial of what was happening to him—but I think if the roles were reversed, I would have become wishful too.

One thing is for sure: we thought he had more time.

A few weeks after my and my dad's GTR driving escapade, and after everything in my office and my last drink, I was at my shop with the team, dealing with some new equipment that no one knew how to handle. Much of the heavy technical work ended with me taking over, if only so if anything broke in the process, it would be my fault and not theirs. So I was talking to an electrician about running some wires when my phone started to ring: Aunty Crystal—my dad's sister. Typically, my phone doesn't get answered while I'm at work, but she lived in my grandmother's house with my dad, so I always made it a priority to answer.

"Your dad had a coughing fit," she said, "and we took him into the hospital."

Looking over the new machine, I wondered, *Why are you telling me this?*

Dad was constantly in and out of the hospital, to the point where it wasn't even an ordeal to mention.

"Okay?" I said somewhat rudely. "If there's more I need to know, tell me . . ."

There was silence on the other end as she tried to muster up the words. She sniffled and, through tears, said, "Now that he's here, they don't think he will be coming out."

I could hear the pain in her voice. And the pain made it real. Thoughts flooded my head. *This is it. I thought we had more time. This can't be happening. It's not real. It's a bad dream.*

"Can I come see him?" I asked.

In April 2020, at the height of the COVID-19 pandemic, it wasn't guaranteed that I would be allowed to visit. Patients in hospitals were dying alone, families had to be separated, and you needed permission anytime you walked into a care center, where they waited with a swab and thermometer gun. If your temperature was even slightly elevated, they wouldn't let you in.

"Yes," she said, "we need to go say our good-byes."

I asked my team to cover for me for the next few days, and as I approached the hospital, my anxiety turned to anger, annoyed at the nurses because, even though he was in critical condition, only a few people could see him at a time. It wasn't their fault. Everyone was in mass hysteria at the time for COVID—so I get it and empathize, but I was still upset.

Being dad's oldest child and daughter-in-law, me and Tiffany were allowed to go in. The nurse gave us masks and guided us to his room. I was doing okay for the moment, but I didn't know what to expect from myself. *Was I going to be strong? Was I going to break down? I've been numb to death before, so how will I react now?*

When we opened the door, we saw more family members in there already crying, and the ball in my throat grew as I fought back tears at the sight of my dad. He was unconscious, his face turned away from us and tubes coming out of his mouth. He was now completely bald, as just a few weeks prior he started to lose his hair in clumps, gasping for air like a fish out of water. It was real; there were no more time extensions, no more signs of last-minute hope, no surgeries, no more analysis.

There was nothing to prepare me for that. Nothing. He was suffering so severely that it was torture for us to watch. Seeing my Hero dying in the most brutal and horrific way possible tore me apart. They were pumping him full of drugs to help ease the anxiety, but when he would wake up briefly, it was clear that they weren't working. The nurses would try to wake him up and let him know his family was there. He would start panicking and reaching for things because he knew every time his vision faded out, he was either going to darkness forever, waking up in heaven or hell reincarnated, or whatever was on the other side (if anything). He was so close to death that he knew it, and every time he woke up was anyone's guess where he would be. He was terrified. It was plain to see, and it killed me.

What's worse is that it was clearly torture. Every time they brought him back, waking him up again, it was worse—the fear in his eyes. The pain. He was foaming at the mouth from his failing lungs producing fluid, and I just sat by his side saying "I love you, Dad" over and over again, in a way we were both unfamiliar with. But I knew I wasn't going to make that mistake again, like the last time he went in for surgery. And I heard him come to and say it back in full, "I love you too." He wasn't going to make that mistake again, either.

These "I love yous" felt like apologies in every letter.

We apologized for trying to be tough rather than being grateful for the opportunity to say it to each other in good health. That's when I realized we're all sides to the same coin. We can live carelessly and ungratefully until the things that matter are in jeopardy, and when we're finally ready to change, it's entirely too late.

I pulled my brother and sister up on FaceTime so that they could see their dad in his final moments. He couldn't talk coherently, and I got mad whenever the nurses or family woke him. I know they all just wanted to say goodbye to him, but I hated seeing that fear in his eyes each time. After my dad faded to unconsciousness again, I looked at my family and the nurses and said, "No one better wake him up again." Not my proudest moment, but we were torturing him for our own sense of closure. We kept waking him up and watching him scan the room and grab for things while shaking, then fade back out. He couldn't even feel me squeezing his hand.

I kept thinking back to a few weeks prior when my dad mentioned suffocation:

"It's funny, but the thing that will kill me is the thing I'm most scared of."

"I hardly think that's funny," I said, "but I get it."

The doctor decided to administer some more drugs to minimize the amount he kept waking up. The nurses had to wake him one last time for permission.

They woke him again and said: "Mr. Shaffer, we're going to give you some more medication to calm your nerves. Are you nervous?"

My father woke up and did something we will all hold near and dear to us forever. Between these big gasping breaths, my dad cracked one of his huge iconic sideways grins that told everyone in the room: "I'm dying in a hospital, suffocating by my own lungs, NO S—T SHERLOCK. Of course, I'm nervous." And we all laughed at the nurse's expense, because he realized how dumb the question was to the point that even a dying man was willing to acknowledge it.

It was the reminder we all needed to remember that my dad was in there, even though he was in awful shape and there were almost no physical similarities to how he's looked for the past forty-seven years. It was still the guy I had always known . . .

The man who gave me a chance.

The man who made sure I didn't follow in his footsteps.

The man who kept me inspired.

The man who encouraged me to seek discipline.

The man who taught me how to ride a dirt-bike.

And I would hug that nurse today, buy him a beer, and support him for life if I saw him again—because that moment we all shared was something I needed to not lose all sense of purpose in life. It showed that we could still see the little beautiful things, even through the pain.

Once they administered the drug, he went to sleep, and we vowed not to wake him. I was battling so much that I felt seeing him like that for too long would kill me, and I had to go just in case he didn't make it through the night.

Seeing my dad's final breath would kill me for two reasons:

First, the vision of my dad flatlining, along with my other struggles, would put me over the edge whenever I heard the wrong tone out in the wild. And second, because he desperately wanted to be a grandfather, and in his final moments, his only goal was to stay alive long enough to see that happen.

The most gut-wrenching part was that my sister was pregnant with his first grandchild, and due any day. The thought of him being too late was just another insult to injury. My wife and I went home and told my grandmother to let me sleep if anything happened while I was gone, and not to call until eight that next morning to give me an update either way. She agreed.

At eight o'clock on April 10th, my phone rang, and it was my grandmother:

"Hey grandson, hopefully you got some rest."

"I did."

"Your father passed away last night."

"Okay."

"Okay? Are you going to be okay?"

"Yeah."

"Are you sure?"

"Yeah."

"Okay, I will talk to you soon and get the next steps figured out."

"Okay, bye."

"Bye."

That was it.

Not a tear, not a moment, nothing.

My wife must have overheard, because she got out of bed and hugged me. I just wanted her to get off of me; I was suddenly furious at the world. I didn't have the emotional maturity to process it, whether to repress it or to let it all out in a fit of blind rage. It was a question that I didn't have the answer to.

Remember when I said no days off, ever?

I wasn't kidding.

But word of my dad's passing traveled fast to my employees. As I walked into work and passed through the front doors, everyone surrounded me, mourned for me, and kept saying, "Sorry for your loss," putting their hands on my shoulder as I tried to make it to my office.

Something had snapped in me, and I didn't know what it was. I wasn't crying; I was in shock. But mostly, I was so angry that I waited so long to start enjoying things with my dad, all because I lacked the value and self-worth to take basic steps toward rewarding myself and possibly improving his life before he got sick. I abused time, ignored blessings, and now the one person besides my wife who made me feel like a kid in the candy store when I shared achievements was gone. I put all happiness on hold for these big future events, like a car, a house, or hunting land for my dad—so much so that I forgot to enjoy my time with him.

And none of it mattered anymore. He was gone.

Those visions, my drive for those things faded away with my father's light. I stopped caring about what I felt I deserved and decided I'm going to live and help others, and I don't care who has anything to say about it. Because that mentality cost me the most precious moments I will NEVER get back. No matter how hard I try, there is no power on this earth strong enough to bring them back. No tool, no amount of money or ritual would allow me to get that time back with him or any other dead friends I miss daily.

One thing that bothered me immediately was that my dad's fate was now sealed, with no chance to improve. He spent all this time worrying about finances, staying in a job he hated, sacrificing the things he wanted, to ultimately never achieve the legacy he always wanted. He would be a blurb in an obituary, remembered by his immediate family and only a few people he interacted with. Nothing hurt me more at that moment than knowing he wanted so badly to be proud of himself, and in the end, there wasn't much to remember him. If I weren't his number one fan and writing about him in my book, you would never know who he was.

And that's how I learned the last lesson I want to leave you with.

Legacy is what lives on in the lives of those we impact.

My dad never imagined I would write his story or tell the world anything about him. He was a person like me, who didn't think they had a story worth telling. He wasn't perfect, but someone who tried to do better. Someone who battled demons and came out the other side stronger. Someone who honestly just needed more time.

Like so many others, he just needed more time.

We don't always get the time we need, but it's up to us to make the most of the time we have. His life didn't have the impact he hoped for or expected. He didn't accomplish the dreams he set out for himself. But what he did do was inspire his children to reach for the things he wasn't able to obtain. He encouraged us to chase those dreams and dare to believe they were possible. When I was a confused kid, he set me on a better path. When I was a broken veteran, he gave me a roof over my head and an ear to listen.

Without words, he showed me love and valor. Maybe in life he didn't take on all the tests of valor he hoped for, but I saw it in him—through and through. I trusted him with my life and loved him with all my heart, and because of that, his legacy lives on.

Because he sacrificed his own dreams for ours.

Because he planted the seeds of trees whose shade he'd never rest in.

Because of who he was, we have the lives that we do.

Because of this journey and all of its adversities, I know who I am now. I realized that I have something rare that motivates me: an obsessive ambition focused on integrity, empathy, and serving others. In other words—legacy.

True success isn't just about financial gain—it's about staying true to your values and continuously striving to make a positive impact. Let your ambition be driven by integrity and empathy, and you will find lasting fulfillment in your journey. Embrace a legacy mindset by focusing on the impact you leave behind; your true legacy is the difference you make in the lives of others. Go out there, build something meaningful, and leave the world better than you found it.

Summary:

- Never take for granted the time you have with your loved ones.
- Say "I love you" to your family and friends regularly, and don't let ego or pride get in the way of expressing your emotions.
- Recognize the fragility of life and let it motivate you to live with purpose, gratitude, and compassion. Be mindful of the legacy you want to leave behind and how your actions affect those around you.

Chapter 22 Exercise

What kind of legacy do you want to leave behind? Circle three to five attributes from the list below that you'd like people to use to describe you after you're gone. Decide on one attribute that you feel you already display, even if not to the degree you wish. Write about how you display this attribute in your life today.

Inspirational	Courageous	Artistic
Charitable	Innovative	Joyful
Visionary	Dedicated	Loving
Pioneering	Humble	Unifying
Honorable	Creative	Supportive
Compassionate	Ethical	Peacemaker
Wise	Committed	Kind
Selfless	Nurturing	Loyal

THE MISSION OF TIL VALHALLA PROJECT

The small choices and little acts of courage add up to big changes. Sometimes those changes are unexpected and catch you off guard. On February 27, 2017, less than a year after creating that first plaque, I made another choice that caught me off guard. I decided to quit my job and drop out of college, solidifying my devotion to Til Valhalla Project (TVP). With the help of my wife, family, and friends, as well as public crowdsourcing from the loved ones of service members, our goal was to create more one-of-a-kind (OAK) memorial plaques. That first memorial plaque I made for Dunston eventually turned into over 3,250 plaques delivered—so far—by Til Valhalla Project. And we're just getting started.

Each plaque is crafted with the same tradition established in that cluttered garage on that dark, drunken night. From the message on the back of each nameplate to providing memorials to the families of Fallen Heroes at no cost, these traditions became the foundation for Honoring the thousands of Heroes and millions more to come. To fund the creation of our memorial plaques without charging the families of Fallen Heroes, Til Valhalla Project produces and sells inspirational clothing that aligns with our message. To this day, OAK plaques cannot be bought by anyone, and they are hand-delivered to families as a complete surprise and at no cost.

Not only did Dunston inspire the plaques, but he planted the seed that would eventually culminate in our mission which has contributed millions of dollars to efforts that reduce the epidemic of veteran suicide and Honor our Fallen. Together, we work hard every day toward a mission that has both saved and changed my life. And in this book, I wanted to show you how. When I shifted my perspective and made my life about living for others, leaving them became a hell of a lot harder. And I firmly believe if you're able to do that, if you're able to make that small choice and take that first step, when the dark thoughts come (and they still do), you'll have those faces, those people, those fighters in your corner. The lives you've helped change, fighting the battles beside you. You're never alone in your battles, and no legacy endures without others.

So, let's do this together.

AFTERWORD

Boy, where do I start?

This book took almost three years to finally come together. There were so many thoughts of imposter syndrome and self-doubt. I believe this happens to any first-time author, but the content within did not become *anything* like I expected it would. I mean, just six years ago I was installing batteries at AutoZone, and now I'm writing a book and have a national company? At first I wanted to talk about reducing veteran suicide, but then it moved on to business, and then an autobiography and a guide, and a self-help memoir, all amalgamating into what you see today. When I put the first words on paper, I was lost—but in the process, I found what I needed.

And what I needed was help. I needed to reach out.

In early 2023, I finally reached out for help and got this book ready for your hands. If I had taken my own advice sooner, maybe I would have gotten it to you years ago—but I'm glad I didn't. My personal growth over those few years have taken the lessons within to new heights.

While writing this book for you, I experienced some of the biggest moments of my life, and one of the biggest scares. My wife woke up one morning after a long stretch of writing with double vision, and we were both terrified, as we had seen just a few years before how fast things can change. We sat in the hospital room for twelve hours, and I got so nervous that I almost threw up. We sat there together, cried, and I got angry all over again, just like I had with my dad. She was diagnosed with an autoimmune disease attacking her eyes' outer muscles. When I tell you that the lessons within this book became real at that moment, I'm not kidding.

I started to take my own advice—and the advice the world was giving me.

I said I didn't take days off because I didn't feel I deserved them. Well, maybe I still don't, but Tiffany does. For a decade, she's been my rock and my safe place, and one currency we'll never get more of is time. So, I spend a lot more time with my family now, and it just so happens that our family is about to get bigger. Toward the final chapters of writing this book, my wife handed me a test with two blue lines. And now towards publishing, my son Cayden is six months old!

How's that for motivation to have a Legacy Mindset?

Writing this book has been a therapeutic process, but the only thing more therapeutic will be to see how many people like you connect with the lessons within. For my veterans, entrepreneurs, car enthusiasts, business owners, family, friends, and anyone else that took the time to parse through these pages, I know we all come from different walks of life, but we can all achieve great things, and I hope to be part of your journey in making the most of the time we have.

Thank you so much for reading this book. If these words have given you anything worth thinking about, pay it forward and inspire someone else who needs it. You never know when your struggles will become someone else's survival guide.

Keep moving forward out there.

—**Korey Shaffer**

ABOUT THE AUTHOR

Korey Shaffer is a US Marine and a visionary entrepreneur who has created several successful businesses and real estate ventures. He is the founder of Til Valhalla Project, an inspiring mission dedicated to honoring fallen military heroes and first responders by surprise-delivering memorial plaques to their families. This noble initiative is funded through impactful apparel that pays tribute, raises awareness, and inspires others.

Korey's journey is one of resilience and transformation. Growing up, he faced challenges fitting in at school and in the broader community. However, his late teen years saw a pivotal change when he discovered the profound rewards of brotherhood and belonging. This experience ignited his passion for joining the US Marines.

Upon returning from combat in Afghanistan, Korey faced significant physical and emotional challenges. These included the loss of one of his closest friends in the service, which could have plunged him into despair. Instead, it became a turning point, motivating him to create his first memorial plaque. This heartfelt endeavor blossomed into a movement, resulting in the creation of thousands of memorials, and setting off a chain reaction of purpose within Korey.

Today, Korey leads Til Valhalla Project with unwavering dedication, ensuring the highest standards of quality and care in memorializing fallen heroes. His efforts contribute millions of dollars to combat veteran suicide, honoring the fallen, and giving back to the community. Recognized by numerous news outlets, Til Valhalla Project continues to expand its reach as one of America's fastest-growing veteran-owned brands.